MODERN ERP

SELECT, IMPLEMENT, & USE

TODAY'S ADVANCED BUSINESS SYSTEMS

MODERN ERP

SELECT, IMPLEMENT, & USE

TODAY'S ADVANCED BUSINESS SYSTEMS

MARIANNE BRADFORD, PH.D.

Associate Professor

Poole College of Management

North Carolina State University

Raleigh, NC

Editor
Betsy Goolsby

Book and Cover Design
Toni Williams

Trademark Acknowledgments
These are registered trademarks in the United States of America and other countries. This book is not sponsored by, endorsed by, or affiliated with any of the below companies.

abas	Microsoft Dynamics
CDC	MicroStrategy
CISA	NetSuite
CISM	Oracle
CGEIT	QuickScore
CRISC	SAP SE
Consona	SAP Business All-in-One
Epicor	Salesforce
Exact	SAS
Expandable	SugarCRM
Fujitsu	SYSPRO
IBM	Tableau
Infor	
ISACA	
LoadRunner	

Credits

Figure 12-2. Copyright © 2012. SAS Institute Inc. All rights reserved. Reproduced with permission of SAS Institute Inc., Cary, NC, USA.

Figure 12-3. Copyright © 2007. SAS Institute Inc. All rights reserved. Reproduced with permission of SAS Institute Inc., Cary, NC, USA.

Figure 12-4. Copyright © 2014. SAS Institute Inc. All rights reserved. Reproduced with permission of SAS Institute Inc., Cary, NC, USA.

This publication contains references to the products of SAP SE. SAP and SAP All-in-One mentioned herein are trademarks of SAP SE in Germany and other countries. SAP SE is neither the author nor the publisher of this publication and is not responsible for its content. SAP Group shall not be liable for errors or omissions with respect to the materials. The only warranties for SAP Group products and services are those that are set forth in the express warranty statements accompanying such products and services, if any. Nothing herein should be construed as constituting an additional warranty.

Clip art used with permission from Microsoft.

Copyright 2015
Dr. Marianne Bradford

ISBN: 978-1-312-66598-9

In memory of my brother Hudson
who never got to write his own book
You were so money

Contents

Preface xv

Acknowledgements xvi

About the Author xvii

Chapter 1: Introduction to Enterprise Resource Planning Systems 1
Objectives 1
Introduction 1
ERP Essentials 2
Who Needs Knowledge of ERP Systems? 4
When Does a Company Need an ERP System? 5
Advantages of ERP Systems 6
Disadvantages of ERP Systems 7
ERP Evolution and Trends 9
ERP Market 11
Summary 12
Keywords 13
Quick Review 13
Questions to Consider 14

Chapter 2: ERP Technology 17
Objectives 17
Introduction 17
Evolution of ERP Architecture 18
Relational Database Management Systems 21
Database Normalization 27
Structured Query Language (SQL) 29
ERP Data 30
Configuration 31
Customization 32
Best of Breed 32
System Landscape 33
Cloud Computing 34
Mobility 36
Summary 37
Keywords 38
Quick Review 39
Questions to Consider 39

Chapter 3: ERP and Business Process Redesign 43

Objectives 43
Introduction 43
Business Processes 44
Common Problems with Business Processes 45
Business Process Reengineering 47
Factors for Reengineering Success 50
Business Process Improvement 52
Business Process Improvement Model 53
Processes in Need of Change 55
Stakeholders for Business Process Transformation..58
Summary 59
Keywords 60
Quick Review 60
Questions to Consider 61

Chapter 4: ERP and Process Mapping..63

Objectives 63
Introduction 63
Systems Diagrams 64
The Process Map 64
Benefits of Process Mapping 66
Gathering Information for the Process Map...67
Process Mapping Roles 67
Steps for Drawing Process Maps..68
Process Map Example – Electric City 69
Extensions to the Electric City Process Map 70
Advanced Process Map Example – Fit Gear 72
Summary 75
Keywords 76
Quick Review 76
Questions to Consider 77

Chapter 5: ERP Life Cycle: Planning and Package Selection...........................79

Objectives 79
Introduction 79
ERP Life Cycle – Planning 80
ERP Life Cycle – Package Selection...89
Summary 99
Keywords 99
Quick Review 100
Questions to Consider 100

Chapter 6: ERP Life Cycle: Implementation and Operation and Maintenance... 103
Objectives 103
Introduction 103
ERP Life Cycle – Implementation 104
ERP Life Cycle – Operation and Maintenance 122
Summary 125
Keywords 126
Quick Review 127
Questions to Consider 127

Chapter 7: ERP Financial Management 131
Objectives 131
Introduction 131
Financial Accounting 132
Management Accounting 137
Asset Management 142
Travel and Expense Management 144
Summary 145
Keywords 145
Quick Review 146
Questions to Consider 146

**Chapter 8: ERP Sales, Customer Relationship Management, and
Knowledge Management 149**
Objectives 149
Introduction 149
Sales Process 150
Point of Sale (POS) Systems 153
Customer Relationship Management 154
CRM vs. ERP 156
CRM Functionality 157
CRM Interaction Channels 159
Social CRM 160
Elements for CRM Success 161
CRM Metrics 162
CRM Analytics 162
Knowledge Management 164
CRM and Knowledge Management 164
Implementing a Knowledge Management System 165
Knowledge Management Metrics 167
Summary 167
Keywords 168
Quick Review 169
Questions to Consider 169

Chapter 9: ERP Supply Chain Management 173

Objectives 173
Introduction 173
What Is Supply Chain Management? 174
Purchasing and Sourcing 175
Supplier Relationship Management 178
Warehouse Management System 180
Transportation Management System 181
Manufacturing 182
Quality Assurance 186
Plant Maintenance 188
Environment, Health, and Safety 189
Supply Chain Technology 190
Summary 193
Keywords 194
Quick Review 195
Questions to Consider 196

Chapter 10: ERP Human Capital Management 199

Objectives 199
Introduction 199
Human Capital Management 200
Employee Self-Service 207
Outsourcing Human Capital Management Functions 208
Summary 210
Keywords 211
Quick Review 211
Questions to Consider 212

Chapter 11: ERP Security and Implementation Assurance 215

Objectives 215
Introduction 215
Internal Control 216
ERP and Internal Controls 218
IT Application Controls 219
IT General Controls 222
Logical Access Controls 225
System Implementation Assurance 227
ISACA Certifications for IT Professionals 230
Summary 233
Keywords 233
Quick Review 234
Questions to Consider 235

Chapter 12: ERP and Business Analytics **237**
Objectives: 237
Introduction 237
Business Analytics 238
Types of Business Analytics 240
Data Stores for Business Analytics 245
Business Analytics Best Practices 247
Corporate Performance Management 248
The Balanced Scorecard 250
Data Governance 252
Summary 253
Keywords 254
Quick Review 254
Questions to Consider 255

Index **259**

Preface

In 2008, I wrote the first edition of *Modern ERP* with the formidable goal of providing an ERP text that was current, easy to read and understand, and vendor-neutral. Immediately I realized that I could do better, and two years later I published the second edition of *Modern ERP*. Based on the number of colleges and universities that adopted that text, the feedback on Amazon, my ranking at Lulu as one of the top sellers, and the absence of complaints in my classroom, I was happy with that edition. However, as could be expected, the marketplace for ERP systems evolved at a fast pace in response to technological innovation and changing business conditions. As a result, I find myself five years later putting out a new edition of *Modern ERP* to ensure that my words stay current, relevant, and valuable for students and practitioners alike.

I have substantially revised each chapter of the third edition to keep pace with advances in the ERP world. This edition is the culmination of two years of writing. In this time, I have spent countless hours reading ERP articles, researching ERP, attending ERP seminars and conferences, and talking to ERP professionals about the latest developments. I've been lucky enough to have formed a strong network of professionals who use ERP systems, support ERP systems, and provide ERP consulting. These individuals help me keep up to date on what's really going on and fill in gaps in my knowledge. These professionals (as well as some educators) have also been gracious enough to read the material in this book and give feedback in the form of suggested additions, corrections, and deletions.

New material has been added to the third edition including coverage of topics such as cloud computing, mobility, and business analytics and an expansion on topics of ongoing importance such as ERP security, ERP risk management, databases, and supply chain. New graphics and screenshots have been included to further aid in the learning process.

I continue to focus on the fundamentals—ERP technology, business process reengineering, ERP life cycle, ERP functionality, security, and intelligence. I also remain impartial to any one vendor's products—what I consider to be one of the main strengths of my book. Every chapter is written with a thorough and up-to-date review of the current state of the market.

Whether you are using this book as part of a university course, to further your career, or simply to increase your knowledge in this area, I hope that the third edition of *Modern ERP* meets your needs. As anyone who has ever used or implemented an ERP system can attest, the size and complexity of many of these systems are enormous. Mastering the twelve chapters in this book provides the reader with the knowledge to successfully take on that challenge.

Acknowledgements

I would like to thank the following professionals and educators who helped review my book.

Chantale Baptiste,
Inexxa Consulting Group

Bob Bucy, SAP Consultant

John "Wes" Dyke, Caterpillar

Sherry Fowler,
North Carolina State University

Donald Frazier, Deloitte Consulting

Tracy Freeman, North
Carolina State University

Greg Gerard, Florida State University

Mike Golden, JaveLLin Solutions, LLC

Stephen Gulliver, University of Reading

Jose Lineros, University of North Texas

Rufus Lohmueller,
Lohmueller Consulting

Lisa Mannion, bioMérieux

Janet L. Marburger, LSI Consulting, Inc.

Matthew McIntyre, Freudenberg–IT

Chris McKittrick,
North Carolina State University

Neal Parker,
North Carolina State University

David Stefanick, IBM

Srinivas Saraswatula, Accuratus, LLC

Ed Thomas, Deloitte

Dawn H. Watts, SPX Corporation

Joe Williams,
North Carolina State University
Benefits Office

James Worrell,
University of Alabama at Birmingham

About the Author

Marianne Bradford is an Associate Professor at North Carolina State University, where she teaches graduate and undergraduate ERP systems in the Poole College of Management. She holds a Ph.D. in Business Administration from The University of Tennessee, an MBA from Millsaps College, and a Bachelor of Accounting from The University of Mississippi. Dr. Bradford has been published in numerous journals including:

- *Journal of Information Systems*

- *Issues in Accounting Education*

- *Communications of the Association of Information Systems*

- *International Journal of Accounting Information Systems*

- *Strategic Finance*

Her research interests include ERP system implementation, identity and access management, business process reengineering, and corporate social responsibility. Her professional experience includes auditor with KPMG LLP and IT auditor with Ernst and Young LLP. Dr. Bradford was named as one of the Top 25 ERP Experts, Blogs, and Influencers to Track in 2010 by Focus Research. Modern ERP has also been translated into Korean.

Chapter
1

Introduction to Enterprise Resource Planning Systems

Objectives

- Understand the essentials of ERP systems

- Recognize when a company would need an ERP system

- Know advantages and disadvantages of ERP systems

- Realize how ERP systems have evolved and identify trends in the market

- Distinguish among the three ERP vendor tiers

Introduction

The introduction of personal computers to the business environment in the 1980s initially led to information systems that were narrowly focused, serving a single, specific function such as accounting or sales. The result was that organizations had disparate systems for their various functional areas. This disparity, in turn, led to duplicate data across the enterprise and an emphasis on departmental boundaries, as data was not shared. In the mid-to-late 1990s, companies began implementing enterprise resource planning (ERP) systems to automate, standardize, and integrate their business processes for effective planning and control. A key feature of ERP systems is the comprehensive database that serves as a single source of the truth. In practice, this means that employees in all departments can look to the ERP system for the information they need and work from the same data. This book is about ERP systems, the information systems paradigm of organizational computing today. This chapter discusses essentials of ERP systems, advantages and disadvantages of ERP systems, ERP evolution, and the ERP marketplace.

ERP Essentials

Enterprise resource planning (ERP) systems are business systems that integrate and streamline data across the company into one complete system that supports the needs of the entire enterprise. ERP systems are designed to enhance all aspects of key operations, such as purchasing, accounting, manufacturing, and sales, by taking processes and functions that were previously disjointed and supported by various **legacy systems**, or older, standalone, disparate business systems, and seamlessly integrating and coordinating them. The foundation of an ERP system is a well-structured database that serves the operational and decision-making needs of the entire enterprise.

By supporting the information requirements of more than one functional area, ERP systems are considered **cross-functional** in nature. ERP systems are also considered **process-centered**; that is, the application enables a clear, complete, logical, and precise view of the organization's business processes, or how it does its vital work. A **business process** is a collection of activities that together add value. Business processes span multiple departments and in many cases traverse the boundaries of the organization, sharing information with partners, suppliers, and customers. Two of the major business processes that most companies have, and which ERP systems support, are "perform order management" and "procure materials and services." Other key processes that ERP systems support are presented in Figure 1-1.

Figure 1-1: ERP-Supported Business Processes

ERP Modules

ERP systems are sold in **modules**, or groups of related programs performing a major function within the system, such as accounting or manufacturing. Modules are individually purchased based on the needs of the company. Most ERP software is flexible enough that businesses can implement a module (or modules) without purchasing and implementing the entire package. The modular organization of ERP systems adds to their flexibility. For instance, a distribution company that doesn't do manufacturing can license and implement financial, purchasing, sales, and inventory modules and have a solution "tailored" to its needs. If, at a later time, the company expands into manufacturing, it can license additional modules to support this new functionality. A benefit to ERP vendors of modular design is that it allows them to put together product offerings for specific industries. For instance, by adding modules for food safety and quality management, a generic ERP system can become a niche competitor in the food industry.

Vendors use modules as pricing units. The more modules a company implements, the more costly the system becomes. Generally, ERP providers will give their customers discounts if they purchase additional modules. Companies do not have to purchase all modules available from an ERP vendor; however, implementing more modules leads to greater integration, which in turn can lead to a greater return on investment. These benefits should be weighed against the costs and organizational resources needed for implementation when deciding upon a strategy for ERP.

Core ERP includes modules for financials, human capital management (HCM), and logistics. These modules are actually suites encompassing various sub-modules. For example, the financial suite will typically include sub-modules for accounts receivable, accounts payable, and general ledger. The HCM suite will generally comprise sub-modules for payroll, benefits, personnel management, and talent management.

ERP systems have historically been seen as **back office systems**, meaning they are used to integrate "back office" functionality such as accounting, finance, purchasing, HCM, and order fulfillment. Now, ERP systems have evolved to more than back office systems, encompassing front office, customer-facing modules as well as modules that facilitate the supply chain. These additional customer relationship management (CRM) and supply chain management (SCM) modules are considered part of the broader ERP system, or **extended ERP**. Other modules that are part of extended ERP include analytics, product life cycle management, business performance management, and many others. These modules are an opportunity for companies to complement core ERP and integrate even more functionality. Figure 1-2 presents typical modules in an ERP system for a manufacturing company.

Figure 1-2: Typical Modules in an ERP System for a Manufacturing Company

Operations and Supply Chain		
Plant Maintenance	Purchasing	Quality Management
Sales and Distribution	Shop Floor Management	Transportation Management
Manufacturing	Warehouse Management	Advanced Planning
Financial Accounting		
General Ledger	Cash Management	Accounts Payable
Accounts Receivable	Fixed Assets	Financial Consolidation
Management Accounting		
Cost Center Accounting	Product Costing	Budgeting
Profit Center Accounting	Activity-Based Costing	Profitability Analysis
Human Capital Management		
Personnel Management	Payroll	Learning Management
Time and Attendance	Benefits	Recruitment Management

Who Needs Knowledge of ERP Systems?

Business professionals interact with ERP systems in various roles, including as end user, auditor, and consultant. End users work with ERP systems on a daily basis in their particular business context. For example, shipping personnel use the ERP system to view logistics information, purchasing personnel maintain supplier data, accounting staff close the books at the end of the month, finance executives view cash requirements, and human resources (HR) staff maintain employee records. Even those employees whose jobs do not require them to use the ERP system on a daily basis interact with ERP for self-service activities such as billing time to jobs, requesting time off, or signing up for training classes.

Financial statement auditors need to understand their clients' ERP systems for the annual audit. They collect reports such as the trial balance and general ledger from the ERP system, as well as other relevant data such as customer account balances that are used to substantiate accounts receivable on the balance sheet. Internal auditors can help organizations maximize the performance of the ERP system by becoming an active part of the implementation project team. They provide expertise in internal control practices, compliance requirements, and business processes. An auditor highly trained in auditing information systems is called an **IT auditor**. These specialized auditors verify the effectiveness of the ERP system's **application controls**, which are programmed controls in the ERP software that maintain the accuracy, reliability, completeness, security, and privacy of the data. An example of an application control would be the "three-way match" whereby a purchase order is matched with the corresponding goods receipt and supplier invoice in the ERP system. Other evidence that IT auditors collect includes the physical controls over the data center that houses the ERP servers and controls over authentication into the ERP system.

Given the widespread adoption of ERP systems, consultants with both business and IT experience are highly sought after to serve as system implementers, also known as integration partners. Numerous activities take place during an ERP implementation with which an integration partner can assist, including, but not limited to, business case development, package selection, business process analysis, project management, testing, and training. Consultants might also be needed for customizing the software, which requires programming skills. However, because these systems are extremely complex and support the information requirements of the entire enterprise, traditional software developers and programmers, who know mostly about technology and little about business, are not as valuable as they once were. The most important criteria necessary for a successful ERP consultant are knowledge of the client's business processes and deep knowledge of the chosen ERP package.

When Does a Company Need an ERP System?

Because every company is different, there is no single indicator that says, "You need ERP now!" However, companies that benefit most from ERP systems often face similar problems and frustrations. Developing a business case starts with identifying the business's challenges, or "pain points." Typical business challenges that can be solved with an ERP system include:

- Too many business problems and unanswered questions – A new system might help a company better determine its exact financial performance. It could help managers decide what levels of inventory should be kept or what it costs to make an item. Other questions an ERP system could answer might include: Why are our customers dissatisfied? Why are we regularly missing promised delivery dates? Why can't we accurately forecast and plan production requirements? Why are our shipping costs so high?

- Changing business model – Software purchased years ago may no longer effectively support the company's new business model. A company may delve into a new line of business, go global, or need more internal controls and procedures in its systems. Any one of these can render a legacy system ineffectual.

- Desire for growth – Existing processes and systems may be unable to manage a growing number of end users and/or transactions or support a merger or acquisition, which is best handled with standardized business processes and integrated data across the organization.

- Need for advanced functionality – A company's existing software might not be able to handle new business procedures and practices.

- Too many business systems supporting processes – When companies have many different systems that are "pieced together," this situation can wreak havoc on the processes meant to ensure that the company is running smoothly. Running many different systems in the company also means that IT maintenance can become a nightmare. Customizing these systems, upgrading them, and applying patches and updates can be complex and can deplete critical time and resources.

- Lack of compliance – Government and institutional compliance requirements continue to grow and evolve. Navigating through numerous legal, regulatory, and supply chain mandates has never been tougher. These mandates include published accounting standards such as the International Financial Reporting Standards (IFRS), international trade standards such as the North American Free Trade Agreement (NAFTA), and legislation such as the Sarbanes-Oxley Act (SOX), which requires implementation and documentation of internal controls, procedures, and processes.

Advantages of ERP Systems

ERP systems provide many advantages to companies. One of the main advantages is data integration. As mentioned earlier in the chapter, one result of the advent of desktop computing was that the same data was often housed in different departmental systems. The inability to keep information synchronized between systems often meant that multiple versions of data resided within the organization. In ERP systems, data is captured once and shared across the enterprise, reducing the risk of inaccuracies and redundancies in data and eliminating time wasted in checking, rechecking, and reconciling data. ERP systems even simplify the error correction process; if a mistake is made, it only has to be corrected once. Data integration gives stakeholders the ability to gain better visibility into business operations. The enterprise has a single version of "the truth," and all users benefit because they share access to—and responsibility for—information that is current, complete, and accurate.

Another advantage of ERP systems is real-time access to information, which improves collaboration and communication across the enterprise. With ERP systems, once data is entered, it is readily available online and in real time to all users in all departments (who have the authority to view or edit the data). The time lag that used to arise when documents sat in in-baskets waiting to be rekeyed into another system is eliminated, along with much of the paper documents involved. Information is available sooner, and interdepartmental communication improves. For example, in a company that has an ERP system, suppose a purchasing agent processes a purchase order for raw material. Once that event is committed in the system, the production department will know the material is coming, and thus production planning becomes  more accurate. Customer service representatives will have complete and up-to-date information needed to provide intelligent support to customers on the status of their orders. This real-time, immediate access to enterprise information can help improve operations, corporate governance, and management of enterprise risk, creating a horizontally "joined up," process-centered company and ultimately improving productivity, insight, and optimized business processes.

An ERP system also requires that the company share a common process and data model covering broad and deep operational end-to-end processes such as those found in manufacturing and the supply chain. This standardization improves coordination within the organization and across the organization, making it easier to interact with internal and external stakeholders.

ERP vendors design their solutions around processes based on industry best practices. A **best practice** is a business process that is generally recognized as more effective and/or efficient than others in a particular industry. When managers of a company select an ERP package to implement, they are "buying into" a particular ERP vendor's view of best practices and relying on the system to support their efforts to embrace these practices. Matching best practices to organizational needs is what differentiates one ERP package from another and is a key contributor to the ultimate success of the implementation. Larger ERP vendors, such as SAP and Oracle, have thousands of best practices programmed into their software. These vendors support enormous research and development efforts to identify best practices in various industries and incorporate them into their solutions. As a result, the cycle of finding, codifying, and delivering best practices to customers allows the ERP vendor to increase its customer base by offering specific versions of their software called **vertical solutions** (or **industry solutions**). Figure 1-3 presents a complete list of vertical solutions offered by Oracle in its E-Business Suite.

Figure 1-3: Oracle's Vertical Solutions

Aerospace and Defense	Industrial Manufacturing
Automotive	Insurance
Chemicals	Media and Entertainment
Communications	Natural Resources
Consumer Goods	Oil and Gas
Education and Research	Professional Services
Engineering and Construction	Public Sector
Finance Services	Retail
Health Sciences	Travel and Transportation
High Technology	Utilities

Source: Oracle.com

Another advantage of ERP systems is that an ERP vendor's modules look and act the same. This similarity makes it easy for users to work in multiple modules. With a single interface and similar navigation, employees will encounter less friction and greater ease in using the ERP system versus working in multiple disparate systems.

Finally, ERP systems can reduce operational costs and increase revenue. Companies that implement ERP do so to gain efficiencies such as lower inventory costs, production costs, or purchasing costs. Similarly, companies implement ERP to transform parts (or all) of the business to improve revenue-generating processes, including time to market, marketing and sales, and customer service.

Disadvantages of ERP Systems

Implementing an ERP system involves much more than a simple installation of off-the-shelf software. It is a complex, time-consuming undertaking that can often involve a myriad of problems along the way. Many of the issues encountered during implementation pertain to what is called the "soft stuff" (people issues) as opposed to the "technical stuff" (software/hardware issues). For example, top management can be a major problem if managers do not set a convincing "tone at the top" that the ERP system is a priority or if they don't allocate enough resources to implementation.

Lack of employee participation can also be a problem if employees are not educated early on about the organization's motivation for investing in an ERP system or if their opinions and feedback are not taken into consideration during the implementation process. Sometimes, ERP systems are met with resistance or even overt hostility. Employees may be quite comfortable with the legacy systems that they have used for decades. They may oppose the additional training, process modifications, and organizational change that inevitably occur or they might complain that the system is difficult to use, too restrictive, or inflexible. They may blame the system for problems that are really just cultural or caused by a lack of user acceptance. Resistance to the ERP system can lead to employees developing counter-productive "work-arounds," in which they do not use the system as intended, perhaps reverting to their old systems and processes. At times, frustrated or fearful of organizational change, they may even attempt to sabotage the system by intentionally interjecting errors or making excessively complicated demands of the system in order to hinder its implementation or operation.

An example of sabotage in an ERP implementation occurred during the SAP implementation at FoxMeyer Drug Co. in the 1990s. Warehouse workers, threatened with the loss of their jobs due to the closing of warehouses, damaged inventory being transferred to the new distribution center. Because of a debilitating morale problem among workers, lots of merchandise was dumped into trucks and arrived at the distribution center with packages damaged or broken open or otherwise unsalable as new product, resulting in an enormous shrinkage in inventory. While this is an extreme example, situations like this can arise from inadequate education and training of employees. Companies should not only educate their employees (the "why") but also train their employees (the "how") in order to ensure a smooth transition when migrating from legacy systems to an ERP system.

Organizations that successfully implement ERP systems often employ change agents to help minimize the people issues during and after implementation. **Change agents** bring to the table skills in **change management**, or the systematic approach to dealing with change, from the perspective of both an organization and the individual. When change management is done well, people feel engaged in the change process and work together towards a common objective, realizing benefits and delivering results. Change management will be discussed in more depth in Chapter 6.

Another disadvantage of ERP systems is their price tag, especially for software from the well-known, larger ERP vendors such as SAP and Oracle. An ERP system and its implementation process may well be the most expensive investment a company ever makes. For large companies, ERP systems can cost millions of dollars and take years to implement. Smaller companies generally incur fewer implementation costs, but they can experience the same type of implementation problems. Furthermore, once implemented, the ERP system needs constant "care and feeding" to maintain its stability, currency, and compatibility with a wide range of ever-changing software applications it may interface with as well as the hardware it is installed on. Many ERP professionals liken this to being on an "ERP treadmill"—once on the treadmill, a company must keep pace with constant changes in the technology. Since ERP maintenance costs are incurred year after year, this component may end up costing more in total than the initial software, database, and implementation.

While the "soft stuff" usually makes or breaks an ERP implementation, the technical problems can also be a challenge. ERP systems are sophisticated and complex, and implementing them requires, in many cases, hiring expensive consultants to help. Companies often struggle to take command of the technology and to leverage that technology into measurable and maintainable business process change. Customers with more simplistic business requirements may find that the various features, options, and setup requirements add a level of difficulty not previously experienced.

The standardization of business processes discussed as an advantage can also be a disadvantage if this structure is different or runs counter to the firm's culture or expectations. Thus, it is crucial that a company perform its due diligence when choosing its ERP system.

Also, because ERP systems are off-the-shelf software packages and are available to any company (for a price!), the issue may be raised that best practices in ERP systems level the playing field between a company and its competitors. Since implementation of an ERP system requires that a company adhere to the best practices in the software, a company could lose the advantage of a unique (and perhaps better) business practice that differentiates it. In these cases, it might be worthwhile to customize the software rather than change the process to match the ERP software. The advantages and disadvantages of customizing ERP software are discussed in Chapters 2 and 6. Also, it should be noted that IT is only an enabler; a company must still be good at its **core competency**, or those unique capabilities that are essential to achieving a competitive advantage. Technology alone cannot make a company successful if its underlying business strategy and core competencies are flawed.

Because of these reasons and more, companies should not take the decision to implement an ERP system lightly. Successful implementations require that all employees—from functional users to IT staff to top management—be motivated to work closely together to advance the organization's mission. Those companies considering an ERP system should perform their due diligence in choosing the appropriate solution as well as partnering with knowledgeable consultants who can lend their expertise to various aspects of the implementation.

ERP Evolution and Trends

The term "ERP" was coined by Gartner, Inc., a leading technology research and advisory company, but its roots date back to the 1960s. During this period, discrete manufacturers used inventory management and control packages to manage their inventory. Software engineers created programs to monitor raw materials and guide plant supervisors on what to order and when replenishment was necessary. A host of inventory-related reports helped manage this process. In the 1970s, these programs evolved into **material requirements planning (MRP) systems**, which is software that manufacturing companies use to plan production and calculate more precisely what materials they require, at what time, and in what quantities. MRP generates schedules for production operations and the raw material purchases needed based on finished goods requirements.

In the 1980s, MRP developed into **manufacturing resource planning (MRP II) systems**, or solutions that provide an integrated method of operational and financial planning for manufacturing companies. While MRP stops at the receiving dock, MRP II incorporates the value stream all the way through the production facility to the shipping dock where the product is packaged and sent to the customer. That value stream includes production planning, machine capacity scheduling, demand forecasting and analysis modules, and quality tracking tools.

From there, MRP II evolved into ERP. The main difference between MRP II and ERP systems is that MRP II systems are often standalone applications, whereas ERP systems comprise MRP II plus many more modules. While MRP II systems manage the computing needs of the manufacturing environment, ERP systems manage the resources of the *entire* enterprise (and in many more industries).

In the mid-to-late 1990s, the Year 2000 (Y2K) issue and the desire of many firms to upgrade to client-server technology were the initial drivers behind the adoption of ERP systems. Most of the early adopters of ERP systems were very large companies such as those in the Fortune 500. Now, ERP systems have become a "must have" for all types and sizes of organizations that need to gain the advantages of greater information management in order to remain competitive in this fast-changing global landscape.

In the 2000s, ERP evolved into "extended ERP" or ERP II, which includes 3-tier or *n*-tier architecture running on a web platform and integrating with additional modules such as product life cycle management (PLM), supply chain management (SCM) and customer relationship management (CRM). Figure 1-4 presents the evolution of ERP from the 1960s to 2000s.

Figure 1-4: Evolution of ERP Systems

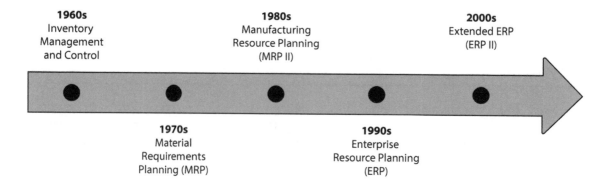

ERP Market

The ERP market is a billion-dollar industry and growing. Although specific numbers are hard to quantify, there is no question that a significant percentage of the world's financial transactions touch an ERP system in one way or another. ERP vendors can be organized by tier, or vendor groupings based on certain characteristics. Figure 1-5 presents various criteria for distinguishing between the three tiers. **Tier 1 ERP vendors** sell ERP solutions to large, multinational corporations with more than 1,000 employees and revenues greater than $1 billion (collectively known as the **enterprise space**). Tier 1 ERP systems are typically very costly due to their vast capabilities, which include being able to handle the operations of a conglomerate with multiple global subsidiaries. Only a few ERP vendors have the size, resources, and functionality to meet these needs. In order to compete with Tier 2 vendors, Tier 1 vendors have been making a serious down-market push by offering simplified versions of their software and versions for niche markets. They also have developed mid-market pricing and implementation strategies to make their products more appealing to the mid-market buyer.

Figure 1-5: Characteristics of ERP Vendor Tiers

Tier 1	Tier 2	Tier 3
High complexity	Medium complexity	Limited functionality
Highest cost of ownership	Medium cost of ownership	Lowest cost of ownership
Many industry solutions	Fewer industry solutions	Fewest industry solutions
Large companies	Mid-market companies	Small to mid-sized companies
Global functionality	Global functionality	Few locations

Source: Ultra Consultants

Collectively, Tier 2 and Tier 3 vendors target **small- to medium-sized enterprises (SMEs)**. **Tier 2 ERP vendors** sell ERP solutions that are designed for mid-market companies, which usually range in size from $50 million up to $1 billion in annual revenues and have between 250 and 1,000 employees. These vendors have products and services designed for single or multiple facilities. They address many of the requirements of larger companies, but their applications are less complex than Tier 1 solutions. Their systems also come with a lower price tag than a Tier 1 ERP system because their software license costs and maintenance fees are lower. Generally these solutions are easier to implement and support than a Tier 1. Often, the Tier 2 vendor focuses on fewer industries, whereas a Tier 1 vendor provides systems for many vertical markets. Recently, the much more crowded Tier 2 vendor segment has started to push up-market, with ERP products that are increasingly powerful, scalable, and suitable for larger companies.

The larger ERP vendors cannot be everything to everybody, so there is a constant opportunity for smaller, more nimble competitors to fill the void with more focused, industry-specific applications. **Tier 3 ERP vendors** sell products that are designed for smaller companies that range in annual revenues from $10 million to $50 million and have fewer than 250 employees. While their products have limited breadth, they offer depth in a particular industry. Their customers have few locations and less complexity, and their solutions usually have the lowest total cost of ownership.

Figure 1-6 presents sample ERP vendors in each of the three tiers. As can be seen, there are fewer vendors in Tier 1 than any other tier. One reason for this is that over the years, vendor consolidation has taken place. Two software giants, SAP and Oracle, dominate the Tier 1 space, with Microsoft beginning to edge into this territory with its Dynamics AX offering. SAP (which stands for Systems, Application, and Products in Data Processing) is the world's largest enterprise software company in terms of software and software-related service revenue. Oracle, the second-largest Tier 1 vendor, has traditionally been known for its expertise in databases; however, they also sell an ERP system of comparable size, Oracle E-Business Suite. Beginning in 2003, Oracle aggressively acquired a number of high-value software companies, including ERP vendor PeopleSoft (which had previously acquired JD Edwards, another ERP vendor). Thus, Oracle's ERP offerings consist of three ERP solutions, plus a relatively new "fused" version: Oracle Fusion. As these two titans battle one another for the prime enterprise accounts, they are polarized to some extent. While Oracle focuses more on services, government, telecommunications, and utilities, SAP is strong in capital-intensive manufacturing and the oil, gas, and chemicals sectors. However, these vendors continue to go head to head in most industries, including retail, government, manufacturing, and banking.

Figure 1-6: Sample ERP Vendors

Tier 1	Tier 2	Tier 3
Oracle	abas	Consona
SAP	CDC Software	exact Americas
Microsoft AX	Epicor	Expandable
	Fujitsu	SYSPRO
	Infor	Microsoft NAV
	NetSuite	SAP Business All-in-One

Source: Ultra Consultants

Summary

An ERP system is an integrated business system that comprises modules that can be used to manage all business processes and data within an organization. These systems typically include modules for accounting, sales and distribution, inventory and purchasing, human capital management, manufacturing, and supply chain. Business professionals interact with ERP systems in various roles, including as end user, consultant, and auditor. Benefits of ERP systems include data integration, real-time access to information, standard business processes and interfaces, a shared data model, industry best practices, and reduced costs and increased revenue. Disadvantages of ERP systems include their high cost, time-consuming implementation, employee resistance, and the burden of constant maintenance and upgrades. The ERP market is a billion-dollar industry and is characterized by tier, which is a way to classify ERP software market characteristics. Companies interested in purchasing an ERP system should be aware of the many solutions available and pick one appropriate for their company size and industry as well as one that fits their business requirements.

Keywords

Application control	IT auditor
Back office system	Legacy system
Best practice	Manufacturing resource planning (MRP II) system
Business process	
Change agent	Material requirements planning (MRP) system
Change management	Module
Core competency	Process-centered
Core ERP	Small- to medium-sized enterprise (SME)
Cross-functional	
Enterprise resource planning (ERP) system	Tier
	Tier 1 ERP vendor
Enterprise space	Tier 2 ERP vendor
Extended ERP	Tier 3 ERP vendor
Industry solution	Vertical solution
Integration partner	

Quick Review

1. True/False: A best practice is a business process that is generally recognized as more effective and/or efficient than others in a particular industry.

2. True/False: ERP systems evolved from customer relationship management systems.

3. True/False: A business process is a collection of activities that together add value to the company.

4. ERP systems are sold in _____, or groups of related programs performing a major function within the system, such as accounting or manufacturing.

5. ERP software for a particular industry is known as a(n) _____ solution.

Questions to Consider

1. What is an ERP system?

2. How are ERP systems different from legacy systems?

3. What are advantages of ERP systems? Disadvantages?

4. How do ERP systems support industry best practices?

5. What are the differences among the three tiers that describe the ERP market?

References

Aptean. (n.d.). Enterprise resource planning (ERP) software is usually packaged in functional "pieces" that can be implemented in various combinations. Retrieved from http://www.aptean.com/en/Solutions/By-Application-Area/Enterprise-Resource-Planning-ERP/Resources-Folder/ERP-Software-Modules

Markus, L., Tanis, C., & Van Fenema, P. (2007). *Multisite ERP implementations.* Communications of the ACM, *43*(4), 42–46.

NetSuite Inc. (n.d.). What is ERP? Retrieved from http://www.netsuite.com/portal/resource/articles/erp/what-is-erp.shtml

Oracle Inc. (n.d.). Oracle industry solutions. Retrieved from http://www.oracle.com/us/industries/index.html

Plex Online. (n.d.). Ten critical questions to ask a manufacturing ERP vendor. Retrieved from http://www.plex.com/wp-content/uploads/2012/05/10Q.pdf

SAP. (2013). *Investor relations: Business in brief.* Retrieved from http://www.sap.com/about/investor/inbrief/index.epx

Sarva, S. (2012). Laying the foundation for ERP implementation success. Retrieved from http://www.theiia.org/intAuditor/itaudit/archives/2008/june/laying-the-foundation-for-erp-implementation-success/

Taylor, E. (n.d.). MRP vs. MRP II. Houston Chronicle. Retrieved from http://smallbusiness. chron.com/mrp-vs-mrpii-15365.html

Ultra Consultants. (n.d.). ERP vendors. Retrieved from http://www.ultraconsultants.com/erp-vendors/erp-vendors/

Wailgum, T. (2008, April 17). ERP definitions and solutions. Retrieved from http://www.cio.com/article/40323/ERP_Definition_and_Solutions

Chapter 2

ERP Technology

Objectives

- Understand the evolution of ERP architecture

- Become familiar with relational database terminology, database relationships, and types of data stored in databases

- Distinguish between customization and configuration of ERP software

- Understand the ERP system landscape

- Identify criteria for choosing between on-premise and cloud computing

- Recognize ERP mobility issues

Introduction

The broad scope of ERP systems impacts users throughout an organization and extends to its customers, suppliers, and business partners. As the core of an enterprise's business systems, an ERP system must be available to users and function properly without unscheduled service outages. Operations can quickly shut down with disastrous results if the ERP system is not accessible. Upgrades, patches and fixes, configuration changes, server maintenance, and interfaces between systems must be addressed throughout the system's life cycle. Supporting hundreds or thousands of simultaneous users with various processing and reporting requirements demands sophisticated and flexible software supported by state-of-the-art technology. Since the information processing needs of an organization depend on its ERP system, understanding the technology supporting this comprehensive, integrated system is critical. To fully explain the complexity of ERP systems, this chapter begins with the technical evolution of modern ERP systems, including three-tier client-server architecture. Next, we review theory on relational databases, as this is where the data accessed by ERP systems is stored. This section is followed by a discussion of configuration versus customization of ERP systems. Finally, this chapter explores issues surrounding ERP system deployment, including cloud computing and mobility.

Evolution of ERP Architecture

Mainframe Architecture

In Chapter 1, we discussed legacy systems, or older information systems that may not easily "talk" to each other. These systems are typically not based on current industry best practices and instead are "stove-piped," meaning they focus on a certain functional area, versus being cross-functional. For example, a "sales system" might not talk to the "accounting system"—thus the order-to-cash process becomes fragmented. Furthermore, customer data will likely need to be input into both systems, creating data redundancies and potential discrepancies.

Most legacy systems are built upon **mainframe architecture**, meaning that all computing intelligence resides within a central host computer that processes data and displays the output on "dummy terminals," or workstations with little to no processing power. Users interact with the mainframe computer through a character-oriented terminal that captures keystrokes and sends the data to the host computer. Mainframes have been around since the mid-1960s, and until the 1990s, they provided the only adequate means of handling the data processing requirements of large businesses. Some companies still maintain legacy systems built upon mainframe architecture.

Client-Server Architecture

In the early 1990s, with the broad adoption of personal computing, client-server computing emerged as an alternative to mainframe computing. **Client-server computing** is a computing model in which tasks and workloads are partitioned between the **client**, which makes service requests, and the more powerful **server**, which responds to the requests. These requests, along with the responses to requests, are performed over a network (see Figure 2-1). The server is often called the back-end application, and the client is called the front-end application; together they form a **two-tier architecture**. Many ERP vendors use this terminology for their client software. For instance, SAP's client is called the "SAP Front End." This type of computing model is known as **distributed computing** because it consists of multiple software components on multiple computers that together run as a single system.

Figure 2-1: Two-Tier Client-Server Architecture

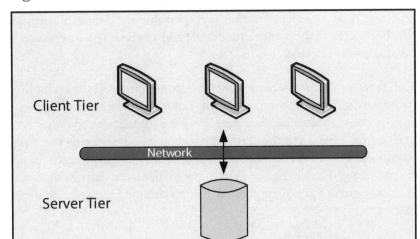

The sharing of processes between the client and the server is the foundation for defining thin and fat clients (and thin and fat servers). Figure 2-2 demonstrates two options for client-server architecture. Option 1 shows a fat client/thin server arrangement. A **fat client** handles presentation logic and business logic. **Presentation logic** is the software logic that displays data to the user and accepts input from the user. This type of logic manages the user navigation experience through a **graphical user interface (GUI)** so that the user can interact with the computer through icons, drop-down lists, and menus. **Business logic** specifies how business transactions are processed and what data needs to be accessed from the data storage device. This component also validates the data, applies the majority of the business rules, such as a mandatory credit check on a customer, and manages communication between the GUI and the data access logic. The **data access logic** refers to the communication with the database, which is responsible for data storage and retrieval on the physical storage device.

Figure 2-2: Options for Two-Tier Client-Server Architecture

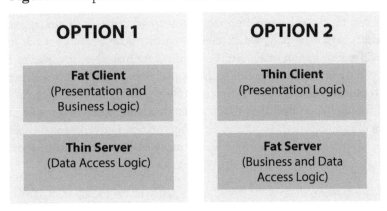

Source: N. Kale

Option 2 shows an alternative for client-server architecture. In this scenario, a **thin client** handles only the presentation logic, and the fat server is responsible for the both business logic and data access logic. In short, a fat client is more functional and requires less interaction with the server, while a thin client does the opposite.

An advantage of client-server architecture is that it becomes practical for multiple clients to update data simultaneously. Client-server computing also improves the security of data since users are unable to change or delete data unless they have specific authorization to do so. Also, the workload is distributed among the clients and the server; by scaling the server to be more powerful than the client, many clients (users) can access the server at one time. By giving each employee a personal computer and centralizing data on the server, two-tier architecture extends more computing power to end users. This advance in technology created the opportunity for hundreds of new ERP vendors to enter the market.

Three-Tier Client-Server Architecture

Although an improvement over mainframe technology, client-server architecture still could not meet the increasing demands for access to information. The overhead of maintaining the connections between the clients and the server limited the number of clients that could access the server. In addition, when every client machine contains applications (see Option 1), it is critical that all client computers run exactly the same software version. These problems were solved with **three-tier client-server architecture**, which places one or more application tiers between the client tier and the data access tier (see Figure 2-3). Each tier only contains code that belongs in that layer. Therefore, the presentation logic resides in the presentation tier, the business logic in the application tier, and the data access logic in the database tier. In the early 1990s, SAP, the leading ERP vendor, based its SAP R/3 version on three-tiered architecture. The "R" refers to real-time computing and the "3" denotes the three tiers.

Both two-tier and three-tier architectures have their relative advantages. For instance, two-tier applications are easier to build and, because of their lower complexity, are cheaper to deploy. However, when the system uses the internet, the performance of two-tier architecture can suffer. Because more data has to be transferred to the client in a two-tier system, the speed of the network and the hardware can have a substantial impact on the performance of the application. Three-tier architecture provides better security, which can be enforced uniquely for each tier if the security requirements are different. Maintenance on the architecture may also be easier in three-tier systems since the architecture separates responsibility into loosely coupled layers. Each tier can only receive requests from and return requests to certain tiers as shown in Figure 2-3. Because of this separation of responsibility, maintenance becomes more understandable and manageable. The database can also be changed without affecting the client. Possibly the main advantage to three-tier architecture is its scalability, as servers and clients can be added more easily as the business grows.

Figure 2-3: Three-Tier Architecture

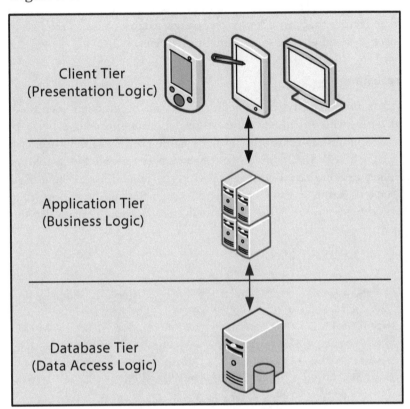

Relational Database Management Systems

Before ERP systems, when business data was supported by legacy systems, data was often duplicated. For instance, imagine a scenario in which sales, marketing, and accounting departments have separate systems, each needing customer data. This situation gives rise to any number of complications. For example, when a customer's address changes, the new information must be changed in each system, which takes time and is costly and error prone.

ERP systems use **relational database management systems (RDBMS)** to store enterprise data. Since data is only entered once and shared across departments and business units, the potential for errors and data duplication is reduced. Modern RDBMS provide many features, including transaction mechanisms to enable concurrent access of the database, stored procedures to enforce business logic, and security to limit access to parts and/or features of the database.

Many companies make the choice of an RDBMS to use with their ERP systems based on licensing concerns as databases have different annual maintenance costs. For instance, an Oracle database can be more expensive than other databases. However, large enterprise customers will typically choose

IBM DB2 or Oracle since the performance is better, the offerings are more mature, and the size and scale of the database are much larger. Small and mid-sized companies more often choose Microsoft SQL Server. Other factors that can affect a company's database choice are previous experiences with and allegiances to certain database vendors or platforms.

Database Terminology

In an RDBMS, data on an **entity**, or something that can be uniquely identified, is stored in a two-dimensional **table**, which is a collection of related data entries consisting of columns and rows. Tables are also known as **relations**, thus the name "relational database." Figure 2-4 shows a simplified view of a SUPPLIER table. A **field**, which is represented by a column in the table, is designed to maintain certain data about every row in the table. Fields define the items of data a user will input, such as Name or Pay_Terms. The rows in the table represent **records**, which are groupings of related fields. In the figure below, each record would contain data fields related to a particular supplier.

Figure 2-4: Supplier Database Table

SUPPLIER

Supplier_No PK	Name	Street	City	State	Phone	Pay_Terms
101023	High Tower Inc.	444 West St.	Raleigh	NC	(919) 338-8783	2/10 Net 30
103486	Paper Are Us	2865 Highway 70	Durham	NC	(919) 937-2124	2/10 Net 30
106555	Downton Smith	1 Peachtree St.	Atlanta	GA	(404) 768-4442	Net 30
109444	Office Stuff Co.	47 Lee St.	Austin	TX	(512) 473-9900	1/10 Net 30

Entity Integrity Rule

When designing a database, each record must be identified by a unique attribute, known as the **primary key (PK)**. Primary keys are usually a type of code, either numeric or alphanumeric. In the table above, the Supplier_No must be unique for every row, identifying a supplier and the data associated with that supplier. Databases enforce the unique identifier for each record, a rule known as the **entity integrity rule**. This rule also requires that the PK not be empty, or null. A common practice in databases is for the RDBMS to assign the next sequential value for a primary key when a new record is inserted into a table. That way we know that each primary key will be unique.

Table Relationships

Where a relationship between two tables exists, the tables are connected with fields in common. For example, a SUPPLIER table and a PURCHASE_ORDER table are related in that each purchase order must be associated with a supplier. Therefore, we can add the Supplier_ID field to the PURCHASE_ORDER table to show that the two tables have a relationship. Doing so will allow users to run reports and queries on both tables together. When one table, such as the PURCHASE_ORDER table, includes a field that points back to a PK in another table, such as the Supplier_ID in the SUPPLIER table, that field is known as a **foreign key (FK)**. It is called "foreign" because it points to a PK in a different, or foreign, table and establishes and enforces a link between the data in the two tables.

An off-the-shelf ERP system from a Tier 1 vendor could easily have 100,000 tables. That's a lot of tables! Compare this to building a typical Microsoft Access database, which might consist of a dozen or so tables. As discussed, tables in an RDBMS are connected through the common data elements of primary and foreign keys. Where the database designer identifies a relationship between tables, the common keys are connected by the database software's internal programming.

An **entity relationship diagram (ERD)** is a graphical representation reflecting the database entities and the relationships among those entities. The ERD diagram is most often used as the method for communicating between database designers and end users when developing databases. In database terminology, a relationship is called a **cardinality**, and it indicates the number of occurrences (none, one, or many) of an entity in relation to another entity. Listed below are the three types of relationships in a RDBMS and an example ERD for each.

One-to-Many Relationship – In this type of relationship, each record of one table can be associated with zero, one, or many records in another table. These relationships are very common in databases. Consider the two tables: SUPPLIER and PURCHASE_ORDER. We could have zero purchase orders, one purchase order, or many purchase orders associated with a certain supplier. However, a particular purchase order must be associated with only one supplier. Hence, the relationship is a one-to-many with the "one" side of the relationship being the supplier and the "many" being the purchase order. In one-to-many relationships, the PK of the "one" side of the relationship becomes the FK in the "many" side of the relationship (not vice versa). The "crow's foot" notation is commonly used to represent the "many" side of the relationship. See Figure 2-5 for an example of a one-to-many relationship. Notice that there are two purchase orders for supplier number 101023, but that the supplier is only listed in the SUPPLIER table once. Notice the two vertical lines on the "one" side of the relationship. This means that each purchase order is associated with a minimum of one and a maximum of one supplier. The circle at the end of the line on the inside means that a supplier could have zero purchase orders associated with it. This generally means that suppliers could be added into the ERP system database without purchases made to them yet.

Figure 2-5: One-to-Many Relationship

SUPPLIER

Supplier_No PK	Name	Street	City	State	Phone	Pay_Terms
101023	High Tower Inc.	444 West St.	Raleigh	NC	(919) 338-8783	2/10 Net 30
103486	Paper Are Us	2865 Highway 70	Durham	NC	(919) 937-2124	2/10 Net 30
106555	Downton Smith	1 Peachtree St.	Atlanta	GA	(404) 768-4442	Net 30
109444	Office Stuff Co.	47 Lee St.	Austin	TX	(512) 473-9900	1/10 Net 30

PURCHASE_ORDER

Purchase_Order_No PK	Order_Date	Delivery_ Date	Total_Cost	Supplier_No FK
100	2/10/2015	2/20/2015	$644.31	101023
101	2/28/2015	3/2/2015	$76.80	101023
102	3/5/2015	3/16/2015	$398.00	106555

One-to-One Relationship – In this type of database relationship, each record in the first table is associated with only a maximum of one occurrence in the second table, and each record in the second table is associated with a maximum of one occurrence in the first table. Thus, one-to-one relationships are single-valued in both directions. These relationships are not nearly as common as one-to-many relationships, but they do occur. The key criterion of the possible need for a one-to-one relationship is a table that contains a field that is only used for a certain subset of the records in that table. In Figure 2-6, an employee can only have one parking permit and a parking permit goes with only one employee. Also, an employee does not have to have a parking permit (he or she could ride a bike to work!) thus the circle (zero) to show the minimum occurrence on the line next to Employee_No FK in the PARKING_PERMIT table. The relationship can be assigned to either the EMPLOYEE table or the PARKING_PERMIT table, but because not all employees have parking permits, it makes sense to put the Employee_No in the PARKING_PERMIT table (not vice versa).

Figure 2-6: One-to-One Table Relationship

PARKING_PERMIT

Permit_No *PK*	Parking_Lot	Employee_No *FK*
133459	Dan Allen Deck	000976533
133460	Brooks Lot	000676371
133461	McKimmon	000222277

EMPLOYEE

Employee_No *PK*	First_Name	Last_Name	Hire_Date
000976533	James	Edwards	6/7/2004
000764736	Florence	Henderson	5/22/2008
000676371	Mary	Bradford	11/10/2009

Many-to-Many Relationship – In this relationship, which is more complicated than the others, a record in one table is associated with more than one record in a second table *and* a record in the second table is associated with more than one record in the first table. Consider two tables: INVENTORY and PURCHASE_ORDER. An inventory item can be on many different purchase orders, and a purchase order can have many different types of inventory on it. The result is a many-to-many relationship. In relational databases, direct many-to-many relationships between tables are not allowed. To handle a many-to-many relationship, a separate table, called an **associative entity** (or **junction table**), separates the many-to-many relationship into two one-to-many relationships. Each record in the associative entity table contains FKs from the two tables it joins. Together, these two FKs become the PK in the associative entity in order to make each record unique. These two fields together are called a **concatenated key**, or **composite key**. Figure 2-7 illustrates this idea with an associative entity table called LINE_ITEM that represents the line items of purchase orders. The concatenated key in the LINE_ITEM table is Purchase_Order_No and Inventory_No, which together are the PK of the LINE_ITEM table. Note that this new table allows purchase order #100 to contain two inventory items and two different purchase orders to contain black office chairs (Inventory_No 77889). Also, note that it is possible for an inventory item not to be associated with a purchase order.

Figure 2-7: Many-to-Many Table Relationship

PURCHASE_ORDER

Purchase_Order_No PK	Order_Date	Delivery_ Date	Total_Cost	Supplier_No FK
100	2/10/2015	2/20/2015	$644.31	101023
101	2/28/2015	3/2/2015	$76.80	101023
102	3/5/2015	3/16/2015	$398.00	106555

LINE_ITEM

Purchase_Order_No PK	Inventory_No PK	Quantity_ Ordered
100	33888	19
100	77889	3
101	33976	10
102	77889	2

INVENTORY

Inventory_No PK	Description	Unit_of_ Measure	Unit_ Cost	Quantity_on _Hand
33888	Pens Ball Point, Red	Box	$2.49	77
77889	Office Chair Black	Each	$199.00	14
33976	Universal Color Paper	Ream	$7.68	27

Referential Integrity Rule

The **referential integrity rule** is a database constraint that ensures that relationships between tables remain valid and consistent. When one table is linked to another table through a PK/FK, the concept of referential integrity dictates that you may not add a record to the table that contains the FK unless there is a corresponding PK in the linked table. This rule helps prevent user errors and results in a more accurate and useful database. For example, suppose that a PURCHASE_ORDER table includes a FK of Supplier_No that points to the Supplier_No, which is a PK in the SUPPLIER table. The referential integrity rule would prevent an end user from adding a new purchase order to the PURCHASE_ORDER table containing a Supplier_No that is not present in the SUPPLIER table. Referential integrity rules would also guarantee that changes cannot be made to the Supplier_ No PK in the SUPPLIER table if those changes invalidate the link to the Supplier_No FK in the PURCHASE_ORDER table. In other words, any attempt to delete a row in the SUPPLIER table or to change the Supplier_No value will fail if the deletion or changed PK value affects the PURCHASE_ORDER table through the Supplier_No FK. To successfully change or delete a row in a SUPPLIER table, you must also change the Supplier_No in the PURCHASE_ORDER table or delete the record in the PURCHASE_ORDER table. A properly normalized RDBMS, discussed next, also produces a more accurate and useful database.

Database Normalization

Database designers employ a sophisticated process called **database normalization** to structure fields and tables in a database. The normalization process involves eliminating redundant data and ensuring that data dependencies make sense by storing only related data in a table. The overall goal of normalization is to isolate data so that additions, deletions, and modifications to a field are made only in one table and then propagated throughout the rest of the database through relationships. There are multiple rules for normalizing a database, although only the first three rules will be discussed in this text. Each new rule enforces the preceding rules and applies stricter guidelines to the design of tables. When the first rule is followed, the database is in "first normal form (1NF)" and so on.

First Normal Form

First normal form (1NF) deals with the "shape" of a record type. Under 1NF, all records must contain the same number of fields, there must be no repeating groups, and no one field (column) can contain multiple values. Although the STUDENT table below does not contain variability in the number of fields, and fields do not contain multiple values, it is not normalized because there are repeating groups for Subjects.

STUDENT DATA (Not Normalized)

Student_No	L_Name	Age	City	Subjects	State	Zip_Code
049658	Bradford	22	Raleigh	Accounting	NC	27608
				IT		
764300	Goolsby	20	Raleigh	Graphic Design	NC	27609
875893	Keller	24	Cary	Spanish	NC	27511
				Accounting		

The STUDENT table below is in 1NF because every field contains one value, we have eliminated the nulls in fields by making sure each repeating group attribute contains an appropriate data value, and all records have the same number of fields. Additionally, we can identify a PK. In this example, the PK must be a concatenated PK comprising Student_No and Subject fields so that each row is unique. Generally, names are not used as PKs.

STUDENT

Student_No PK	L_Name	Age	City	Subject PK	State	Zip_Code
049658	Bradford	22	Raleigh	Accounting	NC	27608
049658	Bradford	22	Raleigh	IT	NC	27608
764300	Goolsby	20	Raleigh	Graphic Design	NC	27609
875893	Keller	24	Cary	Spanish	NC	27511
875893	Keller	24	Cary	Accounting	NC	27511

Second Normal Form

In **second normal form (2NF)**, the table is in 1NF, and all fields refer to or describe a PK value. If the PK is based on more than one field, each non-key field must depend on the whole of the PK, not just one field of the PK, a situation known as a **partial dependency**. Each non-key field that doesn't support the entirety of the PK should be moved to another table. In the 1NF table above, Subject does not depend on Student_No so we need to pull this field out and put it in its own table. We make this new table to eliminate the partial dependency. The Subject and Student_ No fields together must comprise the PK of the SUBJECT table to make each record unique.

STUDENT

Student_No PK	L_Name	Age	City	State	Zip_Code
049658	Bradford	22	Raleigh	NC	27608
764300	Goolsby	20	Raleigh	NC	27609
875893	Keller	24	Cary	NC	27511

SUBJECT

Subject PK	Student_No PK
Accounting	049658
IT	049658
Graphic Design	764300
Spanish	875893
Accounting	875893

Third Normal Form

In **third normal form (3NF)**, the database table meets 2NF requirements and every non-key field is dependent only on the PK. In the STUDENT table above, the address fields of City and State are dependent not on Student_No, but on Zip_Code. This leads to a situation called a **transitive dependency**, in which one or more fields in a table are not dependent on the PK, but are instead dependent on another value in the record, known as a **determinant**. Thus, these fields must be moved to another table. In our example, City and State will be moved to a new table, and the PK of the new table is the determinant, Zip_Code.

STUDENT

Student_No PK	L_Name	Age	Zip_Code FK
049658	Bradford	22	27608
764300	Goolsby	20	27609
875893	Keller	24	27511

ZIP_CODE

Zip_Code PK	City	State
27608	Raleigh	NC
27609	Raleigh	NC
27511	Cary	NC

Structured Query Language (SQL)

The special purpose programming language for communicating with an RDBMS is called **Structured Query Language (SQL)**. ERP end users need not understand the specifics of SQL because the language is hidden from them. SQL is actually being issued when the end user interacts with the ERP system through the GUI. However, it is important to understand what is happening behind the scenes.

The most common operation in SQL is the query. **Queries** are user requests for information from the database. The RDBMS is responsible for planning, optimizing, and performing the physical operations necessary to produce the query result. In SQL, a query is performed using the SELECT statement. The SELECT statement retrieves data from one or more tables. The basic SELECT statement is as follows:

```
SELECT column1, column2 ...

FROM TABLENAME

WHERE condition
```

Using this syntax, we can write a simple query to obtain information from the INVENTORY table in Figure 2-7:

```
SELECT Inventory_No, Quantity_on_Hand

FROM INVENTORY

WHERE Unit_Cost > 100
```

This query would return the below:

Inventory_No	Quantity_on_Hand
77889	14

There are many more SQL commands, but an in-depth discussion is outside the scope of this book, which is intended not for programmers but for end users of ERP systems.

ERP Data

ERP systems store three main types of data: master, transaction, and configuration. The first type, **master data**, is relatively permanent data collected on entities in the business. These entities are the critical nouns in the organization and generally fall into four groupings: people, things, places, and concepts. Examples of master data reflecting the four groupings include data describing employees, inventory items, departments, and licenses. Although master data remains fairly stable over time, it can be changed.

Transaction data are the records of day-to-day business events. While master data is not volatile and rarely changes its attributes, transaction data is highly volatile. Examples of transaction data include purchase orders, sales invoices, and payroll disbursements. For instance, the PURCHASE_ ORDER table would need master data from the SUPPLIER and INVENTORY tables in order to determine who the order goes to and what items are on the order.

A third type of data in ERP systems is **configuration data**. This type of data enables a company to tailor a particular aspect of the ERP system to the way it chooses to do business. For example, an organization can select its fiscal year end, default currency, and default language from various options allowed by the ERP system. Configuration data also includes setting up enterprise structural details such as number and type of plants, sales organizations, warehouses, and distribution channels.

Configuration

An advantage of ERP software is that it is inherently flexible—customers have choices as to how the software works. Because of this flexibility, ERP vendors can sell the same package to many companies by accommodating configuration options in operations, allowing them to expand their market and cut unit costs. **Configuration** is the process of selecting parameters that enable a company to tailor a particular aspect of the system to the way it chooses to do business. System integrators or members of the project team with knowledge of the ERP system will configure the system during implementation. The configuration options that are chosen are stored as configuration data in configuration tables.

To illustrate configuration, a screenshot of NetSuite, a popular cloud-based ERP vendor for small to medium-sized enterprises (SMEs), is shown in Figure 2-8. The screen shows the configuration of accounting preferences. Notice that when a customer orders over the approved credit limit, the ERP system will just "warn" sales personnel. However, NetSuite can be configured to "enforce holds," which would prevent a sale to a customer if the sale causes the accounts receivable balance to go over the credit limit. Other configurable options on this screen include using reversing entries for audit trail purposes instead of voiding entries, and allowing (or disallowing) journal entries in closed accounting periods. The options on the screen are examples of configuration because they change the way the ERP software behaves within the bounds of what is allowed.

Figure 2-8: NetSuite Accounting Preferences

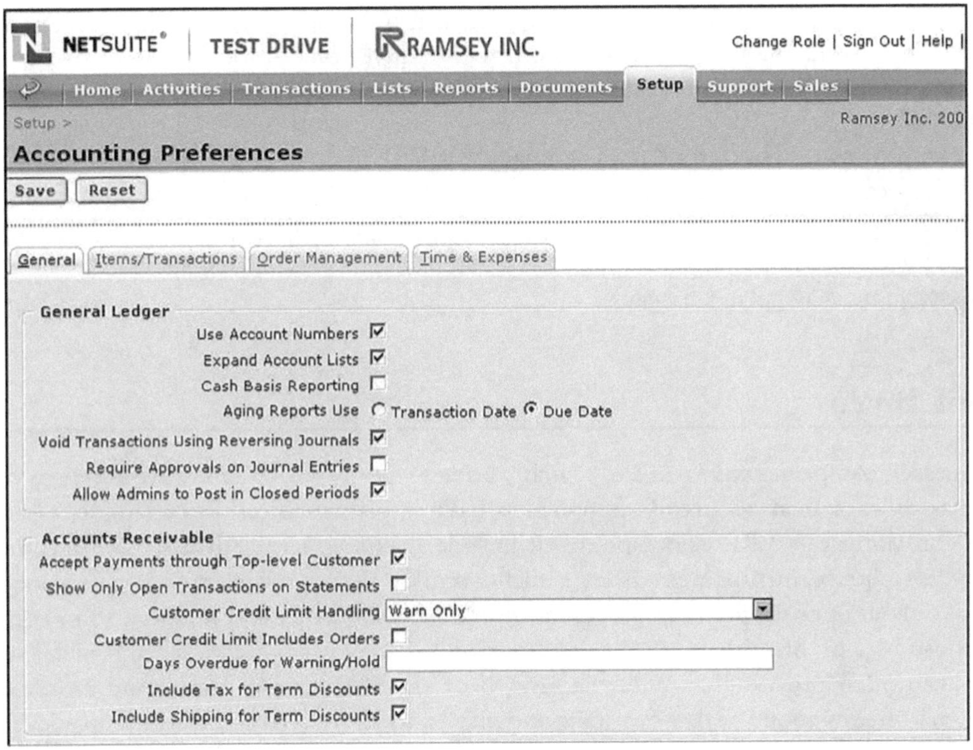

Customization

It's rare that an ERP system's processes, screens, fields, and reports meet a company's requirements completely—especially if the company is a large multinational with complex operations. Issues often arise that fall outside the bounds of what the ERP software will allow a company to do through configuration. These issues include:

- A missing field

- A missing form

- The need to link two tables that are not currently linked

- A missing step in a workflow

- A missing piece of functionality

These issues would typically involve customization by someone with programming expertise. **Customization** is the process of fitting the ERP software to the specific needs of the organization by adding code to the ERP software. Customization is typically done when all attempts to find a solution through configuration have been exhausted. Since customization involves employing experienced programmers, which costs money and takes time, it should be kept to a minimum. For instance, SAP is written in a programming language called ABAP (Advanced Business Application Programming). Companies that need to customize their SAP solution will need to hire experienced ABAP programmers to write the code.

Larger companies are more prone to customize their ERP systems than are smaller companies—most likely because of three reasons: 1) they have the technical expertise to program and maintain the code, 2) they have the monetary resources to fund customizations, and 3) their operations are more complex or unique, thus warranting a deviation from standard ERP code. ERP customization is discussed in more detail in Chapter 6.

Best of Breed

In some cases, companies will "mix and match" modules from various enterprise software vendors, in what is called a **best of breed** approach to ERP implementation. For example, a retail and distribution company's ERP landscape might include PeopleSoft for HR, SAP for all other core modules, warehouse management from a niche vendor that provides warehouse management solutions only (as opposed to a full ERP solution), and a cloud-based CRM solution. Some companies may choose best of breed because they are looking for lower-cost solutions, and niche software vendors can often provide this. With the growth of the SME market, more and more software vendors are offering modules that can "plug and play" into ERP systems. Other companies may opt for a best of breed systems strategy for the promise of differentiation. They employ this approach in order to obtain (what they consider to be) the overall best combination of systems that will set them apart from their competitors. Generally speaking, if the company chooses this route, it's best to only purchase best of breed solutions that support competitive business practices.

However, the promise of differentiation should be weighed heavily against the inevitable integration issues. Modules from various vendors will have to "talk to each other." Sometimes this is easily done, but other times companies must develop or purchase middleware. **Middleware** is software that facilitates sharing data and business logic across systems and requires a certain degree of IT support to set up and maintain. Deciding on a systems strategy is complicated, and unfortunately, there is not a "right answer." It's important to have an information systems strategy in place that looks at all available options, including best of breed. This strategy should take into account the overall business strategy and existing information systems and consider costs, risks, and projected business benefits. Figure 2-9 outlines the pros and cons of the best of breed strategy.

Figure 2-9: Pros and Cons of a Best of Breed Strategy

Pros	Cons
Can result in cost savings since best of breed solutions might be less expensive than their ERP module counterpart	Can result in inconsistent information across departments
More opportunity for differentiation from competitors	Takes time to interface systems
Best of breed solution may have stronger, more in-depth functionality in certain areas	More time and resources spent on software selection, project management, and upgrades

Source: Panorama Consulting

System Landscape

The ERP software and database cannot be installed until a system landscape is in place. A system is an installation of ERP software and related components on a server or servers. This is also called an **instance**. The **system landscape** is the "layout" or "architecture" of the servers. To complete a system landscape, companies will purchase multiple servers and install the ERP system and database several times. Figure 2-10 shows a basic ERP system landscape, which is generally divided into at least three systems. The first system is called **development (DEV)**. In the DEV environment, the ERP system is installed along with the database. It is in this environment that consultants configure and customize the system per the company's requirements. It is common to bring up the DEV system first so that work can begin on configuration and customization as quickly as possible. As the entire system landscape is put into place, the DEV instance is retained for future configuration, customization, and maintenance activities during the life cycle of the ERP system.

At periodic intervals during implementation, the customizations and configurations for the various modules being implemented will be transported (copied) to another ERP environment called **quality assurance (QA)**. QA is where the customizations and configurations will be tested by end users or members of the project team during implementation. After the end users and team sign off on the changes in QA, the configurations and customizations of the system are transported to **production (PRD)**, which will be the live system users will work with. Mature organizations that run an ERP system may also have dedicated environments for training, post-production support, disaster recovery, or data conversion. As well, there may be multiple **sandboxes**, which are areas in the DEV environment where members of the implementation team will explore configuration and customization options.

Figure 2-10: ERP System Landscape

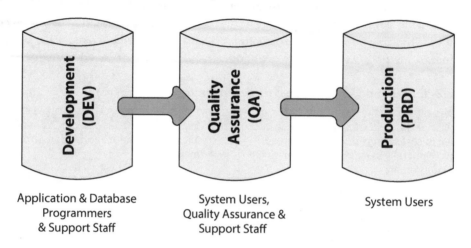

Application & Database Programmers & Support Staff | System Users, Quality Assurance & Support Staff | System Users

While organizations benefit from the simplicity of having just one production system, the reality is often quite different. Sometimes, when a company is geographically dispersed or operates as a number of distinctly autonomous business units, separate environments for the ERP software are required. For example, a global company may determine that they cannot use the same ERP system configured and customized for locations in both the U.S. and China, so they maintain totally separate environments for each country. However, ERP experts will suggest that when separate environments emerge it can mean that: 1) there is a problem with the design, execution, or management of global processes; 2) the system is going to be really expensive and become fragmented quickly; or 3) another system change may be right around the corner.

Cloud Computing

The internet boom in the early 2000s and the earlier introduction of the web browser led to web-based computing. In this computing model, the data and the software code are hosted in a data center, and end users access applications through a web browser. The dramatic improvement in cost of ownership, ease of use, and convenience of web-based computing led many ERP companies to rethink and redevelop their products, much like they did when client-server architecture replaced mainframes.

Building on the tenets of web-based computing, cloud computing has emerged as the next paradigm shift in ERP systems. In **cloud computing,** the ERP system and associated data are managed centrally (in the internet "cloud") by the ERP vendor or a third-party service provider and are accessed by the customer on demand. ERP customers don't have to invest in or upgrade their servers, operating systems, databases, data centers, backup equipment, or programming environments. All the relevant data and applications are stored and maintained remotely. Many of the traditional ERP vendors have now developed a version of their software for use in the cloud. Also, new ERP and best of breed vendors have emerged and are delivering their software only through the cloud. Some solutions, such as CRM, are typically delivered through the cloud.

In cloud computing, companies make periodic payments (usually monthly) to the vendor or service provider for the software, infrastructure, and maintenance. This remote delivery model, known as **software as a service (SaaS)**, makes it easier to budget for the ERP system, since the periodic payments are known in advance. In SaaS, it is important to negotiate a **service level agreement (SLA)** with the service provider. The SLA must spell out clearly what is being delivered, how the service level is to be measured and by whom, and what penalties will ensue if the service level is not met (for example, 99.6 percent uptime measured by standard X, else Y; downtime not to exceed Z in a certain number of months). The SLA is what really matters when outsourcing a mission critical application such as an ERP system.

Cloud computing can be contrasted with an **on-premise** ERP implementation, in which the ERP system is installed locally on a company's own servers. . Generally, larger companies and companies who have already adopted ERP have on-premise installations, as cloud computing has only recently become a popular means of using ERP. Companies that have on-premise ERP systems leverage their own IT resources and develop their own business process expertise versus depending on an outside organization to do this for them. Often, companies will choose an on-premise implementation when their business environment involves highly sensitive data, numerous application changes, and a large user base with rapidly-changing user demands.

Typically, ERP cloud deployments are much faster than on-premise because of the time saved in not having to procure and install the IT infrastructure. Cloud-based ERP systems are also easier to scale as a company grows and adds more employees; on-premise installations may not offer the flexibility to add many new users without adding additional hardware. Oftentimes, cloud deployments are less expensive than on-premise deployments. However, in a recent study, it was revealed that 60 percent of respondents said they only received between 0 percent and 20 percent cost savings, while the remaining 40 percent said they received more. Therefore, companies would be wise to estimate cash expenditures over a reasonable number of years when comparing cloud computing to the costs of an on-premise implementation. Figure 2-11 presents criteria for choosing between cloud and on-premise ERP solutions.

Figure 2-11: Cloud vs. On-Premise ERP Solution: How to Choose?

Cloud ERP	On-Premise ERP
Company does not want to invest or support an IT infrastructure for the ERP system; prefers to make predictable periodic payments	Company already has an ERP system in house
Upgrades and enhancements are the responsibility of the cloud-based vendor; customizations are automatically carried forward in an upgrade	Company needs a high-degree of customization and security is a concern
Company is in growth mode, but still wants to match internal costs against fluctuating business conditions	Company is well-established and can confidently make a five-year commitment to an ERP software investment
Company wants to be up and running quickly with minimal implementation time	Company is prepared to undergo a lengthy implementation process
Company has multiple sites or many geographic locations, but does not want to build or support remote access to an existing network	Company has multiple sites across geographic locations and has a supporting network infrastructure
Company may not have the resources and technical expertise in house for on-premise ERP	Company employs an experienced IT staff to maintain the ERP system
Company core competence is not maximum network performance and security	Maintaining an ERP system may not be a company's core competence but it will make it a priority
Company is not able to meet its desired uptime	Company is able to meet its desired uptime

Source: Sage Software Inc.

Mobility

Recently, there has been a push by ERP vendors toward mobile computing, or **mobility**, which refers to the ability to access data and information from a computing device wherever and whenever needed. The growth in mobility has been fueled by the growth of cloud-accessible software and the proliferation of faster and smarter phones and tablets, which an increasing number of businesses are providing to their employees as everyday work productivity tools. As the choices among tablets and smart phones expand, these devices will get smarter and cheaper, and mobile operating systems will multiply.

Mobility is increasingly being used for data entry points to ERP systems. However, not every task in an ERP system is appropriate for mobility. Companies should let strategy drive what modules and features would be suitable for mobile solutions before wide-scale deployment, keeping in mind the needs of the three key constituents for mobility use: employees, vendors, and customers. Generally, functionality for the ERP "on-the-go" or "occasional" user, who requires minimal data entry and display, makes more sense in a mobile format. This is why mobile ERP applications for time and expense reporting and sales-related activities such as contact management and order entry were among the first ERP mobile applications developed. Serving the needs of those outside the organization, while reducing costs and improving process speed, should also be considered. Thus, applications for improving customer self-service make sense in a mobile format. Companies need to consider mobile solutions that offer the advantage of ERP performance while maintaining flexibility, scalability, and a fully integrated end-to-end solution. If companies do not take the time to develop a purposeful mobile strategy before throwing money at applications and devices, they may incur costs and maintenance headaches without a clear return on investment.

A strategic approach to mobility should also include security concerns. Mobile devices can face a wide variety of threats, including inadequate technical controls and poor security practices among consumers. For example, users often do not configure passwords for their mobile devices. If the device is stolen or lost, there is the risk that sensitive data could be accessed by unauthorized users. Additionally, data sent over a Wi-Fi network using http (rather than https) is not encrypted, making it easy for the data to be intercepted. Additionally, mobile devices typically do not come loaded with security software, making the user vulnerable to malware such as viruses and spyware. Operating systems and applications for mobile devices may also be out of date. Although application developers may update their software to fix security vulnerabilities, it is up to the carriers to test and transmit the updates, which could take time. These security issues, plus more, should be carefully thought through before deploying mobile devices to use with ERP systems.

Summary

The technical environment of ERP systems has evolved from mainframe-based systems to two-tier client-server and then to three-tier client-server architecture, the latter consisting of the presentation, application, and database tiers. At the heart of the modern client-server system is the relational database management system in which data is stored in two-dimensional tables which are connected together through keys in common. The types of data stored in the database tables include master, transaction, and configuration data. Configuration data enables the ERP system to look and act a certain way. Companies might also choose to customize their ERP system to create a competitive advantage, but doing so is costly and time consuming and carries a certain amount of risk. Prior to implementation of the ERP system, a company should set up a system landscape, which consists of the ERP application and database on various servers, each providing a different function. Servers are generally set up for development purposes, quality assurance, and production, which is the live system. However, if a company chooses to use cloud computing, the vendor or a third-party provides the IT infrastructure, which oftentimes decreases implementation time and can be less costly overall. Mobility applications for ERP systems are fast becoming the norm, but companies should determine which tasks are appropriate for mobility and make sure that security concerns are addressed.

Keywords

Associative entity	Junction table
Best of breed	Mainframe architecture
Business logic	Many-to-many relationship
Cardinality	Master data
Client	Middleware
Client-server computing	Mobility
Cloud computing	On-premise
Composite key	One-to-many relationship
Concatenated key	One-to-one relationship
Configuration	Partial dependency
Configuration data	Presentation logic
Customization	Primary key (PK)
Data access logic	Production (PRD)
Database normalization	Quality assurance (QA)
Determinant	Query
Development (DEV)	Record
Distributed computing	Referential integrity rule
Entity	Relation
Entity integrity rule	Relational database management system (RDBMS)
Entity relationship diagram (ERD)	
Fat client	Sandbox
Field	Second normal form (2NF)
First normal form (1NF)	Server
Foreign key (FK)	Service level agreement (SLA)
Graphical user interface (GUI)	Software as a service (SaaS)
Instance	Structured Query Language (SQL)

System   Three-tier client-server architecture

System landscape   Transaction data

Table   Transitive dependency

Thin client   Two-tier architecture

Third normal form (3NF)

Quick Review

1. True/False: A concatenated key is a key that consists of two or more fields that together uniquely define a record.

2. True/False: A best of breed ERP solution is one that mixes and matches modules from more than one ERP vendor.

3. _____ is the industry term that means paying for software on a periodic basis.

4. The type of data in an ERP system that is the result of business events is known as _____ data.

5. _____ requires that programmers develop extra code to make the software perform in ways the vendor had not originally intended.

Questions to Consider

1. Explain the differences between mainframe and client-server architecture.

2. What are the advantages of storing data in a relational database?

3. What are the three types of database relationships? Give an example of each.

4. Discuss the advantages and disadvantages of customizing ERP software.

5. List reasons a company would want to employ cloud computing for its ERP system.

References

Aldrich, J. (2014, July 11) Is a best-of-breed ERP system right for your organization? Retrieved from http://panorama-consulting.com/is-a-best-of-breed-erp-system-for-you/

Basics of Computer.com. (2012). *Client server architecture*. Retrieved from http://basicofcomputer. com/ client_server_architecture.htm

Coronel, C., Morris, S., & Rob, P. (2013). Database systems: Design, implementation, and management. 10th ed. Boston, MA: Cengage Learning.

Cooney, M. (2012, September 21). 10 common mobile security problems to attack. Retrieved from http://www.pcworld.com/article/2010278/10-common-mobile-security-problems-to-attack.html

Ektron, Inc. (2011). Chapter 23 – Three-tier architecture. In *Ektron Reference Version 8.5, Doc. Rev. 2.0*. Retrieved from http://documentation.ektron.com/cms400/v85/webhelp/Developer85/ Architecture/ThreeTier_Intro.htm

Focus Research. (2012). *Focus experts' briefing: ERP in the age of mobility*. Retrieved from http://www.inside-erp.com/research/erp-in-the-age-of-mobility-26997?mid=&tfso=13718&r=B2B RegMailingCS

Howitz, C. (n.d.) What is 3-tier (multi-tier) architecture and why do you need it? [SimCrest Round Table Blog]. Retrieved from http://blog.simcrest.com/what-is-3-tier-architecture-and-why-do-you-need-it/

Kale, N. (2013). ERP system and enterprise architecture. In *Readings on enterprise resource planning*. Retrieved from http://web.calstatela.edu/faculty/pthomas/CIS301/Nitin.pdf

Marston, T. (2012, October 14). What is the 3-tier architecture? Retrieved from http://www.tonymarston.net/php-mysql/3-tier-architecture.html

NetSuite. (n.d.). *How cloud ERP compares to on-premise ERP*. Retrieved from http://www.netsuite.com/portal/resource/articles/on-premise-cloud-erp.shtml

Panorama Consulting Solutions. (2013). *2013 ERP report*. Retrieved from http://panorama-consulting.com/resource-center/2013-erp-report/

Relevate SA. (2013). *Why customize your ERP?* Retrieved from http://www.revelate.com/products/revelate-erp/why-customize-your-erp

Sage Software Inc. (2011). On-demand or on-premise: understanding the deployment options for your business management system. Retrieved from http://norcalerp.com/wp-content/uploads/2013/12/sageerpsolutions-deployment_options_wp.pdf

Studytonight (n.d.). Normalization of database. Retrieved from http://www.studytonight.com/dbms/database-normalization.php

Syed, I. (2011, February 1). On premise vs. hosted ERP solution: How to choose. Retrieved from http://blog.sageerpsolutions.com/on-premise-vs-hosted-erp-solution-how-to-choose/

Taub, J. (2011, March 25). Understanding the mobile computing trends before moving forward. [ERP SoftwareBlog]. Retrieved from http://www.erpsoftwareblog.com/2011/03/understanding-the-mobile-computing-trends-before-moving-forward/

Wright, M. (2013, September 13). 2-tier vs. 3-tier application architecture? Could the winner be 2-tier? [Nitroblog]. Retrieved from http://www.nitrosphere.com/2013/09/20/2-tier-vs-3-tier-application-architecture-could-the-winner-be-2-tier-2/

ERP and Business Process Redesign

Objectives

- Be aware of goals for business processes

- Identify types of problems with business processes

- Compare and contrast business process improvement and business process reengineering

- Explain the relationship between business process reengineering and ERP

- Summarize the steps in business process improvement

Introduction

Modern companies face unbridled competition, rapid technological innovation, increased customer demands, and globalization. Firms that do well in this environment are those that optimize their business processes in pursuit of greater efficiency and customer value through the smarter use of human capital and technology. This chapter discusses two methods that organizations use to transform their business processes: business process reengineering and business process improvement. Business process reengineering entails radical, dramatic changes like those that take place during an ERP implementation. Incremental, gradual changes to processes, known as business process improvement, can also have a significant impact on the ongoing efficiency and effectiveness of an organization. Many companies use both techniques to make changes to their business processes over time. This chapter summarizes the body of knowledge surrounding business process reengineering and business process improvement. The goal of this chapter is to help the reader recognize issues with processes that can wreak havoc on productivity, efficiency, and customer value and identify steps that today's competitive companies take to overcome these problems.

Business Processes

A **business process** can be defined as a series of activities that are linked together to convert inputs into a product or service output. Business processes involve coordinated activities that serve a useful purpose and comprise people, procedures, technology, and infrastructure. Some processes constitute a firm's core operations, such as the provision of products or services to customers. Other processes provide a supporting role, such as those in accounting and human resources. Business processes can be simple or complex based on the number of steps or number of systems involved, and they can be short or long running, the latter involving multiple dependencies. Processes can also be formal or informal. Formal processes are documented and have well-defined steps. For example, a company might have documented processes for granting credit to customers or sourcing products. Informal processes are those that have been developed organically by employees and may not be written down. Formal processes are optimal for a variety of reasons. One advantage of formal processes is that employees can get work accomplished faster by following set processes and procedures, allowing managers to spend less time supervising. Formal processes can also improve the consistency of product and service delivery. Additionally, formal processes are important when there are legal or financial reasons for following particular steps. Finally, formal processes lead to accountability. If there are no rules, no one is held accountable, since there is no right or wrong way to do something. Without formal documented processes in place, inconsistencies in the way the process is executed could lead to negative outcomes for the organization and the customer.

However, just because a company may formalize its business processes does not mean those processes are best in class. An organization is only as effective as its business processes, so successful companies spend lots of time analyzing and optimizing their processes to meet the following criteria:

- Cost efficiencies – Processes should enable employees to get work accomplished faster, thereby reducing the cost of products and services while improving the firm's competitive advantage and profitability.

- Customer satisfaction and differentiation – Processes should help a company better serve its customers as well as provide clear and visible differentiation in the marketplace, thus protecting profit margins and pricing power.

- Standardization – Processes should be standardized across the organization wherever and whenever possible. Well-developed standards reduce errors and allow for more uniform interaction with customers, suppliers, and other business partners. Process standardization also makes it easier for new employees to learn and adapt to various work environments and tasks. Finally, standardization creates new opportunities for global process consolidation, referred to as **shared services**, or the provision of a service by one part of an organization or group where that service had previously been found in multiple parts of the organization or group. Today, most companies employ a shared services model for finance, human resources and information technology.

- Value-added activities – Processes should add value. A **value-added activity** typically has three characteristics: 1) It accomplishes something the customer cares about and is willing to pay for; 2) it converts, or physically changes, an input to an output; and 3) it is imperative that it is done right the first time.

- Improved agility and speed – Processes should be nimble so the company can anticipate, manage, and respond to changes in the marketplace.

Common Problems with Business Processes

Companies should be alert to problems with their business processes. When business processes go unchecked for any length of time, problems can emerge resulting in lost profits, skyrocketing costs, and poor customer service. During an examination of these processes, the answer to the question, "Why do we do that?" is often, "We've always done it that way." Obviously, this response is not ideal! Companies should always seek out ways to optimize their processes, especially as they grow, diversify, globalize, and try to remain competitive all at the same time.

Figure 3-1 presents a list of common problems with business processes. All of these issues involve non-value-added work and its ensuing costs and therefore are linked to the "bottom line." For example, downtime can result when a bottleneck stops the process flow. When workers are being paid with no resulting productivity, profits are lost. The last process issue, **segregation of duties** violations, relates to a company's **internal controls**, or policies and procedures put in place to safeguard the integrity of data and avoid risks. Although it might not seem that internal controls could affect profit, they can if an employee is allowed to have access to assets (for example, inventory) and, at the same time, maintains accountability for those assets. This lack of segregation of duties could enable the employee to steal from the company and cover it up.

Figure 3-1: Common Problems with Business Processes

Authority ambiguity	Having two or more people provide approval may be unnecessary, reeks of bureaucracy, and increases the cycle time of the process.
Bottlenecks	When a number of information flows lead to a single activity, the process may be hindered by insufficient resources dedicated to the roles and events downstream. Bottlenecks can limit the performance or capacity of the entire system, delaying or completely stopping the process.
Cycle time	The cycle time is the time consumed during the entire process flow; it should be at the heart of performance measurement, providing focus on the length of time the process takes from start to finish.
Data duplication	When multiple groups involved in a process begin maintaining their own separate information systems, variations of the same data often appear in multiple places.
Handoffs	The transfer of responsibility from one role to another creates the opportunity for mistakes, miscommunication, and delay.
Intermediaries	Words such as "pass it by me" include an intermediary and often an unnecessary step.
Manual steps	Technology and systems could be implemented in place of manual steps, which add to cycle time and create errors.
Old ways	Technology and systems are available but not used because employees have not been trained (or have been trained and do not want to use new systems). Employees revert to "the old ways of doing things."
Paper records	Storing data in electronic form is optimal since the data then becomes easier to share. Management should question whether the current process is adding, maintaining, or eliminating paper records.
Quality control	Quality control refers to the process of another person checking work rather someone checking his or her own work. Is the quality control really needed? Can the work be mistake-proofed to make it impossible for the defect to pass on? Prevention is better than detection.
Rework	Management should seek to minimize the necessity of spending time fixing errors or remediating problems by investigating the source of the errors and making modifications to the process to eliminate the potential for errors.
Role ambiguity	A lack of clarity about the expectations, norms, and behaviors associated with a particular job can lead to process inefficiencies.
Segregation of duties violations	Employees should not be in the position both to perpetrate and to conceal fraud. The activities in a process that should be segregated among employees include: 1) custody of assets, 2) authorization or approval of related transactions affecting those assets, and 3) recording or reporting of related transactions.

Source: M. Smith

Business Process Reengineering

In the 1990s, the term "business process reengineering" came into vogue as a result of a number of articles and bestselling books by Dr. Michael Hammer, whose major work was titled *Reengineering the Corporation: A Manifesto for Business Revolution*. **Business process reengineering (BPR)** is the fundamental, radical redesign of business processes that an organization undertakes to achieve breakthrough performance in key measures of cost, quality, speed, and service. It consists of the methods that companies use to transform their business processes in a major way. The ideas for BPR grew out of Hammer's research in the 1980s, when he noticed that a few high-profile global companies had drastically improved their performance. Upon further study, he discovered that these companies were not changing their **core competencies**—the capabilities critical to a business in achieving competitive advantage—but instead were optimizing their business processes in order to make them more efficient and customer-centric. These companies were successful at reducing process cycle times, mountains of paper, mistakes, and rework, as well as bringing out key knowledge held captive in desk drawers by individual workers.

How do we define radical change? One research study suggests that radical changes are those that result in excess of 60 percent improvement in key performance indicators; major changes are those that result in 30 to 60 percent improvement; and incremental changes are those that result in less than 30 percent improvement. This way of determining what "radical" means is somewhat arbitrary, but Hammer's meaning is clear: To be considered true reengineering, an organization must experience a breakthrough transformation. Two ways to accomplish BPR are clean slate reengineering and technology enabled reengineering.

Clean Slate Reengineering

Clean slate reengineering involves starting over from scratch and completely redesigning a process. This type of reengineering tends to foster innovation and creativity because the BPR team is typically burdened with fewer bounds and constraints. Asking, "If we had no limitations, what would this process look like?" encourages a free flow of ideas and can result in unique processes that can be difficult for competitors to imitate. The benefit of clean slate reengineering is that this creativity can result in a competitive advantage.

The current process being analyzed is called the **"as is" process**. Next, process designers will go through a learning process to create a vision for the future design of the new business process, known as the **"to be" process**. Michael Hammer proposed eight BPR principles that can be used to guide process designers in the development of a "to be" process (see Figure 3-2).

Figure 3-2: Business Process Reengineering Principles

BPR Principle	Description
Have those who use the output of the process perform the process	Reduce or eliminate handoffs
Empower workers	Give employees information so they can make decisions
Treat geographically dispersed resources as though they were centralized	Centralize data through a common database
Link parallel activities instead of integrating their results	Do not wait until the end of a process to merge results
Organize around processes, not tasks or functional areas	Use ERP systems, technology, and best practices
Use self-service so that employees and business partners can access information and perform routine tasks	Move costs and accountability for work to the beneficiary of the process and eliminate the need for interaction with a company representative
Put the decision point where the work is performed and build controls into the process	Use automated controls in the process and transfer the responsibility for checking from management to the worker
Capture information once and at the source	Enter data one time where it originates and then disperse it to those who need it

Source: M. Hammer

Once the "to be" process is developed, process designers will create a plan of action based on the gap between the "as is" and the "to be" processes, technologies, and structures. It is then a matter of implementing the proposed solution. Oftentimes, clean slate reengineering can result in recommendations to replace some or all of an organization's existing business systems. However, it is not until *after* the company has spent time redesigning one or more processes that it determines what system it needs. At that point, the company would search for a system that "brings to life" the proposed new processes.

An example of a company that underwent clean slate reengineering is Harley-Davidson. In the 1990s, it sought to reengineer its purchasing process. The BPR team surveyed purchasing personnel and found that 85 percent of their time was being spent on non-strategic activities such as reviewing inventory, expediting orders, and entering data. The goal was to have 70 percent of time spent on activities such as developing supplier relationships, analyzing supplier performance, and improving quality, cost, and timing measures. After nearly a year and a half of examining the "as is" process, they designed a completely new "to be" purchasing process. Only then did the company search for an ERP solution that could deliver the functionality it had envisioned. Harley-Davidson's purchasing process suffered from many of the process issues listed in Figure 3-1. Furthermore, many of Hammer's BPR principles in Figure 3-2 were used to dramatically transform the company's purchasing process.

Clean slate BPR does have some disadvantages. First, clean slate is very costly—usually only first movers in an industry and large companies with deep pockets can afford clean slate reengineering. Clean slate reengineering also requires that experts devote time to documenting processes, developing requirements, and creatively designing a superior process. Additionally, clean slate reengineering can take many months—if not years—to accomplish. And, this time frame just refers to the time spent in developing the new process. Applying technology to automate the new process—thus adding more efficiency—is an additional project on top of the process redesign.

Critics of reengineering point to the many clean slate failures of the 1980s and 1990s. The radical change forced on employees by top management was not always welcomed by employees with open arms, especially when many clean slate initiatives led to lost jobs. Often, CEOs or consultants hired to "fix" a company sought to improve short-term performance by quickly reducing headcount. In these cases, companies tried to gain cover for these headcount reduction efforts by calling them "reengineering," although these initiatives were really downsizing. Many true reengineering projects were therefore met with employee resistance, resulting in efforts that were politically challenging and ultimately risky.

The term "reengineering" has now been resurrected in the context of ERP system implementations. ERP systems evoke radical change and cannot be successfully implemented unless the company also drastically changes its business processes to match the best practices in the software. Now, reengineering generally refers to "technology enabled" reengineering.

Technology Enabled Reengineering

Instead of starting over from scratch, most companies today in need of radical change to their business processes embrace ERP systems and other technologies as the means for transformation. This form of reengineering is known as **technology enabled reengineering**—the technology enables the reengineering. Because the technology imposes constraints on the resulting business operations, this type of reengineering is also referred to as **constrained reengineering**, meaning that the information system's design "constrains" the process design.

When a company implements an ERP system, it is using technology enabled reengineering. The last thing a company should do is implement an ERP system and keep its old processes in place. Doing so would be analogous to "paving the cow paths," a euphemism that refers to using new technology to automate an old process. All you will wind up with is an expensive old process!

An advantage of technology enabled reengineering using ERP is that the system provides a roadmap for transformation by eliminating many of the difficult decisions required when designing processes from scratch. Also, since other companies have implemented the same system, the risk of whether the process designs are feasible is reduced. However, the fact that other companies have access to the same ERP system can also be a disadvantage. When many companies in an industry use the same ERP system, this situation can theoretically level the playing field. To combat this disadvantage, companies implementing ERP systems must make sure to keep unique processes that provide them with a competitive advantage even if doing so requires customizing the ERP system for these processes.

BPR and ERP share a central philosophy—both aim to reduce costs and improve customer satisfaction while increasing profits and stakeholder value. Both require changes to the way people work and to the processes organizations employ to achieve business goals. The key goal of both BPR and ERP is to break through functional silos toward a process orientation. Adopting ERP best practices requires fundamental changes in the way employees do their work and the way companies interact with their customers, suppliers, and business partners. Neither BPR nor ERP has a perfect record. Both efforts carry risks, as we've discussed. These risks should be acknowledged and addressed for a successful BPR/ERP initiative. Figure 3-3 shows the difference between clean slate and technology enabled reengineering.

Figure 3-3: Clean Slate versus Technology Enabled Reengineering

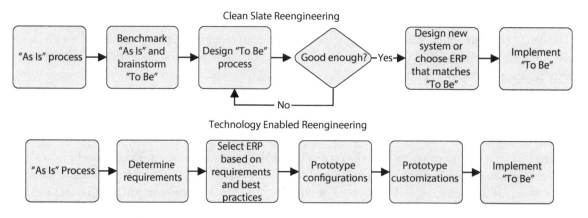

Factors for Reengineering Success

BPR requires sustained management commitment and leadership, a defined scope, managed expectations, and an alignment of rewards and recognition with the new business processes. Success also occurs more often when the dots are connected between a reengineered process and customer and shareholder value. Other factors leading to BPR success include:

- Scaling up and down – Processes redesigned in one division of a company should be able to work across the entire company. However, it should be noted that processes that suit a larger division might become a burden to a smaller division. For example, if a company has a small division and implements processes that support its largest division, those processes may burden the small division with license and operational support costs to the extent that the advantages of BPR are lost. In addition, the organization must plan for local regulatory requirements, often on a country-by-country basis.

- Thinking outside the functional box – If a company reengineers in silos, it tends to harden those silos, hindering subsequent BPR efforts and creating problems upstream or downstream. BPR techniques should be used to get rid of silos and instead focus on process.

- Looking at other companies for similar solutions to similar processes – Lessons learned from other companies could save time and money and help with setting budgets, plans, and expectations. While companies should not assume that they can copy another company's processes and get identical results, proven processes often eliminate a number of risks and uncertainties.

- Recognizing that a process is just one aspect of success – Employees and their capabilities, experience, adaptability, motivation, and values are important factors in success as well as marketplace realities and customer perceptions.

- Delivering sooner rather than later – According to Dr. Hammer, "There is no such thing as slow major change." If a project lacks momentum, it begins to lose credibility and employees become apathetic. Others will object, or worse, try to undermine the project's success. Setting and meeting short-term goals help to overcome this behavior by providing quick wins that can motivate those involved. Interim deliverables also provide a great opportunity for feedback and refinement.

- Considering the competition – Companies should factor the competition into their BPR plans and consider the following questions: Will the competition follow? Can they follow? How fast will they follow? Will they be able to do it better? Ideally, companies want to choose a vector that distances them so much from the competition that the competition has a difficult time following. If they do this, they will achieve competitive differentiation, which potentially means higher profit margins. However, the time will come when competitors do catch up. It is not a question of "if" but "when."

- Remembering the employee – If BPR is part of a cost-cutting initiative, there is a high probability that it will result in downsizing. According to research, BPR failures are often caused by paying insufficient attention to the human factor. Questions to consider regarding employees during a BPR initiative include:

  o If employees must be let go, will there still be the experience and capacity to continue without a hiccup? Will employees carry valuable corporate knowledge to competitors?

  o Will downsizing impact the loyalty of those who remain? Experience can be priceless—and so can loyalty. Can employee loyalty ever be regained once lost?

BPR is not the same as downsizing. Downsizing should only be considered after exploring ways to reassign employees to other parts of the organization. This is where understanding employee capabilities, experience, adaptability, motivation, and values becomes so important. Mishandling these issues will negatively impact morale and performance.

Business Process Improvement

Another method companies use to upgrade their business processes is called **business process improvement (BPI)**, which involves gradual improvement to business processes over time. Whereas BPR is radical and revolutionary, BPI is incremental and evolutionary. While BPR is necessary for a successful ERP implementation, BPI is simply not enough. The scope and intensity of a BPI project is much smaller than a BPR effort, but the goals are very similar: strive for business processes that are streamlined, standardized, and of superior quality in order to better serve customers, increase employee morale, and improve the company's ability to anticipate, manage, and respond to changes in the marketplace. A general rule is that if an existing process is somewhat close to expectations, maybe it can be improved. If not, then maybe the current process is fundamentally broken and radical change is necessary.

Companies use various methods to improve their processes, including Six Sigma, Lean Thinking, and Total Quality Management. Regardless of what methodology is used, the goals and objectives of a BPI initiative must be determined and expectations should be put in writing and communicated to all stakeholders involved. Similar to BPR, a BPI initiative takes time, resources, patience, and expertise, and the project should be organized with clearly defined roles. Figure 3-4 presents a general description of key roles for BPI and their primary responsibilities. Similar roles could also be used in a BPR initiative.

Figure 3-4: Organizational Roles for Business Process Improvement

Sponsors	Project Leaders/ Change Agents	Champions
Senior leaders who: • Sanction the business process work and the resulting outcomes • Align the key stakeholders • Create or support an environment that allows change to happen	The project members who: • Facilitate change • Provide support and expertise • Assist with identification of improvements	The members of the organization who: • Believe in the improvement project and demonstrate support in public • Reach out to personnel who do not support the change and try to influence them • Contribute expertise and experience

Source: The Frame Group

Business Process Improvement Model

Figure 3-5 presents a model for BPI. The first step is that an organization must identify specific goals and objectives of the business process improvement plan. A process improvement team should also be assembled, including project leaders, change agents, and champions. High-level sponsorship should also be obtained from senior leaders in the company. The next step is to compile a **process inventory**, which identifies key business processes in the organization, including their sub-processes and activities. Processes can be identified by reviewing the work done by departments, analyzing job descriptions, or talking to colleagues to ascertain their roles and responsibilities.

Figure 3-5: Business Process Improvement Model

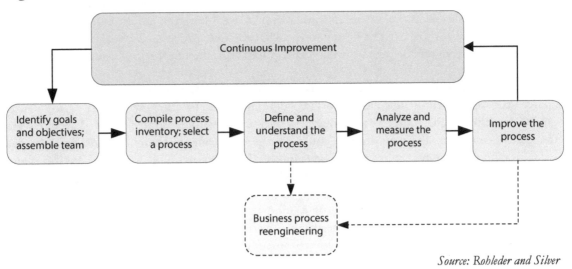

Source: Rohleder and Silver

From this process inventory, the BPI team can determine and prioritize a list of processes in need of change. Those processes that are core competencies, or customer facing, or will net the largest return if improved should be ranked first. The feasibility of making improvements to these processes should also be considered. Often, benchmarking with competitors can help determine those processes in need of improvement. As a result of these steps, the first process will be selected for improvement.

Next, the BPI team must obtain information about the process from process owners and experts. It is usually necessary to include knowledgeable sources from various departments for the complete view of a process. The team should also document the "as is" process so that everyone involved understands how the process currently works. The process documentation should include all activities, decisions, and resources required and should be verified with stakeholders to make sure it correctly reflects the existing process.

The next step is to analyze the process to pinpoint any problems. Figure 3-1 lists common process issues that can result in higher-than-necessary costs and long cycle times. The team should attempt to take current measurements of the process. It will be useful to again elicit feedback from users to make sure all problem areas are noted. Additionally, the organization should carefully consider potential benefits to be realized from improving the process.

Once the current process has been analyzed and measured, is it time to make improvements. The team should use brainstorming techniques, while challenging everything. New prototypes of process flows, policies and procedures, and reporting requirements should be developed. The team should also be aware of where mistakes can occur in the new process and design internal controls to prevent these errors. Team members should use technologies and tools to automate steps where appropriate and create new metrics to show if the process works as planned. When implementing changes, the team should have a communication plan in place. Managers, employees, and sometimes customers or suppliers will need to be reminded what the new process is, why it is needed, how things will be different and better, and what will happen when the new process is in operation.

Practicing the new process is one way to build a detailed understanding of how it will work. This practice scenario, which includes a step-by-step demonstration of the new process, is frequently called a "**walkthrough**." Often, companies will pilot a new process especially if difficulties are expected. For instance, the new process could be piloted in one company location, in one sales region, or with one group of customers. The team should also be available to answer questions and provide support to those stakeholders whose jobs or roles changed.

Lastly, the company should embrace the new mindset and drive continuous improvement. This process of continuously improving processes is referred to as **business process management (BPM)**. Rather than thinking of process improvement as a project that has a beginning, a middle, and an end, it should be envisioned as an ongoing activity that is tied to all technology and business activities critical to enterprise operations. At regular intervals, the team should gather data on the performance of the new process to measure its success.

It should be noted that BPR may be required instead of BPI at two points (see dashed lines in the model). When defining and understanding the process, the team may realize that the process is chronically and fundamentally broken. At this point, process innovation (BPR) might be necessary. Additionally, if improvement techniques are applied and the process continues to be of concern, BPR is generally the next step.

Processes in Need of Change

Companies should keep the "Three Cs" (customer, core, and competition) in mind when determining processes in need of change. First and foremost, processes should make it easy for customers to do business with a company so they keep coming back. In addition, processes that are part of the company's core competency should be as efficient as possible. Finally, companies must strive to have competitive processes. With the Three Cs in mind, suitable targets for BPI and BPR initiatives include the following types of processes.

Customer-Facing Processes

Organizations should consider the impact that processes have on customer-perceived value. When considering a customer-facing process, companies should answer these questions: Who is the customer? What is the customer willing to pay for? What does the customer receive? Are we meeting expectations? The team should figure out how well the company is satisfying its customers and consider ways to increase customer satisfaction. To measure the value of a process, companies should compare current levels of process performance to customer expectations. For instance, customer focus groups or surveys can yield data on perceptions of the company's customer service responsiveness, accuracy, assurance, and empathy.

Core Competency Processes

As discussed earlier, a company's core competency transforms generic inputs into uniquely developed products or services, yielding a competitive advantage. A core competency may be an area of specialization where a company possesses inimitable knowledge that allows differentiation from its competition. It may also be a large operation with sufficient economies of scale that the magnitude of the capital required to become competitive acts as an entry barrier to competitors. A core competency may also be a brand that sends universally favorable messages throughout the market. The study of these core competencies and others forms the heart of business strategy.

While core competencies vary by company, location, and industry, they are considered a firm's "bread and butter." To determine how well a core competency is performing, oftentimes companies use **benchmarking** to measure and compare their processes against strong competitors that have the same core competency in order to identify quality gaps and specify programs or action plans to meet or exceed the competition. Key areas of interest in benchmarking include financial performance, efficiency, asset utilization, reliability, and service quality. For example, a company might want to compare  its sales volume or customer churn rate against key competitors or the industry average. With these types of measurements in hand, a company can determine what processes, including activities and systems, it can change in order to increase its revenue.

High Volume, Low Margin Processes

High volume, low margin activities are usually a symptom of operating in a highly competitive market with considerable price pressure. Suppliers in these markets are usually poorly differentiated and offer a commodity product. Several characteristics of this type of market include:

- High revenue – The high sales volume generates substantial revenue and thus is extremely important to the company's cash flow. However, this revenue does not necessarily translate to profit or large profit margins.

- Efficient and controlled – The low profit margin increases the need for efficiency and magnifies the detrimental impact of defects.

- Capital intensive – The need for efficiency requires capital assets and sophisticated production facilities.

- Inventory costs – The high volume might drive up inventory storage costs if production and purchasing are not synchronized.

Together, these characteristics combine to drive up operational leverage. With sufficient volume, even tiny improvements can result in remarkable gains.

High Defect, High Reward Processes

Each time a process incurs an error or defect, costly material and labor that would otherwise be committed to other revenue-generating activities are wasted reworking the defect. Quality defects have significant costs associated with them—some of the most obvious being money, time, resources, and lost reputation.

Because quality is such a major driver of revenue and expense, companies should consider opportunities to improve quality. As mentioned in Figure 3-1, quality control is checking someone's work such as testing manufactured products to uncover defects. **Quality assurance**, on the other hand, attempts to improve and stabilize processes to avoid, or at least minimize, issues that lead to defects in the first place. While quality assurance is a proactive managerial tool focused on defect prevention, quality control is a reactive tool for product quality. In processes with high defects and high rewards, tackling the cause of the defects in the first place using quality assurance methods will be more effective over the long term.

High Skill, Time Intensive Processes

Not surprisingly, time intensive processes that consume highly skilled workers are expensive. Companies will try to aggressively control these processes, employing technologies or simplifying the process, to empower the same people to perform the job faster or to use lower-paid workers to perform the process or part of the process.

High Complexity, Specialized Resource Processes

Everyone has heard of "KISS," or "keep it simple, stupid."
Another similar mantra is "less is more." Some businesses tend
to embrace complexity and the market advantages that complex
solutions garner. A firm's marketing message may say something
along the lines of, "We are very clever and have dreamed up this
complex solution to your complex challenges." The difficulty
here is one of escalating complexities. When a customer's need
is complex, the solution becomes complex, and the processes
that produce the solution may also become complex. As a result
of this complexity, processes may require highly paid specialists,
growth may be difficult as complex processes may involve diseconomies of scale, and errors and
defect rates may climb unacceptably.

One further manifestation of this tendency toward complexity is the way companies often seek
to differentiate their products by adding features and components because otherwise the products
would seem too ordinary. By moving away from KISS, businesses lean toward riskier activities that
threaten the likelihood of success. BPR can focus on all of these tendencies in an effort to replace
complex activities with simpler ones.

Processes Built around Obsolete or Changing Technology

Quite often, keeping legacy systems around because of the cost of implementing an ERP system
and fear of the resulting change will trap a company into less-than-optimal business processes
and obsolete business models. Companies need to evaluate their current business models and
define where they want to be in the future. Most likely, their legacy systems will not be effective in
supporting this desired business model, as older systems suffer from outdated software code and
are not built on current best practices. Companies should look to design new business process
models around their strategic value propositions. These new models can then be automated into
a new customer-focused architecture. Most likely, systems are available that closely match those
models. The objective is to use systems as an opportunity to transform processes. Advantages
include flexibility and scalability, standardization of processes, new features and a more user-friendly
interface, normalized data structures, and simpler and more effective corporate and IT governance.

Stakeholders for Business Process Transformation

Businesses operate for the sake of stakeholders. From the minimally invested stockholder to the last
customer and out to the ends of the supply chain, each of the stakeholders below has an interest in
business process transformation. Plans for BPI and BPR should include an analysis of the impact

to these parties as well as plans to help mitigate any negative consequences swiftly and successfully. Failure to plan for key stakeholders can cause a company undergoing a transformation to quickly lose valuable time, support, and money. They could also lose reputation—arguably the hardest thing to win back.

Customers

The most frequently repeated mistake is the failure to directly involve customers in BPR or BPI efforts. Most companies think they already know what the customer really wants and needs—and are very surprised if and when the customer actually suggests anything differently. Processes that focus on the relationship with the customer help with customer satisfaction, retention, and profitability.

Employees

Some employees fill a day no matter how much (or how little) they have to do. If their time is not dedicated to value-added activities, their employer gains less output with the same fixed employee cost. This reduces margins, profitability, and the company's ability to meet customers' expectations. Some people are "self-starters" who will invent and create more effective ways to do things, adding value both financially and strategically. When given more time to think, some people will perform at higher levels. Others will get wrapped up in "pet projects" that add little or no value. In fact, some of these projects could detract value. If the change initiative frees up time for employees, what will be the response? Hopefully a good one.

Information Technology Staff

IT staff have an important role in process transformation efforts that rely on IT. These are the team members who will need to run the IT infrastructure that supports new systems implemented and provide technical support after the systems go live. The key to successful redesign is to constantly question why a certain task is done, what are better ways of doing it, who should be responsible, and which technologies best support the redesigned process. The IT staff has a keen ability to contribute to the project's success by helping answer these questions.

Executive Suite

Business process change initiatives need a high-level sponsor of sufficient status to underscore the importance of the project so employees will understand how committed the company is to making the necessary changes. Executive sponsors must often stake their reputation on the project's success and should be willing to address issues and objections from peers or subordinates who might be resistant to change. The higher the rank of sponsors, the less likely objections from employees will derail the project.

Business Partners

Change implies disruption, and a company's business partners are often wary of any interference in their relationship with the firm. Placating these concerns requires a willingness to share information about the impending changes and to address issues that arise during the project. Business partners may also have to enact their own changes to avoid any adverse effects caused by the necessary disruptions. However, a change in one company's processes is often an opportunity and impetus for its business partners to take advantage of new, more efficient activities.

Suppliers

Suppliers are often beset with uncertainties about demand for their products. Acting with imperfect information, they tend to overproduce and overcharge in an effort to protect themselves from uncertainty. If a new process can provide better information to suppliers, they in turn may be able to effect greater accuracy and efficiency in their own operations and potentially pass those savings along to their customers.

Other Interested Parties

As processes are transformed and systems are integrated, internal controls within those processes can be designed to better support security and privacy requirements from laws and regulations such as HIPAA and the Sarbanes-Oxley Act of 2002. Shareholders, creditors, regulatory bodies, and the general investing public all benefit when companies they invest in, lend to, or regulate have a strong internal control structure in place so that fraud and errors are prevented.

Summary

If not properly managed, business processes can become inefficient and ineffective over time and can eventually become riddled with issues such as bottlenecks, manual steps, mounds of paper, outdated systems, and long cycle times. This chapter discussed two methods that companies use to change their business processes to make them become more competitive. One method, known as business process reengineering (BPR), is a fundamental, radical redesign in business processes to achieve dramatic improvements in key measures of quality, cost, speed, and customer satisfaction. Implementing ERP systems enables companies to dramatically reengineer their business processes to match best practices built into the software. Business process improvement (BPI) is a second method used by companies to enhance their business processes, but this method is an incremental approach to change. Companies will most likely undergo both types of process change at some point in their life cycle. An analysis of "as is" processes is paramount to beginning any type of redesign initiative. Benchmarking, creatively designing new processes, and implementing technology solutions are techniques used in business process redesign efforts. Key stakeholders affected by a process change initiative includes customers, employees, suppliers, IT staff, the executive suite, and other interested parties.

Keywords

"As is" process	Manual step
Authority ambiguity	Old ways
Benchmarking	Paper records
Bottleneck	Process inventory
Business process	Quality assurance
Business process improvement (BPI)	Quality control
Business process management (BPM)	Rework
Business process reengineering (BPR)	Role ambiguity
Clean slate reengineering	Segregation of duties
Constrained reengineering	Segregation of duties violation
Core competency	Shared services
Cycle time	Technology enabled reengineering
Data duplication	"To be" process
Handoff	Value-added activity
Intermediary	Walkthrough
Internal control	

Quick Review

1. True/False: Business process reengineering is defined as gradual, incremental changes to business processes.

2. True/False: A drawback to clean slate reengineering is that it can inhibit innovation and creativity.

3. True/False: Using an ERP system to reengineer is an example of technology enabled reengineering.

4. The BPR principle of _____ transfers the cost and accountability for work to the beneficiary of a process.

5. The _____ process reflects how work is currently accomplished and the _____ process shows an improved or reengineered process.

Questions to Consider

1. How does reengineering relate to ERP?

2. Explain the pros and cons of clean slate versus technology enabled reengineering.

3. What is the difference between BPI and BPR?

4. List and describe several problems with business processes.

5. Describe the steps in the BPI life cycle.

References

Austin, R., Sole, D., & Cotteleer, M. (2003). *Harley Davidson Motor Company: Enterprise software selection.* Boston, MA: Harvard Business School Publishing.

Bashein, B., Markus, M., & Riley, P. (1994). Preconditions for BPR success. *Information Systems Management, 11*(2), 7–13.

Davenport, T., & Stoddard, D. (1994). Reengineering: Business change of mythic proportions? *MIS Quarterly, 18*(2), 121–127.

Diffen. (2013). Quality assurance vs quality control. Retrieved from http://www.diffen.com/ difference/ Quality_Assurance_vs_Quality_Control

Hammer, M. (1990). *Reengineering work: Don't automate, obliterate. Harvard Business Review, 68*(4), 104–112.

Hammer, M., & Champy, J. (2006). *Reengineering the corporation: A manifesto for business revolution.* New York, NY: HarperBusiness.

Harmon, R. (1996). *Reinventing the business: Preparing today's enterprise for tomorrow's technology.* New York, NY: The Free Press.

Hefferman, L., & Porter, L. (2010). Process mapping: Dissecting processes for optimal performance [presentation]. Portland, OR: 2010 Annual Conference of WACUBO.

Jarrar, Y. (1999). Business process re-engineering: Learning from organizational experience. *Total Quality Management, 10*(2), 173–186.

Klein, M. (1994). The most fatal reengineering mistakes. *Information Strategy: The Executive Journal, 10*(4), 21–28.

Manganelli, R., & Klein, M. (1994). *The reengineering handbook: A step-by-step guide to business transformation.* New York, NY: AMACOM Books.

Mind Tools Ltd. (n.d.). Improving business processes: Streamlining tasks to improve efficiency. Retrieved from http://www.mindtools.com/pages/article/improving-business-processes. htm

O'Leary, D. (2000). *Enterprise resource planning systems.* Cambridge, UK: Cambridge University Press.

Page, S. (2010). *The power of business process improvement: 10 simple steps to increase effectiveness, efficiency, and adaptability.* New York, NY: AMACOM.

Porter, L. D. (2013, May). *Process mapping: Dissecting processes for optimal performance.* Presentation given at 2013 CUPA-HR Midwest Region Conference, Columbus, OH.

Rohleder, T. & Silver, E. (1997). A tutorial on business process improvement. *Journal of Operations Management, 15*, 139–154.

Seppanen, M., Kumar, S., & Chandra, C. (2005). *Process analysis and improvement.* New York, NY: McGraw-Hill Irwin.

Smith, M. (2010). BOLO (Be on LookOut) list for analyzing process mapping. Retrieved from http://www.isixsigma.com/tools-templates/process-mapping/bolo-be-lookout-list-analyzing-process-mapping/

Tonnessen, T. (2000). Process improvement and the human factor. *Total Quality Management, 11*(4-6), 773–778.

The Frame Group. (2012). Business Process Improvement. Retrieved from http://www. framegroup.com.au/Portals/0/Documents/Capability%20Sheets/Level%202%20 sheets/Frame%20Business%20Process%20Improvement.pdf

Tradewinds Group, Incorporated. (2004). Business process reengineering and improvement. Retrieved from http://www.tradewindsgroupinc.com/Tradewinds_Business_Process_ Improvement_ White_Paper.pdf

Chapter 4

ERP and Process Mapping

Objectives

- Recognize the importance of process mapping

- Understand the difference between "as is" and "to be" business processes

- Become familiar with process map symbols

- Distinguish among the various roles used in process mapping

- Know the steps involved in mapping a business process

Introduction

As an organization grows, processes can become more complex and over time may become ineffectual. Eventually, management must take a long hard look at its business processes to determine if they need to be redesigned. Many times system diagrams are used to illustrate business processes so they are well understood by all. This chapter focuses on one system diagramming method, the process map, which is widely used in conjunction with ERP implementations and BPR and BPI initiatives. The benefit of using a process map is the strong logical flow that includes all the activities and contingencies of the process as well as the roles involved. In this chapter, we will learn the benefits of developing process maps, the symbols used in process maps, and some tips on drawing them. We will also learn how to use process maps to identify process issues that would benefit from BPR or BPI techniques. There are two types of process maps—the "as is" map, showing the current state of the process, and the "to be" map, showing the desired state of the process after redesign or an ERP implementation. A company needs to understand both before embarking upon an ERP implementation.

Systems Diagrams

"A picture is worth a thousand words." This well-known saying can be used to explain why systems diagrams are so widely used in business. A **systems diagram (SD)** is a graphical representation of a **system**, which is a group of parts that are connected and work together. Systems diagrams are used in businesses for many reasons, including to describe business processes, to assess internal control procedures, and to evaluate, design, or change information systems.

In this fast-paced world, it is imperative to get your point across quickly and concisely. Often, it is easier to show how something works or how ideas or events are connected by drawing a diagram of it rather than writing a narrative or trying to explain it verbally (we've all used the back of a cocktail napkin to explain something we couldn't get across in a conversation!). Often your audience has an easier time thinking systematically and logically about a problem that has been illustrated.

It's important for business professionals to be able to read SDs—to extract information from them and interpret what that information means. It is also important to be able to draw SDs to capture ideas and interpretations of a complex situation. The next section will elaborate on a popular SD method, the process map, which is used by many companies to visually display their business processes.

The Process Map

The earliest known process-oriented systems diagram, the process chart, was developed in the early 1900s to find a faster way to lay bricks. Starting in 1921, the process chart was rapidly integrated into the field of industrial engineering, where it was used by companies such as Procter & Gamble. Over time, the process chart morphed into an SD method known as a process map, which was developed by General Electric in the 1980s to assist them in improving their manufacturing processes. A **process map** is a graphical technique that documents inputs, outputs, activities, and decision points in order to effectively tell the reader the step-by-step procedures for a specific business process.

Also known as **cross-functional flowcharts** or **swim lane diagrams**, process maps have been used in all types of companies and industries and have gained widespread acceptance by leading global organizations seeking to analyze, design, and improve business processes. This SD technique divides a process into a series of steps, or activities, and identifies the role responsible for each step. A **role** is the party responsible for an activity in the process and can be an external entity, such as a customer, supplier, or business partner, or an internal entity, such as a customer service representative or a purchasing manager.

Process maps allow the preparer to visually illustrate and convey the essential details of a process (in a way that written procedures cannot) by replacing many pages of words with boxes and arrows. They can be developed at a high-level, macro perspective, or they can be drawn to focus on the smallest units of work, thereby providing a detailed, micro perspective. They are good for conveying to the reader "what we do around here." Specifically, process maps indicate what is happening, where and when it is happening, who is doing what, and how inputs and outputs are handled.

Process maps allow the reader to understand how the process is currently operating; additionally, they enable the reader to think about how the process can be improved. The first type of map is the **"as is" process map**. Mapping out current processes will help a project team develop requirements for an ERP system and make necessary changes to their processes. For ERP implementations, the "as is" map will be used as the starting point for mapping the existing processes into configurations of the ERP system. Processes will undoubtedly need to be changed to match the best practices in the ERP software. The team should identify and map unique, competitive, "as is" processes that will need to be supported by the new ERP system. If they are not, then a company could lose its competitive advantage. For BPI initiatives, the exercise will help generate responses such as "Do we still do that?" "You mean, you guys don't review that report after all?" or "Why are we doing it this way?" As the team reviews the "as is" maps, it will begin to question "why?" and may find opportunities for change

The second type of process map, the **"to be" process map**, is a visual representation of the redesigned process, which is more efficient and effective. This future-state process is developed to reflect changes that need to be made to the process. If the process is to be reengineered through ERP, the "to be" processes should already be documented by the ERP vendor to show best practices in the software. This helps potential customers to more easily understand how the various ERP systems they are evaluating work. Their "as is" process maps can be compared to processes supported by ERP systems under consideration to identify how current business processes must be changed to fit with the ERP system's best practices.

Figure 4-1 presents process map symbols and descriptions. While these symbols can be sketched out, it is easy to create more professional process maps with flowcharting applications such as Microsoft® Visio or SmartDraw. Novices may find process mapping rather awkward and challenging at first. However, as a well-known organizational theorist once said, "You don't learn to process map. You process map to learn." In other words, the development of the process map is not the end goal; the information obtained from the map is.

Figure 4-1: Process Map Symbols and Descriptions

	Activity	Activities are depicted in process maps with rectangles. Every process has a series of steps (both value-added and non-value-added) that help transform inputs into outputs.
	Decision point	Decisions points are depicted with diamonds. Processes may involve choices that result in different outcomes.
	Process flow line	Directional arrows connecting symbols show the flow of data, information, or physical goods.
	Start/Stop	An oval should both designate the trigger to the process and any termination points. There may be multiple termination points if decisions exist in the process.
\<phase\>	**Phase**	Often, a process may involve multiple sub-processes that need to be visually separated to distinguish them. Phases should be labeled to denote each sub-process.
	On-page connector	When the visual appeal of the map is marginalized, on-page connectors, represented as circles, are used to reduce clutter. These circles are cross-referenced using the same letters of the alphabet.
	Off-page connector	When the process map spans multiple pages, an off-page connector is used. These connectors are cross-referenced using page numbers.

Benefits of Process Mapping

The ability to draw a process map is an invaluable skill for anyone involved with the analysis, design, or redesign of business processes. Well-constructed process maps provide a number of benefits including:

- Planning for the ERP system by defining the "as is" business process and clarifying the changes necessary to transform the current process into a more efficient, streamlined "to be" process

- Determining whether "as is" measures of performance are appropriate and potentially developing new performance measures for the "to be" process

- Identifying responsible parties, the points in the process at which they are involved, and their impact on upstream and downstream activities

- Highlighting workflow inefficiencies such as bottlenecks, excessive handoffs, duplicate work, and unproductive utilization of resources

- Understanding where internal controls are in the process or dictating where they should be

- Orienting and training new employees or retraining existing employees

- Serving as an integral part of the company's policies and procedures documentation

Gathering Information for the Process Map

Gathering information to create a process map can be an arduous task, especially as the number of activities and roles increases. There are three basic methods used to obtain information needed to map a process. The **self-generate method** is used when the preparer personally knows the process. He or she can draw a preliminary process map and then ask others who are knowledgeable about the process to give their input on its completeness and accuracy. This method is typically faster than the other methods because it involves less people. However, its usefulness is limited to the process knowledge possessed by the analyst.

The next method used for information collection is the **one-on-one interview method**, in which each person involved in the process is interviewed separately and sequentially. After the interviews, the process map is circulated to those interviewed so they can review its completeness and accuracy. This method works well if the interviewer has good questioning and listening skills. It is also helpful if the interviewer has some knowledge of the process in question.

The last method, the **group interview method**, is usually more effective than the other two methods. In this method, everyone involved in the process is asked to participate together as a group to generate the process map. When everyone has to agree on the way the process works, the outcome is typically more accurate. Additionally, the high degree of participation that this method requires increases the ownership that the group feels regarding the process map, and more importantly, the process itself.

Process Mapping Roles

Process mapping is best performed by a team of people, including those who actually perform the processes as they currently are. It should be a small team—no more than five or six people—and in addition to the users, it should include some people who are familiar with process mapping and ERP. The following key roles are generally employed during process mapping:

- **Process map facilitator** – Promotes and focuses the discussions and provides an unbiased, objective point of view. The facilitator should be insightful and able to recognize when a process step may be based on assumption and not fact. Also, the facilitator should be on guard for someone who continually says, "This will not work."

- **Process owner** – Maintains responsibility for the proper completion of process steps and has authority over the process, its interfaces, and the changes that will take place.

- **Subject matter expert** – Knows the process intimately and provides knowledge and expertise.

- **Process implementer** – Executes recommendations and implements changes such as new procedures and systems.

- **Process evaluator** – Tests the "to be" process and helps determine new metrics for its evaluation.

Steps for Drawing Process Maps

Process maps portray activities in sequential order and can be drawn horizontally or vertically. Horizontal process maps (shown in this chapter) represent time from left to right, whereas vertical maps represent time from top to bottom. Steps for creating process maps include the following:

- Have a defined purpose for mapping a process and explain it to those participating.

- Identify the scope (beginning and ending) of the process and label it at the top of each page. Avoid the mistake of making the scope too broad.

- Agree on the level of detail to be displayed.

- Determine the roles participating in the process. These roles are shown as bands across or down the page and are called **swim lanes**. Swim lanes organize activities into groups based on who is responsible for the various steps within the process being mapped.

- Identify the **trigger**, which denotes the start of the process. For horizontal maps, the trigger, designated with an oval, should be placed in the top swim lane all the way to the left.

- Organize the process map so that activities move either to the right, down, or up. Avoid lines that move to the left.

- Use active verbs for activity descriptions such as "enter," "inspect," or "input." Activities such as "send" and "receive" can generally be excluded because these activities are represented by the process flow lines (that is, the flow of data into a rectangle means that the data/ information/goods has been sent by a sender and received by the recipient).

- Do not combine completely separate/unrelated steps in an activity.

- Write a description of the data, information, or physical flow on the process flow line.

- Ask questions within the decision symbols. Label the decision outcomes with "yes" or "no" or similar. Put decisions in the swim lane of the role making the decision.

- Capture information about which systems or ERP modules support the process and note their names within activity or decision symbols.

Process maps should follow the conventions listed above, but they should also look professional. Figure 4-2 lists tips for constructing process maps that are visually appealing and easy to understand.

Figure 4-2: Tips for Drawing Professional Process Maps

Make sure every area of the map contains approximately the same amount of detail
Take notes while mapping and create a glossary of acronyms so that information generated in the process mapping session is not lost or later becomes ambiguous
Ensure that swim lanes retain the same role throughout the map even if the map spans multiple pages
Terminate the process in the swim lane where the process ends
Make similar shapes the same size
Try to collocate those swim lanes that have the greatest number of interactions with each other
Avoid using names of individuals in process maps as people can come and go; roles remain more consistent
Minimize space between symbols and ensure that spaces are as uniform as possible

Process Map Example – Electric City

An example process map describing the "as is" order-to-cash process at Electric City is shown in Figure 4-3. The narrative of the process is as follows:

After a customer browses merchandise, he or she fills out an order form. A sales clerk enters the order into the MTS 900 sales system. The sales clerk then prints out a picking ticket and hands it to a warehouse employee. The warehouse employee locates the items in the warehouse and places them on a conveyor belt for the sales clerk to give to the customer. If the items are not in stock, the process terminates. If the items are in stock, then the customer inspects the merchandise. If the customer decides to purchase the merchandise, he or she pays for it, and the sales clerk processes the sale and payment in MTS 900. The sales clerk then gives a receipt to the customer.

Steps for Drawing the Electric City Process Map

After having a defined purpose for mapping the process (such as planning for an ERP implementation), the first step in drawing the process map is to identify the scope. Here, the process is Electric City's order-to-cash process, which is labeled at the top of the map. Next, we identify the roles involved in the process, which will become swim lanes: customer, sales clerk, and warehouse employee. The next step is to identify the trigger. The narrative states that potential customers browse the merchandise first. However, this is not the trigger. The trigger is the point at which a "customer" to the process (which happens to be Electric City's customer) first interacts with the process. This involvement occurs when the customer completes an order form. The next activity is when the sales clerk enters the order information into the MTS 900 sales system.

Figure 4-3 identifies the three distinct decisions in Electric City's order-to-cash process. The decision points appear in the swim lane of the role that is making the decision. Additionally, the process flow lines are labeled with the outcomes of each decision and descriptions for data/information/physical flows. Termination symbols are also placed in the swim lane where the process ends.

Figure 4-3: Electric City Order-to-Cash Process

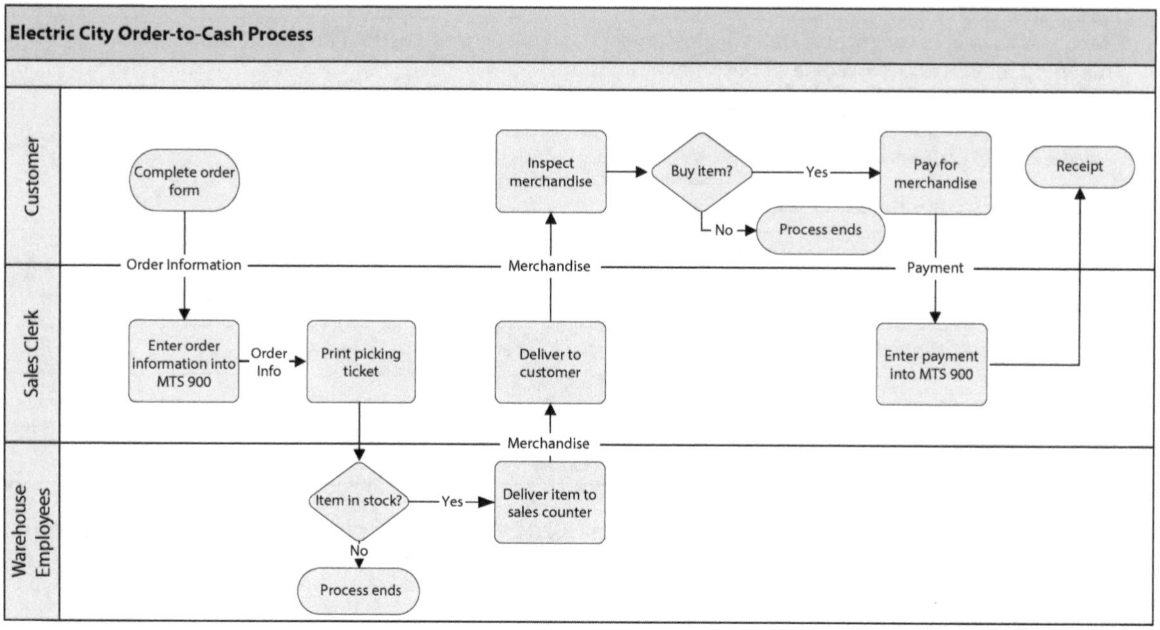

Extensions to the Electric City Process Map

The Electric City example includes the basic symbols we have discussed. However, the process map palette can be broadened, depending on the environment being documented and the level of task detail shown. For instance, in a manufacturing environment, symbols can be used to denote delays, such as queue times or setup times, inspection of parts, rejection of parts, and storage of parts. Using these symbols to document the flow of materials from receiving dock through the manufacturing process to storage can show excessive delays, handoffs, and other types of inefficient movement of goods. Isolating these problems through the use of process mapping can lead to improvements in **flow time**, or the distance a part travels, and cycle time, which was discussed in Chapter 3. Once management identifies these issues, it can seek to mitigate them through BPI or BPR.

Business processes can be mapped at a high level, as shown in the Electric City example, or expanded to show greater detail at successively lower levels. More detailed maps often uncover process flaws, difficult or time-consuming interactions, or inefficiencies. For instance, at a high level, manufacturers engage in exactly the same processes:

- Inbound logistics – Firms buy goods and services from their upstream supply chain

- Internal operations – Firms process these things to add value to them

- Outbound logistics – Firms sell things to their customers

This high-level process may not provide sufficient detail to identify the root of problems and where improvements can be made; each of these high-level activities could be explored in more detail to identify potential issues. Process maps can also be expanded by associating task instructions with specific process events. For example, the activity "Deliver Item to Sales Counter" in Figure 4-3 could be accompanied by documentation that articulates the steps and specific instructions used by the warehouse employees to perform this activity (see Figure 4-4).

Figure 4-4: Detailed Documentation for "Deliver Item to Sales Counter"

Date	August 25
Process Owner	Warehouse Supervisor
Customer	Sales Clerk
Step	Instructions
1	Retrieve picking ticket from sales clerk.
2	Using MTS 900, enter item number into item number field; determine availability of item.
3	If item is not in stock, notify sales clerk. Otherwise, locate and retrieve item using bin location in warehouse system.
4	Tape picking ticket to item and place on carousel "A" for heavy items, carousel "B" for light items.
Dependencies	Warehouse System
Inputs	Picking Ticket
Outputs	Item to Sales Clerk

Advanced Process Map Example – Fit Gear

An advanced process map for Fit Gear's bi-weekly payroll of plant employees is presented in Figures 4-5 and 4-6. This process map includes the phase symbol, which is called the "separator" in Microsoft® Visio. The phase symbol, described in Figure 4-1, is used to delineate sub-processes within the overall process to make it easier to read the process map. The narrative of the process is as follows:

Fit Gear plant employees use a timecard machine to clock in and clock out during a two-week period. At the end of the second week, the receptionist collects the timecards from the plant and makes sure she has the correct number of cards (75 cards for 75 employees) and that they are complete (for example, did someone forget to clock out?).

If there appears to be a problem, she tries to resolve it with the employee. She then corrects the timecard for the employee and gives the timecard data to the plant supervisor. The plant supervisor signs off on hours for all plant employees and returns the cards to the receptionist. The receptionist then enters the time for each employee into an Excel spreadsheet, which is emailed to the payroll clerk.

The payroll clerk enters the bi-weekly time (including sick, vacation, and leave) into the TEMS Payroll System. The payroll clerk also enters any updates to the HR master data (for example, change in address, change in exemptions) into the system.

The payroll clerk prints a payroll register and reviews for correctness. If there are errors, he resolves them in the system. Next, the payroll register is reviewed by the HR manager for correctness. If she finds additional issues, the payroll clerk resolves them in the system as well. The payroll clerk then prints paychecks, and the receptionist distributes them to the plant employees.

Figure 4-5: Fit Gear Bi-Weekly Payroll Process for Plant Employees (Page 1)

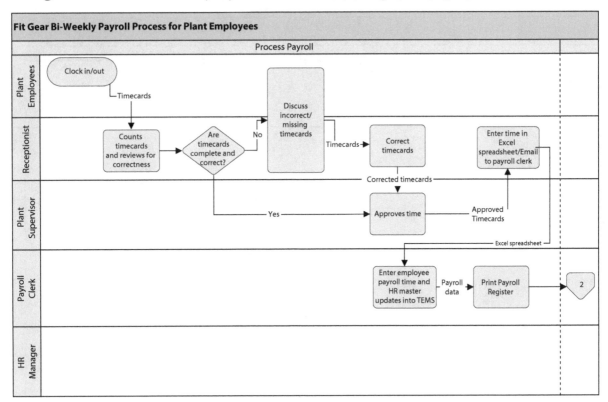

Figure 4-6: Fit Gear Bi-Weekly Payroll Process for Plant Employees (Page 2)

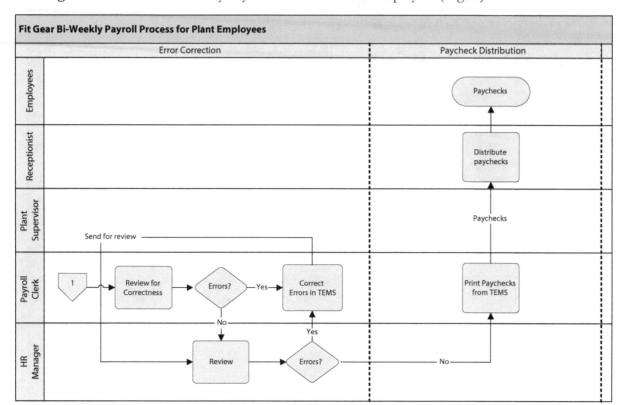

Process Issues and Suggested Process Redesigns for Fit Gear

Fit Gear's "as is" payroll process may look efficient at first glance, but it actually includes an assortment of problems that should be either reengineered or improved, depending on the nature of the change. After reviewing types of process issues in Figure 3-1 and reengineering principles in Figure 3-2, an analyst might arrive at a few suggestions for redesigning the payroll process, including the ones below:

- *Cycle time* could be improved by using *self-service* for HR master data updates (employees could have controlled access into TEMS to change their address, exemptions, and so forth). This also relates to the BPR principle of *having those who use the output of the process perform the process.*

- The payroll clerk should not enter HR master data updates. This is a *segregation of duties violation.* The employee through self-service or the HR manager should be entering HR master data updates.

- It is inefficient to use a manual time card system and then re-enter the time into Excel then the TEMS Payroll system. Employees could enter the time directly into the ERP system through a time and attendance interface or through an electronic time clock. Data should be *captured once at its source* and *data duplication* should be avoided.

- The receptionist is performing *manual steps* and *rework*. Also, the inclusion of the receptionist in the process causes *handoffs* between her, the plant supervisor, and the payroll clerk.

- Printing and distributing manual paychecks can lead to internal control problems. Fit Gear should use direct deposit. Continuing to use paper paychecks may represent an *old way* of doing things.

- The *old way* of processing payroll is inefficient. One new way of handling payroll and HR is through outsourcing. Companies can outsource processes that are not their core competence and save money doing so.

- The payroll clerk does not need an approval from the HR manager. This is a *segregation of duties violation* and also a non-essential *quality control* step. The payroll clerk should be *empowered* to make decisions.

Summary

One way an organization can gain a better understanding of its processes is by diagramming them. This chapter focuses on a process-oriented SD method, the process map. A process map defines inputs, outputs, activities, and the roles involved in the process. Although process maps can be used to illustrate complicated processes, they entail few symbols and are fairly simple to draw and read. Oftentimes, experienced facilitation is required to get the best results during process mapping using the group interview method. There are many benefits of process mapping, such as uncovering bottlenecks and other non-value-added work, as well as documenting employee roles for training purposes. "As is" process maps can establish a starting point from which the eventual "to be" process design can begin.

Keywords

Activity	Process map
"As is" process map	Process map facilitator
Cross-functional flowchart	Process owner
Decision point	Role
Flow time	Self-generate method
Group interview method	Start/stop
Off-page connector	Subject matter expert
On-page connector	Swim lane
One-on-one interview method	Swim lane diagram
Phase	System
Process evaluator	Systems diagram (SD)
Process flow line	"To be" process map
Process implementer	Trigger

Quick Review

1. True/False: Process mapping is primarily used to model relational databases.

2. True/False: When collecting information for a process map, the one-on-one interview method is generally preferred over the group interview method.

3. The process map is also known as a _____ or _____.

4. The _____ event is the point in which the customer is first involved in the process.

5. The _____ is responsible for the proper completion of process steps and has authority over the process, its interfaces, and changes that will take place.

Questions to Consider

1. What are the benefits of process mapping?

2. What steps are involved in creating a process map?

3. List the symbols used in a process map and explain their uses.

4. Who are the important roles during process mapping and what do they do?

5. What are some tips for creating professional-looking process maps?

References

Abubakker, H. (2010, February 26). Practical guide to creating better looking process maps. [blog post]. Retrieved from http:// www.isixsigma.com/tools-templates/process-mapping/ practical-guide-creating-better-looking-process-maps/

Andrews, C. (2007). *Drawing a map of the business. Internal Auditor, 64*(1), 55–58.

Argent, D. (2009). Mapping the p*rocess. Paper, Film & Foil CONVERTER, 81*(6), 14. Retrieved from http://www.nxtbook.com/nxtbooks/penton/pffc0607/index.php?startid=14

Aveta Business Institute. (n.d.). Six Sigma projects – Five benefits of process mapping. Retrieved from http://www.sixsigmaonline.org/six-sigma-training-certification-information/ articles/six-sigma-projects---five-benefits-of-process-mapping.html

Bradford, M. (2004). *Reengineering a process: A group project using Hammer's reengineering principles and process mapping techniques. Compendium of Classroom Cases and Tools for AIS Applications (C3), 2*(1).

Cook, R. (2013). Process mapping the processes. Retrieved from http://it.toolbox.com/blogs/ inside-erp/process-mapping-the-processes-57110

Damelio, R. (1996). *The basics of process mapping.* New York, NY: Productivity Press.

Hefferman, L., & Porter, L. (2010). Process mapping: Dissecting processes for optimal performance [presentation]. Portland, OR: 2010 Annual Conference of WACUBO.

Jacka, J. M., & Keller, P. J. (2009). *Business process mapping: Improving customer satisfaction* (2nd ed.). Hoboken, IL: Wiley.

Paradiso, J., & Cruickshank, J. (2007). Process mapping for SOX and beyond. *Strategic Finance*, *88*(9), 30–35.

Process Mapping Associates Inc. (2007). Process mapping. Retrieved from http://www.processmaps.com/ mapping.html

Seppanen, M., Kumar, S., & Chandra, C. (2005). *Process analysis and improvement*. Boston, MA: McGraw-Hill Irwin.

Smith, M. (2010, February 26). BOLO (Be on LookOut) list for analyzing process mapping. iSixSigma. [blog post]. Retrieved from http://www.isixsigma.com/tools-templates/process-mapping/bolo-be-lookout-list-analyzing-process-mapping/

The Open University. (n.d.). Systems diagramming. Retrieved from http://www.open.edu/openlearn/ science-maths-technology/computing-and-ict/systems-computer/systems-diagramming/content-section-1

ERP Life Cycle: Planning and Package Selection

Objectives

- Identify factors that affect an organization's readiness for ERP

- Describe activities that take place in the planning stage of the ERP life cycle

- Recognize the various cost components of an ERP system

- Describe activities that take place in the package selection stage of the ERP life cycle

Introduction

An organization typically uses its ERP system for ten to thirteen years before retiring it and implementing something new. During this time, a company will go through various stages. These stages can be thought of as a life cycle, encompassing many activities, from planning to the much longer phase of operation and maintenance, which ultimately results in the system being replaced. At this point, the life cycle starts all over again. Although experts vary on the nomenclature for the ERP life cycle stages, one classification is as follows:

- Planning

- Package selection

- Implementation

- Operation and maintenance

A solid understanding of the tasks, decisions, and roles involved in each stage of the life cycle is critical for managing a successful ERP implementation. This chapter focuses on the first two stages of the ERP life cycle: planning and package selection. The planning phase involves many activities, the most important of which is ensuring that top management vocally champions the project and puts a good project team, project manager, and steering committee in place. The package selection stage also comprises many steps and should culminate in choosing the ERP system that best fits the company's functional and technical requirements.

ERP Life Cycle – Planning

An ERP system can be one of the most expensive investments a company will ever make. It is not uncommon for large, global companies to spend tens of millions of dollars on an ERP system including software licensing, hardware, IT infrastructure, implementation costs, and maintenance. There is a significant risk of failure if a company approaches the ERP implementation without the adequate prioritization, commitment, and attention to detail required for such a massive undertaking. Considering the size of the investment and the associated risk, proper planning is imperative to the success of the ERP project. Poor planning can lead to missed opportunities, costly mistakes, or even failure, depending upon how massive the problems are and how long they continue. Too often, a common outcome of the planning process is that key executives will think and rethink decisions made early on in the life cycle—a situation known as "analysis paralysis"—thus wasting precious time and increasing the overall cost and duration of the project before it even officially begins. In the worst-case scenario, the initiative becomes so "wrapped around the axle" that it is categorized as a failure and the system is never fully implemented. The following sections outline tasks that should be thoughtfully and carefully executed in the planning phase of the ERP life cycle to help ensure a successful implementation.

Organizational Readiness for ERP

One of the first tasks that should be conducted during the planning stage is determining whether the company is, in fact, ready to embark upon an ERP implementation. A review of the following key assessment points will help determine an organization's readiness for ERP.

- The first question should be: "Is this the right time for change?" Sometimes the answer to this question is a resounding "No!" If the company has withstood a lot of turmoil in the past few years, such as staff layoffs or management shakeups, now might not be a good time to begin such radical change.

- It's important to gauge the level of business process standardization currently enforced across the company. If each location or business unit has its own unique business processes and accompanying procedures, an ERP implementation is going to be much riskier and will take longer due to the BPR work that must take place to homogenize the operating environment.

- If executive leadership is not strong in its backing of the initiative, it will be far more difficult—if not impossible—to get employees behind the implementation. Clearly, management needs to be honest about whether this project is going to be one of its top priorities.

- The company needs to assess whether its culture is open to the project or if key stakeholders have to be convinced of the usefulness of the ERP system.

These and other issues need to be considered before moving forward since they impact the level of inherent risk in the project.

Project Team

Before planning begins (or progresses too far), executive leaders should appoint a project team. The **project team** plays a crucial role in the success of the ERP project and should be given wide discretion to make most of the important day-to-day decisions regarding implementation. The team's composition should consist of key process owners, end users, managers, and IT staff spanning functional boundaries, locations, and organizational levels of the company. With an optimum mix of personnel as described above, all business areas and organizational layers should have a voice in the process and feel a sense of ownership. The project team will likely also include consultants, who lend technical and functional expertise. Co-locating the consultants with the internal members of the project team is conducive to knowledge transfer. Team members should also be able to educate other personnel on their respective functional areas.

The composition of the project team is a major factor for a successful ERP implementation. Therefore, companies should appoint their most valuable and knowledgeable employees—the "best and brightest." If possible, individuals with experience in a previous ERP implementation should be considered first for the project team. Project team members should be made aware of why they were chosen for the project and how they are expected to contribute to its success. Some questions to consider when choosing members of the project team include:

- Does this person understand multiple parts of the business or just his or her own domain?

- Does this person express a willingness to embrace organizational and procedural change?

- Can this person influence others in a positive way?

- Can this person work harmoniously with others, both internal and external to the company?

- Is this person looking for a better way to get things done?

The scope of the implementation often dictates the size of the project team. The usual rule of thumb is to have two full-time resources per functional area and include at least two members from each business unit. However, there are tradeoffs to consider when determining the number of team members. Larger teams will provide more expertise, but are more difficult to manage, take longer to agree on issues, and can provide greater cover for members that are not contributing sufficient effort. Smaller teams may exclude key functional areas and may lack the breadth or depth of knowledge necessary, but are easier to mobilize.

Commitment to the team will undoubtedly conflict with employees' normal job functions, particularly when they are considered indispensable. Participation in the project generally requires a 100 percent time commitment on behalf of the team members (at least during the latter stages of the implementation). A 50 percent contribution to two jobs may breed failure in both!

Perhaps the most important decision the project team will face is the selection of the ERP package itself, which is discussed in more detail later in this chapter. However, before making a final software decision, the project team should formally sign off on the planning stage, signifying that it is complete. Everyone needs to be on the "same page."

Project Manager and Program Manager

The selection of a **project manager (PM)** is critical to the success or failure of the initiative, since this person is responsible for the managing the day-to-day operations of the ERP project and the project team. The PM must be able to communicate a number of important points to the user base, including the objectives and goals of the ERP project; financial, operational, and technical risks associated with the project; time and budget expectations and constraints; and the way the system will change users' roles. The PM must be able to translate business requirements into IT solutions, so it is important that this person understands both business processes and technology. In addition, the PM should understand the impact that the ERP system will have on the business to organize a smooth transition from the "as is" state to the "to be" state. Figure 5-1 lists 10 characteristics typical of a successful project manager.

The project manager reports directly to the **program manager**, who is the person in charge of all ERP projects across the company (if there are more). This person is responsible for overall project governance and the functional and operational aspects associated with the project(s) including, but not limited to, vendor management, change management, and communication with and presentations to the steering committee.

Figure 5-1: 10 Characteristics of a Successful Project Manager

Flexible, but can make tough decisions
Disciplined to stay the course
Quick learner/high aptitude
Capable of guiding and mentoring team
Has ERP experience
Motivator and delegator
Has the backing of top management
Knows the business well
Collaborative spirit and works well with others
Excellent problem solver

Source: Adapted from Gartner, Inc.

Executive Sponsor and Steering Committee

Research has consistently shown that executive leadership is one of the most important ingredients to an ERP project's success. A high-level sponsor should rally support, distribute resources, and delegate management of the implementation. Generally, the CEO is this high-level sponsor, and he or she has a huge impact in getting the word out about the value of the ERP project. He or she will set up a **steering committee** to serve as the highest decision-making authority for the project, and the ultimate success or failure of the ERP project will rest with it. The committee comprises the company's top management, senior consultants, project manager(s) and program manager. The steering committee members are typically not actively involved in the day-to-day running of the project (with the exception of the project managers), but the issues they do manage are monumental to the project. Figure 5-2 presents the steering committee's responsibilities.

Figure 5-2: Steering Committee Responsibilities

Set project objectives
Establish scope and timing
Approve ERP system selection methodology
Select project manager(s)
Approve subject matter experts
Define and prioritize critical success factors and key requirements
Approve potential ERP vendors
Approve ERP vendor short list
Approve ERP vendor finalist
Monitor implementation and resolve scope creep issues

Source: 180systems.com

Project Charter

The **project charter** is a high-level document, the purpose of which is to get the project "green-lighted" by the executive sponsor and board of directors. It outlines the project objectives, business case, stakeholders involved in the project, and a description of how the project will be organized and conducted, including start and end times, budget information, and final deliverables. Some of this information is provided by the project manager, and some information, such as the business case, is provided by the executive sponsor. Once written, the project charter is signed by the sponsor, authorizing the project to commence and funding to begin. The project manager will also co-sign the charter showing that he or she is agreeing to the information contained therein. The project charter is the defining document for the ERP project and can be referred to later if the project seems to be steering off course.

Scope Statement

The **scope statement** is written after the project charter and provides detail about what is included (and excluded) in the project. The statement should include information such as the ERP products and versions that are to be implemented, the business processes that will be reengineered, deployment sites, technical architecture, project management methodology, and key milestones and deliverables. An effective scope statement should be detailed enough so that there are no misunderstandings. For instance, a scope statement might state that the project includes PeopleSoft Financial Management.

But this is not enough. It is necessary to drill down and state exactly which functions within Financial Management are in scope (for example, is a management accounting module to be implemented?) and what locations of the company will use the new module.

The focus of **scope management** is to define and control what is, and is not, included in the project scope statement. If the scope is not clearly defined and managed, the project team may overlook important work, jeopardizing the project success. On the other hand, the team may perform work outside the scope, which consumes valuable time and money. According to research, one of the main reasons ERP projects exceed their anticipated schedule and budget is due to **scope creep,** or the expansion of a project's original goals while it is in progress. Usually scope creep begins as subtle adjustments for additional functionality that, in the aggregate, culminate in a project taking far longer than originally estimated. In the worse case scenario, excessive scope creep could result in the project failing before completion. Oftentimes the adjustments are the fallout of poor definitions of upfront business requirements, organizational non-readiness, changing market conditions, or competing forces within the company. Revisions to the project scope during implementation can cause confusion among project team members and the user base. To prevent "never-ending-project syndrome," the team should draft a scope statement so that the project's boundaries are clear to everyone. The goal of the implementation is to finish on time and within budget while producing satisfactory outcomes (which likely will not happen if the team is constantly trying to hit a moving target!). With that being said, there does need to be a process in place for **change requests** if it becomes overwhelmingly apparent that it is necessary. Any changes to the scope during the implementation must go through a rigorous change control process with the steering committee.

Business Case

One thing is clear: Businesses today rarely implement an ERP system because they just want new technology. They implement ERP systems because they want to realize benefits in the form of productivity improvements, cost reductions, and so forth. However, benefit realization won't happen if there is not a clearly defined business case to guide the team's efforts. A **business case** outlines the business need for an ERP system and the expected resulting benefits. Many companies ignore this part of planning, but they do so at their peril. The detailed business case should be grounded in **business case rationales**, or high-level reasons why a company undertakes an ERP implementation. Business case rationales for ERP systems include:

- Technology rationale – In the late 1990s, many businesses were concerned with Y2K issues. They believed that their information systems would crash when the date rolled over to the year 2000. Faced with an alternative of funding large scale rewrites of nearly obsolete code bases, many businesses chose to implement an ERP system. In addition to the infamous Y2K issue, more current technology rationales include upgrading systems to a client-server model, better visibility of data across business units, and data integration.

- Competitive rationale – ERP systems have generated "buzz" throughout the years, and many companies have implemented them because their competition has them. The possibility of a competitor gaining an advantage because of a superior information system should concern top management, who are often forced to adopt ERP solutions to maintain competitive parity.

- Strategy rationale – ERP adoption can be driven by a specific strategy, such as growth, mergers and acquisitions, diversification, or globalization.

- Business process rationale – Probably the main rationale for companies today, the business process rationale means that companies want to attain best practices in their business processes so they can achieve targeted, specific, and measurable performance improvements such as inventory reductions, improved manufacturing processes, and faster order fulfillment.

In earlier years, the motivation to implement ERP was driven more by the technology rationale. In more recent years, we have seen competitive, strategy, and business process rationales become the primary motivations for ERP. Management can use any or all of these rationales to justify its company's decision to implement an ERP system. The important point here is that they need to have at least one high-level rationale, and the executive sponsors should communicate that rationale to the rest of the company as well as specific benefits.

ERP Benefits

The basic methodology for ERP benefits realization simply involves taking baseline measurements (for example, inventory turnover or order-to-cash cycle time) early in the planning process, comparing them to projected measurements, and calculating the difference. These improvements in measurements are the benefits, and they should be able to be quantified. The culmination of all these benefits should become part of the business case for an ERP system. Quantifiable measurements are known as **business metrics**, and they are used to track and assess the efficacy of specific business processes. After the ERP system has been implemented, the organization needs to continue to track these metrics every few months to actually see if there is continued improvement toward the business case. Companies should also try to employ measurement methods that are not too difficult, time-consuming, or burdensome. Figure 5-3 presents a simple acronym for a business "metric."

Figure 5-3: Characteristics of a Metric

Measurable
Easy to calculate
Timely
Repeatable
Insightful
Controllable

Source: McDaniel, et al.

Organizations realize many benefits by implementing an ERP system. These benefits depend on the project scope and the amount of reengineering involved. For instance, if a company is implementing a module to help with purchasing and inventory management, then benefits such as improving the cycle time of the purchase to goods receipt process or reducing inventory levels will likely be part of a business case. If a production module is being implemented, benefits such as improved goods quality, lower manufacturing costs, increased throughput, less rework, and improved manufacturing schedule compliance may likely accrue. Key benefits for implementing financial accounting include integrated financial data across business units and locations, which helps in better business decisions and a faster period-end close. While some benefits are simple to quantify, others are more difficult, such as improved efficiency through better visibility of data; elimination of manual processes; better collaboration with partners, suppliers, and customers; and greater insight through business analytics.

ERP Costs

ERP costs are much easier to quantify than benefits, since the majority of costs require documented outlays of cash. ERP system costs should be viewed in the context of the **total cost of ownership (TCO)**, or the entire costs that will likely be incurred throughout the project's implementation and several years after the system goes live to capture recurring maintenance costs. Calculating TCO is important for making a fair comparison of different vendor proposals, for negotiating with vendors more effectively, and for budgeting purposes. Unlike the cost of tangible capital assets such as machinery, ERP systems have various cost components that are not readily apparent. It is in the vendor's best interest to downplay the cost of its solutions; it remains up to the customer to identify and validate a more realistic cost picture.

"How much does an ERP system cost?" is not as straightforward a question as some might think. The answer is, "It depends." Typically, an ERP system's price tag depends on the:

- Number of end users (and their respective license type)

- Vendor tier being deployed (Tier 1 software is typically more costly than Tier 2, while Tier 3 would be the least costly)

- Project scope (for example, how many business units are affected, what modules are being deployed)

In the following sections, ERP cost components are discussed in detail. These components include software licenses, database and other software costs, hardware and IT infrastructure costs, implementation costs, and recurring maintenance costs.

Software License Costs

Purchasing ERP software involves licensing expenses that govern its use. Generally, the price of the software depends on the number of end users and the number of modules implemented. For instance, if a company implements modules for purchasing, sales, and financials and has thousands of employees, software license costs will be higher than if the company implemented just financials and has hundreds of users. Also, software prices are generally competitive within a tier.

There are several ways to license ERP software, including named users, heavy versus casual users, concurrent users, and subscription-based. With **named user licensing**, the company identifies the total number of users who will access the ERP system and pays a user license fee for each one. This method is also called "per-seat licensing." Many ERP vendors offer different categories of named users. For instance, SAP offers licenses for SAP Professional (operational-related roles for HR, finance, and so on), SAP Developer (access for development tools to customize the software), and SAP Employee (access for self-services such as time, expenses, and performance evaluations). The Professional license is generically known as **heavy user licensing** for those who use more of the system's functionality and are charged a higher fee, while the Employee license, or **casual user licensing**, is for those who view reports or run occasional queries. Generally, a company would only purchase a few Developer licenses.

Another license type is **concurrent user licensing**, which sets a maximum number of users who would potentially access the system at a given time. In general, concurrent user licensing is significantly less expensive than per-seat licensing. With concurrent user licensing, the buyer pays for an estimated average number of users who will access the ERP system at one time, instead of paying for every potential user of the system. However, it's important to estimate the average number correctly or the company may find that some of its employees can't work because they can't get on the system! Heavy and casual user licensing can also work with concurrent licensing. For example, a company with four heavy users and three more casual users, who just need to look at reports periodically, could likely suffice with five licenses rather than seven.

A large majority of ERP software licensing is perpetual, meaning that employees can use the licensed software for an unlimited period of time. However, many ERP solutions are available as cloud offerings with subscription-based licensing. **Subscription-based licensing** gives users access to the hosted ERP software. The software installation, maintenance, and upgrades are handled by the ERP vendor or an authorized value-added reseller. With cloud solutions, the recurring subscription fee is usually calculated on a per-user, per-month basis, and the customer must renew regularly. If a company is considering cloud computing, the TCO should be compared against on premise deployment costs to determine which overall cost (initial plus ongoing) is higher, using a reasonable time frame for analysis.

A final thought on software licensing is that companies should beware of buying more modules and licenses than they need. It's more economical to add users and functionality over time than to scale back on licenses and "shelfware," or purchased software never used. Companies should be careful of vendors that offer "once-in-a-lifetime" deals on software licenses and extra modules. They may just be trying to meet their quarter- or year-end numbers! Chances are, if a company hasn't thought about the module, it doesn't need it (at least not yet). If a module is something the business is interested in for the future, one tip would be to pre-negotiate the price on future purchases to avoid unanticipated license cost increases.

Database and Other Software Costs

ERP vendors will provide the infrastructure specifications for the type of database needed. The database license cost is usually based on the number of simultaneous users that will log in to the system or the number or type of database servers required. Some vendors bundle the database cost with the software license. The company may also need to purchase operating system software as well as **identity and access management (IAM) software** for administering rights and attributes to manage, enforce, and monitor user entitlements and access activities to the ERP system.

IT Infrastructure Costs and Hardware

Successful ERP system operation demands a solid IT infrastructure to run on. Infrastructure components include servers, storage systems, network components, wiring, cooling and power, and redundancy measures. Although a company might already have these components is in place, they might be near their end of life and need upgrading. The cost of hardware varies depending on the scope of the implementation and computing platform. The vendor should propose minimum specifications for the servers that run the system. Additional user workstations may have to be purchased. It should be noted that much of the hardware costs is eliminated by using cloud computing, since the software runs on the vendor or service provider's servers.

Implementation Costs

Most ERP costs are incurred during the actual implementation of the software. Estimating these costs beforehand can be difficult, but often a multiplier of the software license cost is used. The general rule of thumb is that the ratio of services to software costs is approximately 3:1 for a "consultant light" implementation, meaning for every $1 spent on the software, the customer should plan to spend $3 on the implementation. For a "consultant heavy" implementation, the ratio could reach 10:1.

A company should estimate an upper and lower value and the expected value to get a realistic idea of the potential cost. Very often the ratio of services to software costs provided by the vendor is an indication of the system's ease of implementation. It is important to recognize that implementation costs have more to do with the number and complexity of business processes affected during the implementation than the number of licensed users. The number of users only impacts end-user training during implementation.

Research has shown that many companies drastically underestimate various items during implementation including the cost of using internal resources for implementation tasks. The largest part of the internal cost factor is lost productivity for employees, specifically the project team and subject matter experts, who are pulled from their regular duties to work on the implementation. To estimate internal cost, project planners often calculate the number of **full-time equivalents (FTE)**, which is a measure of how many full-time employees would be needed to accomplish the work performed. For example, let's assume that 13 employees work full time on the project and five employees work half time. Also assume an eight-hour day (which is low for an ERP project!). The daily staffing is:

$$(13 \text{ people x } 8 \text{ hrs.}) + (5 \text{ people x } 4 \text{ hrs.}) = 124$$

$$124 \div 8 = 15.5 \text{ FTEs per day.}$$

Based on 15.5 FTEs, the company could roughly estimate how much internal costs are each day by multiplying this number by average salary and benefits.

In many cases, companies do not adequately detail their business requirements, and later on when they are implementing, they find gaps between their requirements and the functionality present in the system. These gaps must be closed with customization or bolt-on solutions. Given how costly both of these options are to the implementation, steps should be taken to ensure that the right ERP system is chosen.

Many other costs are incurred during an ERP implementation, and these will be discussed in Chapter 6. To help minimize these costs, vendors try to simplify the implementation process for their customers. For instance, SAP has a methodology called Accelerated SAP, or ASAP, which streamlines the implementation process. As mentioned previously, Tier 2 and 3 vendor solutions are usually less expensive to implement and have a quicker time-to-benefit.

Maintenance and Support Costs

ERP spending is by no means over at go-live. Generally, ERP system vendors charge an annual maintenance fee in the range of 18 to 25 percent of the **software contract value**, or the license costs minus any discounts. A maintenance contract entitles the customer to receive software corrections, patches, fixes, and new releases. It also covers system updates and enhancements as the supplier continues to invest in the product and take advantage of new functions and technologies. The contract may also include support services. These services typically include continuous access to a support portal, which includes the ability to review support notes, view all the installation and configuration documentation, and ask technical and functional questions. Different levels of support are generally available. More expensive, premium support might include having a vendor representative onsite during the project implementation as well as post-go-live for a certain amount of time. Premium support might also include extended support past a release's normal maintenance time period.

ERP Life Cycle – Package Selection

The process of choosing an ERP system should never be rushed. Generally, it takes three to six months to get to the decision stage, although 12 months is not uncommon. The end goal is to pick an ERP system that best meets the company's requirements out of the hundreds of choices available. The "best" application for a particular company can be based on many factors, including functionality, affordability, user-friendliness, customizability, and vendor support. These factors and their relative importance will generally vary from company to company, but functionality should *always* be at the top of the list.

The following sections outline key steps for selecting an ERP system. While due diligence should be performed during package selection, spending time evaluating vendors takes time—and time is money. Some companies get too engrossed in the process of package selection and evaluate way too many vendors. The following steps outline how to narrow down the vendor choices to one finalist. Before beginning package selection, the organization should form an **ERP selection team**. This team will include members of management, functional experts, and end users from various departments and business units in the company. While the team could be the same as the project team, sometimes it is a different group, perhaps from corporate headquarters. Often, companies will hire an external consulting company to assist in the package selection process. Throughout the selection process, it is important to build consensus among members of the selection team in order to gain company-wide acceptance of the ERP system that is ultimately chosen.

Requirements Analysis

The detailed analysis companies go through to determine all the technical and operational functionalities they need and desire in an ERP system is called **requirements analysis**. In essence, requirements gathering is a fact-finding exercise. Examples of technical requirements include security, customizability, ease of use, and compatibility with existing operating and database systems. Operational (functional) requirements depend on what business processes are in scope. For instance, if the purchase-to-pay process is in scope, the company would need the ability to enter purchase requisitions and purchase orders, post goods or services receipts, enter and approve vendor invoices for payment, and pay invoices. There may also be industry-specific or country-specific operational requirements that need to be addressed. Furthermore, ERP systems can provide additional functionality the company never contemplated, such as advanced planning and scheduling, business analytics, or governance, risk, and compliance. These additional items may surface during requirements analysis or later, when ERP vendors demo their solutions.

Subject matter experts and process owners are the best source of information for operational requirements, and there are various methods of obtaining the information. One method is to hold a series of workshops in which employees discuss the functionality necessary to do their jobs. These workshops should also focus on "pain points," including areas in the company where work-arounds and spreadsheets are used because the functionality is not present in the current systems. These problem areas can become opportunities for enhanced functionality that improve the business. Questionnaires and brainstorming activities are also useful for obtaining requirements and uncovering problem areas that a new system could address. Many companies also document "as is" processes to help with determining requirements.

It is also important to remember that requirements gathering can be burdensome to already overworked employees. The selection team should stay focused on the goal of gathering accurate requirements in no more detail than would be necessary to compile a focused list of selection criteria. An over-expression of requirements should be avoided, as this will lead to unnecessary expenditures. A successful requirements analysis should capture everything that the current business process does today and compile reasonable "should be" changes that would improve the business processes. The results of requirements analysis are contained in a **requirements document**, which details all functionality needed. An excerpt of a requirements document outlining purchasing functionality is presented in Figure 5-4.

Figure 5-4: Example Requirements Document for Purchase-to-Pay Process

Core business processes requirements

- Requisition processing (entry, canceling, changing, deleting, closing, printing, copying, reconciling)
- Purchase order processing (entry, canceling, changing, deleting, closing, printing, copying, reconciling)
- Receiving report processing (entering, changing, canceling, closing)

Additional requirements

- Organizational security for requisition and receiving reports to restrict additions or updates
- Workflow routings and approval for requisitions, purchase order distribution changes, and over-shipments
- Commitment control in order for accounting transactions entered in the Purchasing module to be reflected in the general ledger

Market Survey

Before choosing an ERP package, the selection team should perform a market survey to determine which vendors' systems might be possible candidates. ERP vendors can be identified from any number of sources, including websites, industry magazines, and trade exhibits. Vendors may also be identified through discussions with customers, suppliers, and other business partners. It is important for companies to consider ERP vendors in the appropriate tier. Based upon the requirements document, industry, and cost considerations, the selection team can eliminate many vendors at this point. Typically, companies will arrive at a list of six to eight "long list" vendors to assess after this phase.

Short Listing

If possible, the selection team needs to narrow down the list to three to four vendors, simply due to the time and manpower it takes to evaluate each one. Companies can pare down their lists by talking to a vendor's product expert, watching overview demos of software online, reading the vendor's product literature, or getting insight from a consultant. Often, "discovery calls" will provide the selection team with better insight into the vendors and their solutions than if they just relied on product brochures and sales literature. When analyzing this information, the selection team needs to identify "deal breakers," which are missing requirements. Any ERP system not fulfilling a predetermined core requirement should be eliminated at this stage.

Request for Proposal

The requirements document forms the basis for preparing the **request for proposal (RFP)**, which is sent to the short-listed vendors so they can indicate what requirements their solution meets. The RFP will also ask for other important information such as the cost of the solution, reference sites, financial viability of the vendor, and its local presence. The RFP should also outline due dates for proposals, the selection and award process, and the estimated award date. It is best practice to have a separate selection process for the integration partner (separate RFP and evaluation). Key questions to be addressed with potential integration partners include their industry focus, software product knowledge, the high-level project plan and methodology, thought leadership (for example, publications and presentations), the number of years of partnership status with the vendor, and implementation references.

It is important to keep in mind that answers to the RFPs should be taken with a "grain of salt" because software vendors want to remain in consideration and will put themselves in the very best possible light. Therefore, responses to RFPs must later be backed up with a live demonstration during which the selection team will check out all self-reported information.

Demo Days

Demo days are when ERP vendors must "walk the walk and talk the talk." Vendors still under consideration after the selection team has reviewed their RFPs are invited to the company for a presentation and demonstration of their software. The presentation content usually includes reasons the vendor believes it will make a good potential business partner. The main event, the demo, should include how the vendor's software specifically meets the requirements of the company. The selection team should ask the vendor to focus on the "must haves," but the "nice to haves" and the "bells and whistles" will also be of interest to the team. It is important when evaluating each vendor to focus on what the vendor can deliver now versus what can be provided in the future. The demo should also include menus, navigation, configuration and customization capabilities, reporting capabilities, and support.

Planning for vendor demo days is important, as Figure 5-5 shows. The nature of the demo should be carefully scripted and sent to each vendor well in advance. What must be avoided is an incomplete demo that requires a follow-up, which is costly for both parties. The demo should consist of a walkthrough of key business processes using the **vanilla software**, or non-customized software. The company should also make sure that each vendor organizes the demo around the company's requirements and uses the company's own data, not generic data supplied by the vendor. The intention is to present the ERP system as if it were in production.

Demo days are also the time to evaluate each vendor's technical capabilities. Solutions typically rely on a small number of underlying technology frameworks, and each will present advantages and disadvantages when interacting with existing or future solutions that the organization may employ. Scalability and interoperability should be discussed. These technical considerations may or may not weigh as heavily as the functional business requirements. The fit between a vendor and the company depends on many factors, including the vendor's technical and corporate direction and the steps they take to drive down TCO. If the vendor is also being considered as the integration partner, its commitment to a successful implementation and post-go-live support should be evaluated.

Figure 5-5: Rules for ERP Demo Days

Explain the business requirements to the vendor beforehand
Agree on the agenda with the vendor well in advance and stick to it
First confirm the "must haves," then the "nice to haves," and lastly the "bells and whistles"
Give each vendor scripts reflecting typical workflows in the business for them to demonstrate with actual company data (not their generic data)
Require that the selection team be on time and attend the same sessions for each software vendor
Notice vendor culture if the vendor is also being considered as the integration partner
Evaluate the ERP software based on requirements as opposed to the vendor's performance during the demo; do not be swayed by flashy appearances or "freebies"
Designate a timekeeper to make sure sessions stay on schedule; leave enough time for a post-demo question-and-answer session
Use a weighted score sheet for scoring and ranking vendors

Each vendor may structure its demo somewhat differently, so the team should use a **weighted score sheet** to assist in making an objective decision and comparing "apples to apples." The score sheet is a checklist of important selection criteria combined with a point system. Weights are assigned to each criterion based on the selection team's determination of the criticality of the issue. Figure 5-6 presents a condensed example of selection criteria and points awarded for the evaluation of three different ERP vendors. Each line in this example would be supported by multiple pages of detailed criteria. On the left side of the figure are functional, technical, and commercial requirements that may be considered when evaluating a vendor. One important requirement is "matched to our growth." A high score on this criterion means that the ERP package will be able to scale up as the company grows. It would be a waste of time and money to implement a solution that would become obsolete in a few years. It is also crucial that the vendor has a long-term product vision and is investing adequate research and development for future releases. Ease of customization is always a key technical requirement that needs to be evaluated for each vendor solution. The last four rows in the figure are selection criteria for evaluating the integration partner.

Figure 5-6: ERP Package Weighted Score Sheet

ERP Selection Criteria	Importance (1-3)	Vendor A		Vendor B		Vendor C	
		Rating (1-10)	Weighted Rating	Rating (1-10)	Weighted Rating	Rating (1-10)	Weighted Rating
Manufacturing functionality	3	8	24	10	30	7	21
Human resources functionality	3	6	18	7	21	8	24
Sales and distribution functionality	3	6	18	5	15	4	12
Financials functionality	3	4	12	7	21	6	18
Purchasing functionality	3	6	18	9	27	3	9
Software license cost	1	5	5	9	9	6	6
Customizability	2	6	12	7	14	8	16
Compatibility with existing applications	1	4	4	6	6	5	5
Scalability	2	6	12	5	10	4	8
Security	3	2	6	8	24	6	18
Vendor commitment to R&D	2	6	12	7	14	8	16
Integration with third-party applications	1	4	4	6	6	8	8
Product commonly used in our industry	2	8	16	5	10	3	6
Support and maintenance costs	2	3	6	5	10	7	14
Ease of use	1	3	3	8	8	10	10
Product used in similar size companies	3	7	21	7	21	2	6
Integrator understands our business	3	5	15	9	27	4	12
Implementation cost	2	5	10	8	16	9	18
Implementation methodology	1	5	5	8	8	7	7
Integrator understands our processes	3	4	12	8	24	10	30
Totals:			**233**		**321**		**264**

Fit/Gap Analysis

After the demos are completed, the team will need to meet in order to discuss each package. The methodology used to compare the company's business requirements with what the ERP systems under consideration offer is known as a **fit/gap analysis**. This analysis should be performed on every package on the short list so that an objective comparison can be made. "Fits" are where the

ERP system matches the company's required functionality. "Gaps" are where there is a mismatch between the ERP system and the company's required functionality. The more functionality "gaps," the less attractive a system is to the customer. Requirements gaps must be closed by customization of the system or implementing additional "bolt-on" solutions, which may pose unexpected costs and delays. For instance, if package "A" has 50 gaps and package "B" has 15 gaps, package "A" will likely create more problems during implementation. However, it should be noted that process "gaps" could be an opportunity to reengineer the process to best practices.

Reference Visits

The selection team may also wish to ask each short-listed vendor for references in order to conduct reference visits. A **reference visit** allows the selection team to see each system under consideration implemented in a real-world environment with live data and actual users versus what has been seen in a demo conducted by the vendor's sales team. During a reference visit, the selection team members have the opportunity to speak frankly with their counterparts at other companies and gain insights into the benefits and drawbacks of the system they are using. Keep in mind that references supplied by the vendors are generally the ones that are very happy with the vendor's software. However, the more objective the reference, the better. Therefore, the team should seek out additional companies that have implemented the short-listed vendor solutions and not rely solely on vendor-provided references.

References should be companies comparable in size, industry, and geographic location using the same software version and, ideally, the same database. These commonalities will boost the relevance of the reference site to the selection process. Companies should request lists of short-term customers (implementation in progress or within the last six months), mid-term customers (one to three years after implementation), and long-term customers (four to six years after implementation). From the reference visits, the team should be able to confirm if the ERP system under consideration is right sized, if it fits the industry well, how good the local technical support is, and how the current version runs. Special notice should be taken of different software versions, particularly when the versions are markedly different. Comparisons with dissimilar versions may have minimal value. Issues to discuss with "like" customer sites include overall satisfaction with the software functionality, system performance, and look and feel of the system. When discussing potential integration partners, questions to ask at the reference companies include:

- Did you go over the original budget? If your implementation took longer and cost more than was estimated, why?

- How is the local vendor support? It can get costly flying consultants in every week!

- Are there any lessons you learned through issues that were not anticipated, but arose after the implementation began?

Vendor Negotiations

After all this hard work, it is finally time to negotiate and procure an ERP system (see Figure 5-7 for negotiation tips). Before commencing negotiations, the customer should make sure that all information collected thus far from demos, reference visits, and fit/gap analysis has been painstakingly analyzed. The steering committee and legal department are primarily responsible for negotiating the purchase of the ERP system and implementation services. There may be multiple vendors and integration partners that are finalists, and not a bad idea to let these parties know that negotiations are taking place with more than one company.

The vendor's initial contract proposal will include the recommended modules and prices for the defined scope. The proposal should also include any annual fees for maintenance and support and software assurance that provides rights to future releases of the system at little or no cost. The company may wish to inquire about a reduced annual fee in exchange for agreeing to a multi-year maintenance contract. The customer may also need coaching on upgrades to hardware, network resources, or supporting software such as operating systems, database capacity, or connectivity requirements. To help make this determination, the proposal should specify this additional information.

It has been said that the price of ERP software is "firmly written in Jell-O." ERP vendors expect their customers to negotiate for the best ERP deal. Therefore, the initial price quote is usually marked up considerably to ensure the vendor makes the most profit possible. Customers should do their due diligence by asking reference companies what price they paid, and of course, leveraging multiple quotes. Offering to serve as a reference can sometimes persuade a vendor to discount its

price. Timing also plays into the price of the licenses. Typically, software providers are more generous with incentives or discounts early on in an effort to gain the customer. Vendors may also provide volume discounts if the company purchases multiple modules packaged as a "suite" of software. However, customers should be wary of paying for modules that will never be used. Often, paying up front for the maintenance contract will induce the ERP vendor to discount it. All potential discounts should be considered because once the deal is signed, the company is locked in—the costs of switching become prohibitive, and the provider knows it.

Talks can break down if both parties merely focus on their own short-term goals while trying to create the best monetary deal for themselves. Sharing with the vendor various ways to work together long-term can affect contract negotiations positively. Viewing ERP vendors and resellers as partners, rather than adversaries, is an important step in reaching the right deal. Communicating clearly and openly about needs, budgets, and challenges is often the best way to reach a "win-win" solution.

The company's CIO, who generally sits on the steering committee, should compare the suitability of the technology with the existing IT infrastructure, and the CFO should evaluate the cost of the system and the vendor's financial health. These parties, as well as the legal team, should also review the vendor contract. Legal experts often remind buyers that boilerplate contracts are designed to favor the vendor. Instead of taking a boilerplate contract as it is written, companies should use it as an opportunity to ask questions about confusing language.

Final negotiations may include rapid interaction as terms, prices, and contractual obligations are discussed at length until the teams from both parties reach an agreement. Keep in mind that if the vendor is also going to serve as the integration partner, the services component is generally the most expensive and least negotiable since experienced personnel are scarce and at a premium. The implementation schedule can also affect the negotiations, which might include built-in incentives and penalties based on timely performance. Negotiating integration services is discussed next.

Figure 5-7: Tips for Negotiating the Best ERP Deal

The starting point	Be aware that the first offer is typically inflated.
Don't stop looking at other vendors	Continue to evaluate other ERP solutions and make sure vendor account executives are aware of this fact. An organization will never have more negotiating power than it does before it signs the deal.
Don't overbuy	Some ERP vendors will offer free features or modules in lieu of a price discount. Unless these are on the company's original list of requirements, do not accept.
Serve as a reference in return for a discount	Before serving as a reference, be sure to consult with the legal team regarding any contractual stipulations and possible repercussions that could arise.
Make the deal sustainable	Business climates change. The company might enter a merger, spin off a business unit, expand functionally or geographically, or divest assets. The deal must cover all these possibilities or the company risks additional fees at each event.
Any deal for "any price" is profitable for the vendor	There are no direct costs linked to a software deal (all associated costs are sunk costs). This means that whatever the price, the deal is profitable for the vendor. In theory the starting selling price could be zero. This gives lots of negotiating power to the buyer. However, typically salespeople can't go below a certain level without permission from a superior.

Source: AlixPartners

Integration Partner Negotiation

While it is important that a company selects an ERP package that has the requisite breadth of functionality to support current and future needs, the truth is that the capabilities of ERP solutions within a given tier and industry are all comparatively similar. There are, however, significant capability differences among integration partners. These differences help explain why nearly every major ERP software vendor can point to both satisfied customers and failed implementations. Culture seems like a frivolous factor, but since an implementation can take years, confidence in a working relationship with the consultants is important.

A company might choose to contract for implementation services with the ERP vendor directly, with a third-party integrator such as Accenture or Deloitte Consulting, or with one of the vendor's value-added resellers (VARs). Of upmost importance is to make sure the integration partner has plenty of experience with the chosen ERP package and the company's industry. A company might contract with the best consultants for the software it chooses, but if the consultants have

never worked in the company's industry, then the company is making a major mistake, as the consultants will not appreciate and understand the nuances of the business. It is also critical to know what types of project management tools, methodologies, and processes the integration partner will leverage to make the implementation more efficient and effective. Generally, with each ERP package there is a "best" methodology used for implementation. The customer should make sure that the integration partner is using a standard, acceptable methodology and has vast experience with it.

The proposal with the integration partner should clearly define what activities are the consultant's responsibilities and what activities are the customer's. For instance, the proposal could state that data is the responsibility of the customer. This means that the customer will extract data out of legacy systems and make sure that it is all correct before the consultant loads it into the ERP system. The proposal might state that testing and customization are the responsibility of the consultant. Delineating responsibilities minimizes confusion and "finger pointing" during implementation and provides input for the project plan.

Also set forth in the proposal should be issue escalation procedures, decision-making, scope management, and risk management. These items are all part of **project governance**, which are the rules and regulations under which an IT project functions. It clearly defines policies, processes, and responsibilities that define establishment, management, and control of projects. Also, the composition of the consulting team should be agreed upon to avoid the "bait and switch" of personnel (that is, sending "newbies" in to learn the company's industry and processes on the company's dime). Training, communication, and change management (helping employees acclimate to the new system) should also be discussed. Travel costs of vendor personnel and consultants can become significant, so the customer may want to establish limits or provide for a way to control them. Once all these issues are fleshed out, the two parties can complete a services estimate along with a statement of work that clearly defines the project as well as the mutually agreed upon roles and responsibilities of the vendor, integrator, and customer. The outcome of all this intense scrutiny is selecting a "winner." Finally, the big day arrives. The contracts are signed and ERP implementation begins!

Summary

There are four stages of the ERP life cycle. This chapter discusses the first two stages: planning and package selection. Planning for ERP involves making sure that there is a strong business case before proceeding. Benefits to be realized should be documented and all cost components considered. The organizational structure should be established for the project including the steering committee, project team, and project manager. The project manager's job is crucial, as this person is involved in the daily supervision of the project. The project charter and scope statement should together firmly outline the goals of the project and detail the deliverables and project milestones. The selection team should perform its due diligence and gather enough information about each package being considered before it makes a final decision. Package selection activities include market surveys, requirements analysis, reference visits, software demonstrations, and fit/gap analysis. The culmination of all this work is to come to mutually beneficial agreements with the vendor and integration partner and form partnerships that are advantageous for both parties.

Keywords

Business case

Business case rationale

Business metric

Casual user licensing

Change request

Concurrent user licensing

ERP selection team

Fit/gap analysis

Full-time equivalent (FTE)

Heavy user licensing

Identity and access management (IAM) software

Named user licensing

Program manager

Project charter

Project governance

Project manager (PM)

Project team

Reference visit

Request for proposal (RFP)

Requirements analysis

Requirements document

Scope creep

Scope management

Scope statement

Software contract value

Steering committee

Subscription-based licensing

Total cost of ownership (TCO)

Vanilla software

Weighted score sheet

Quick Review

1. True/False: The project manager typically reports to the program manager.

2. True/False: Software license costs are typically the largest part of the total cost of ownership for an ERP system.

3. The _____ should include key process owners, end users, managers, and IT staff spanning functional boundaries, business units, and organizational levels of the company.

4. The detailed analysis companies go through to determine all the technical and operational functionalities they need and desire is called _____.

5. A methodology used to quantify the comparison of ERP package functionality to the customer's ERP requirements is the _____ analysis.

Questions to Consider

1. What are the four stages in the ERP life cycle?

2. Explain the four business case rationales for an ERP system.

3. What are some decisions that the steering committee is responsible for regarding the ERP project?

4. List steps in the package selection stage of the ERP life cycle.

5. How can the buyer ensure that an ERP software demo runs as smoothly as possible?

References

Aldrich, J. (2012, July 20). Is a best-of-breed ERP system for you? Retrieved from http://panorama-consulting.com/is-a-best-of-breed-erp-system-for-you/

Aldrich, Jennifer. (2013, May 24). How requirements gathering can improve your ERP selection process. Retrieved from http://panorama-consulting.com/how-requirements-gathering-can-improve-your-erp-selection-process/

AlixPartners. (n.d.). The art and science of ERP selection & negotiation. Retrieved from http://www.alixpartners.com/itaa/IntellectualCapital/TheArtandScienceofERPSelectionNegotiation.aspx

Aptean. (n.d.). ERP system cost. Retrieved from http://www.aptean.com/en/Solutions/By-Application-Area/Enterprise-Resource-Planning-ERP/Resources-Folder/ERP-System-Cost

Beaubouef, B. (2011, February 13). Defining scope for ERP implementations. Retrieved from http://gbeaubouef.wordpress.com/2011/02/13/defining-erp-product-scope/

Business-Software.com. (n.d.). 5 tips to negotiate the best ERP deal. Retrieved from http://www.business-software.com/article/5-tips-to-negotiate-the-best-erp-deal/

Cook, R. (2013, May 3). The payoff: Calculating the ROI on ERP. Retrieved from http://www.inside-erp.com/articles/inside-erp-blog/the-payoff-calculating-the-roi-on-erp-55779

Focus Research (2010). 6 best practices for selecting ERP software. Retrieved from http://whitepapers.technologyevaluation.com/view_document/22741/6-best-practices-for-selecting-erp-software.html

Gartner, Inc. (n.d.) 10 Characteristics of a Successful Project Manager. Retrieved from http://www.datamation.com/entdev/article.php/614681/ERP-Project-Management-Is-Key-To-A-Successful-Implementation.htm

Kimberling, E. (2007, February 5). Assessing your organization's ERP readiness. Toolbox.com. Retrieved from http://it.toolbox.com/blogs/erp-roi/assessing-your-organizations-erp-readiness-14294

Langenhop, C. (2012, December 1). Calculating total cost of ownership (TCO): An important measurement of ROI. CTS Manufacturing Blog. [blog post] Retrieved from http://www.ctsguides.com/manufacturing/calculating-total-cost-of-ownership-tco-an-important-measurement-of-roi/

Management Study Guide. (n.d.). Evaluation and selection of ERP packages. Retrieved from http://www.managementstudyguide.com/evaluation-selection-erp-packages.htm

McDaniel, M., Sullivan, M., & Siegel, R. (2004, December). Using metrics to track progress of community outreach programs. *CEP Magazine*. Retrieved from https://www.aiche.org/resources/publications/cep/2004/december/using-metrics-track-progress-community-outreach-programs

Neely, B. (2012, April 23). An expert's guide to ERP success. Retrieved from http://panorama-consulting.com/an-experts-guide-to-erp-success/

One Hundred & Eighty Degrees Systems Limited. (n.d.). Implementation is all about people. Retrieved from http://www.180systems.com/articles-and-research/erp/ImplementationPeople/

Panorama Consulting Solutions (2013). 2013 ERP report. Retrieved from http://panorama-consulting.com/resource-center/2013-erp-report/

Pearl, M. (n.d.). *How to buy your next ERP system*. Retrieved from http://techexchange.com/library/How%20to%20buy%20your%20next%20ERP%20system.pdf

RFP Evaluation Centers. (2014). *How to write an RFP?* Retrieved from http://www.rfptemplates.technologyevaluation.com/how-to-write-an-rfp.html

Sage ERP. (2010, September 29). The role of the ERP project manager. [blog post] Retrieved from http://blog.sageerpsolutions.com/the-role-of-the-erp-project-manager/

TechAdvisory.org. (2012, June 26). Five crucial questions for ERP evaluation. [blog post] Retrieved from http://www.techadvisory.org/2012/06/five-crucial-questions-for-erp-evaluation-2/

Ultra Consultants. (2012, December 26). Calculating ROI: Just one step toward effective ERP selection. [blog post] Retrieved from http://www.ultraconsultants.com/calculating-roi-just-one-step-toward-effective-erp-selection/

Chapter 6

ERP Life Cycle: Implementation and Operation and Maintenance

Objectives

- Recognize activities that take place in the implementation stage of the ERP life cycle

- Know the various types of ERP customizations

- Identify the steps in data migration

- Describe specific types of testing done during an ERP implementation

- Differentiate among ERP implementation strategies

- Identify the advantages and disadvantages of using consultants during an ERP implementation

- Be aware of issues that must be addressed during the operation and maintenance stage of the ERP life cycle

Introduction

In the previous chapter, we examined the first two stages of the ERP life cycle, planning and package selection. Once these stages are complete, a company is ready to implement the ERP system. Generally, the implementation stage takes much longer than the first two stages combined. Depending on factors such as project scope, extent of customization, internal and external resources devoted to the project, and size and complexity of the company and its processes, implementation can take months—or even years. Once the ERP system is implemented and goes live, the operation and maintenance stage begins, in which the system becomes stable and over time, patches, service packs, enhancements, and upgrades take place. It is essential that everyone involved in an ERP project understand what tasks are required and what issues must be addressed in each stage of the ERP life cycle. Mismanagement of an ERP project can have disastrous financial, legal, operational, and reputational consequences. However, prudent management of the ERP project can translate into great rewards for the company.

ERP Life Cycle – Implementation

Software implementation is a structured approach to integrating software into the workflow of an organization, thereby transforming its business operations. Many of the ERP software implementations in the late 1990s and early 2000s were unsuccessful, but now we know more about how to effectively conduct an implementation. That is not to say that companies don't still experience problems implementing ERP systems. A quick search of the internet using the keywords "ERP failure" yields many reports of calamitous rollouts. Laying the groundwork for success does not start when the first consultant walks in the door. It begins much earlier with strong project sponsorship and clear objectives and goals for the ERP system. The implementation stage of the ERP life cycle involves a number of activities that must be accomplished well for the project to be a success. Each of these activities calls for specific knowledge and skills required by internal and external resources and a carefully thought-out and managed project plan. The following sections describe various ERP implementation activities, starting with installation of the ERP system.

Installation

Software installation is the process of either transferring the software from disc or downloading it from the internet onto the hard drive of a computer. The ERP system, database, and operating system must be installed on servers, creating multiple environments for use during and after implementation. In Chapter 2, we learned that these multiple environments include development (DEV), quality assurance (QA), and production (PRD). Each environment has an important role to play. The software must be configured and customized properly to fit the requirements of the company in the DEV environment and must be tested in QA. Training can take place in one of these environments as well. The focus is to implement the ERP system successfully so that once go-live is reached, the version of the ERP system in PRD is bug free and meets the requirements of the company.

Installation may also include creating or upgrading the technical infrastructure that will support the ERP system. In the case of a hosted ERP system, a service provider, which may be the software vendor, will handle the details of making the system available to the customer based on the terms of the contract. However, many companies still choose to install their ERP systems on premise for various reasons as discussed in Chapter 2. During the ERP contract negotiation process, the vendor should have supplied specifications for the IT infrastructure. It is likely that the company will need to purchase new hardware, update the operating system, increase networking capacity, and upgrade other infrastructure components.

Configuration

ERP systems are designed by software vendors based on the generic needs of many different companies. Because of the many options available within each ERP system, companies spend a lot of time during implementation determining which of these options will be switched on or off, which entails making entries into various tables to make the ERP system meet their particular needs. This process, known as **configuration**, is a major task during implementation. Configuration does not make any changes to the core software code, but instead tailors a particular aspect of the ERP system to the way a company chooses to do business. This process can be complex, and for many software implementations, consultants are usually brought in to help. As ERP software vendors attempt to gain market share, they continue to broaden their target customer base by providing configuration options to address an increasing number of system requirements.

Database tables used for configuration are called **configuration tables** (as opposed to master data or transaction data tables). Project team members can use configuration tools in the ERP software to access configuration tables. This allows them to select enterprise and process settings through an easy-to-use graphical user interface (GUI) built into the ERP system. The following are examples of configuration decisions:

How many different companies (legal entities) need to be reflected in the system?

- What is the default currency and language?

- Who approves customer credit?

- When is the fiscal year end?

- What are the various units of measure for materials (for example, base unit, selling unit, storage unit)?

- What is the transaction limit that certain employees can post before requiring a second approval?

SAP has thousands of configuration decisions that have to be made during implementation, and navigating through them can be a formidable task. For example, when Dell Computers implemented SAP, the configurations alone took over a year to decide upon. For many companies, the array of configuration options offers enough flexibility to allow them to do a **vanilla implementation**. This means that the organization uses only the configuration options available in the ERP system to tailor the software to its business. While this introduces very little "flavor," or differentiation, to companies, these implementations have a better chance of coming in on time and on budget. So what happens when the options the system allows don't exactly fit the business requirements? At this point, the organization may elect to supplement the ERP programming code, a process known as customization.

Customization

Customization involves modifying existing code or adding additional code to the ERP system to make it fit a company's unique needs. As mentioned, ERP applications are designed with common requirements of an industry in mind. However, ERP software does not have an infinite number of configuration options. Inevitably something will crop up that the system doesn't do exactly the way a company needs it to—a particular workflow step needs to be inserted, a report or form written, an interface developed, or functionality added. So, the company will start customizing the software.

The majority of companies implementing ERP systems customize them. In fact, a recent study found that 89 percent of companies surveyed had customized their ERP system. For an ERP system to be "fully customizable," there must be complete flexibility on defining the screens, workflows, data model, and reports. Generally, a company would only want to spend money on customization if it supports a business process or function that is unique or provides them with a competitive advantage. Additionally, a company may need custom functionality due to a compliance, regulatory, reporting, or legislative requirement that the software does not meet. With custom code, you can do just about anything to the ERP system—given enough time, money, and development talent.

Any customizations should be based on the fit/gap analysis, which should have been performed at a high level during package selection but is completed in more detail during implementation. Customization requires developing functional and technical specifications followed by programming, so the company will likely need consultants to do this type of work. The customizations are collectively referred to as RICEF:

- **Reports** – Basic reports are included in an ERP system, but developers may also need to write custom, company-specific reports to replace those native to the sunset system(s) because users still need them.

- **Interfaces** – Interfaces connect two or more different systems so that data can pass back and forth. ERP systems are often interfaced with legacy systems that are retained or with other ERP vendor modules. Interfaces physically extract, transfer, and load data between separate databases, on a less than real-time basis. These customizations can be a major expense during implementation depending on the number needed.

- **Conversions** – A conversion supports the data migration process, which will be discussed later. Programs may need to be written to extract the data from legacy systems and load it into the ERP system. Data must be converted from one format to another and from one system to another.

- **Enhancements** – Enhancements add to the standard code. These customizations make use of **customer exits**, which are pre-defined breaks in the core code where the customer can insert custom programming without fundamentally altering the core code. The majority of ERP implementations involve customer exit enhancements.

- **Forms** – Forms include technical development that deal with taking necessary data from the ERP system and using it for printing customized output documents.

An additional, but rarely used, type of customization is a modification. **Modifications** make changes to the core code, fundamentally altering the software. Because of the invasiveness of modifications, they are rarely done and should be discouraged. Modifications require steering committee approval and must be registered with the software vendor. Furthermore, modifications are written over during an upgrade, which adds time and cost to that process.

While there are advantages to customizing an ERP system, there are also disadvantages. The following are disadvantages to customizing ERP software:

- Creating custom code involves inherent risks that can only be eliminated with exhaustive testing. Too often, quality assurance is undercut in order for the project to come in on time, creating risks associated with "buggy" software. This, in turn, leads to a less stable and reliable system.

- Customization can be expensive because of the time it takes to write technical and functional specifications, program the code, and test for bugs. For instance, SAP customizations are written in a proprietary SQL-like programming language called ABAP. It is highly unlikely that an ABAP programmer exists in-house, so companies implementing SAP may have to hire ABAP programmers to write the code.

- The focus on heavy customization efforts may detract attention from other, more critical aspects of the ERP implementation, such as change management and training.

- Ironically, customizations don't add value by default. Instead, they *subtract* value because of design and programming costs and in the long run, through upgrade, maintenance, and support costs. Firms should ensure that the net result is value-added. Each time a company contemplates a customization, it should assess the business case for it.

- If the customization is a modification of core code, it can limit the company's ability to upgrade the ERP system. The new code will need to be reprogrammed each time the customer wants to upgrade. The process of redoing customizations done for an earlier version of the software during an upgrade is known as a **retro-fit**.

- Customized systems may be difficult to integrate and/or interface with other systems.

107

- The ERP vendor typically does not support code it did not provide.

Regarding this last point, the project team should consider consulting with the ERP vendor regarding customizations. Often the vendor may assist by internalizing efforts to provide unique solutions that would otherwise require customization and instead make them configurable options. This approach may be advantageous to both parties. The company gets what they want more easily, and the vendor may expand their target customer base to attract more companies that need this option as well.

Bolt-on Technology

Companies may need to purchase a third-party software package, referred to as a **bolt-on**, to obtain additional functionality not present in the chosen ERP system. With this approach, the software is "bolted-on" to the ERP system. As a side note, bolt-on vendors may say that their products are "fully integrated" with the ERP system. However, integration implies that solutions use a common database, with minimal file duplication, and the data is updated across the system in real time. So, it is important to understand what the vendor means when they say "fully integrated." It is often the case that the bolt-on will require an interface so the two systems can "talk" to one another. Typical examples of bolt-ons include radio frequency identification and electronic data interchange, which are discussed in Chapter 9.

Conference Room Pilot

Early on, during the package selection stage, the ERP system might have been installed on a server to allow the selection team to practice business tasks with the new software and determine fits and gaps. These "workshops" continue throughout implementation and are known as **conference room pilots (CRPs)**, since conference rooms are typically designated as temporary locations for the work. Key objectives of CRPs include:

- Define and document desired end-to-end business processes and workflows for configuration

- Identify in a detailed manner gaps between the new ERP system and the old system for customization/addition of bolt-ons

- Recognize the impact of the changes on affected departments and individuals and estimate training and change management needs

- Understand the strengths and weaknesses of the ERP software being considered (during package selection)

- Test the system prior to go-live

Data Migration

Early on in the implementation or during planning, the project team should identify all of the legacy systems that will be sunset and consider a data migration strategy. **Data migration** is the process of moving master and transaction data from the legacy systems being retired into the new ERP system. Also referred to as **ETL (extract, transform, load)**, this process can include moving whole data entities or data fields into the ERP system from areas that are being automated for the first time. In most implementations, migration entails a large data conversion, and every effort should be made to assess the quality of these data sources before moving them into the ERP system. However, in many instances, data migration is treated as a low priority, and the implementation suffers as a result. Migrating data, especially master data, is critical to an ERP implementation, as it has far-reaching effects on the accuracy of transactions. The volume of data to be moved into the ERP system (for example, detail or summary level, number of years of historical data needed) takes time and thus increases the cost of the implementation. Companies typically use the following data migration procedures during an implementation:

- **Data extraction** – taking data out of existing legacy systems and databases; requires special utilities obtained through the ERP vendor or a third-party vendor

- **Data collection** – compiling new data not already in digital format; may require that spreadsheets are populated with the required data before moving it into the ERP system

- **Data cleansing/Data scrubbing** – changing the format of the data into what the ERP system requires; involves correcting inaccuracies in the data such as incorrect code numbers, obsolete data, duplications, and misspellings

- **Data harmonization** – standardizing data, often from different sources, into a common format company-wide; examples include standardizing material numbers and customer numbers

- **Data loading** – putting the data into the ERP system; many iterations of testing should be performed on this data prior to and after loading into the ERP system to ensure a successful go-live

When migrating master data, the team should consider breadth of scope. For instance, a company may only want to migrate suppliers that it has purchased from in the last five years, or only active employees. Reducing the scope of data to carry forward supports the simplification and rationalization efforts that many companies undertake with ERP implementations. For transaction data, companies should consider depth of scope. Some companies may only load open transactions (for example, open purchase orders). However, only loading open transactions will restrict a company's ability to perform historical reporting and analysis in the ERP system (although the older data could be moved to a data warehouse for analysis). Therefore, companies should carefully consider how much transaction history to migrate.

For data migration to achieve its objectives, the importance of the data and where the data resides must be fully understood. The natural starting point for developing this understanding is through a dialog with the **data owner**, which is a person or department that approves access to certain data and is responsible for the data's accuracy, integrity, and timeliness. However, as anyone who has tried to find a data owner knows, it can be a daunting task. Determining early on in the project who these data owners are is key to a successful migration strategy.

Also included in the data migration strategy should be the composition of the data migration team. Generally, the team should include the project manager, key stakeholders, business analysts, programmers, and data owners. The strategy should also include tasks and responsibilities for all these individuals. For instance, data owners identify where the data is and what needs to be cleansed, key stakeholders sign off at various stages during the migration process, and business analysts ensure proper definitions of data fields.

Testing

One of the most critical activities during implementation is testing. Testing helps confirm that data has been loaded successfully into the ERP system and that the system behaves as expected. Testing should also be performed on the hardware, network, and entire IT infrastructure supporting the ERP system. Major problems can arise if a thorough testing strategy has not been included in the project plan. The risk of skimping on testing is that the system will go live and not work as anticipated. This can bring a company to a halt pretty fast!

Employees across the company should be enlisted for the various types of testing involved. For quality assurance, this group should be separate from the functional personnel working on configuration or the technical staff working on customization. All errors found during testing should be documented, and a process should be in place to manage how these errors will be fixed, retested, and closed. Additionally, testing should only be conducted on functionality that is stable and not under major development. It is critical to get sign-offs during testing cycles to ensure buy-in and serve as documentation for audit purposes. Specific types of testing include:

- **Data migration testing** – The ERP system must be able to properly use the data transferred from the previous system(s).

- **Data mapping testing** – When the ERP system is interfaced with other systems, data is mapped from one system to the other. This can often be the most difficult type of testing because technology platforms and languages may be divergent and the mode of transport can vary from relatively straightforward point-to-point interfaces to increasingly more sophisticated middleware technologies. Also, corrupt or invalid data may reside in the other systems, which causes display issues in the ERP system.

- **Unit testing** – This is the lowest level of functional testing in which discrete steps in a business process or a single customization are tested against the specification. An example of unit testing is entering a purchase order and saving it.

- **Integration testing** – This type of testing involves checking end-to-end business processes, including any customizations to the system. As transactions are executed, expected results can be compared to actual results. An example of integration testing is simulating the entire purchase-to-pay process.

- **User acceptance testing** – The final round of integration testing prior to go-live, user acceptance testing tasks end users with making sure the system meets their approval and agreeing that it is ready to move to production.

- **Authorization testing** – This is security testing in which user roles and authorizations are verified. Tests for security should include both positive and negative tests to demonstrate that allowed functionality can be accessed by a particular user role or that disallowed functionality is appropriately denied. Authorization testing is important to a secure identity and access management (IAM) infrastructure.

- **Performance load testing** – This type of testing is used to determine whether the ERP system and database can handle the load that will be placed upon it by simultaneous users by testing the response times of key business processes and transactions. These stress tests must pass predetermined acceptance criteria or performance thresholds. Performance testing is often conducted using software to simulate peak volume, such as LoadRunner.

Each type of test requires the testing team to outline the testing procedures it will use and to describe what a successful test would look like. The team should develop metrics that will help measure whether the testing of the ERP system is progressing satisfactorily. Listed below are categories of testing quality and key questions to ask for each.

- Progress – How much testing have we completed? How much is left to test? When will we finish? Is our testing rate improving?

- Coverage – What percentage of the application have we tested? How does this break down across application functions?

- Defects – How many defects have we found, fixed, or reported to the ERP vendor due to "buggy" software? What is the severity of the defects we are finding?

Testing helps ensure that the implementation has been done competently and completely. If testing is done with quality in mind, the ERP go-live will be far less traumatic. It is crucial that tests and test outcomes are documented to reduce the risk exposure to the project team and consultants. A final note about testing is that go-live is not the finish line for testing; it is the starting point. There are probably patches from the ERP vendor waiting to be applied post-go-live, and new defects will inevitably be revealed that were undetected earlier. Testing should be approached as an ongoing process throughout the life cycle of the ERP system.

Change Management

Change management is the body of knowledge that addresses change within the context of an organization. It is a structured approach to getting employees from "Point A" (pre-change) to "Point B" (post-change), where all employees are fully trained and new processes are in operation. An ERP system can be significantly unsettling to employees because it requires a paradigm shift in the way the company operates and how they perform their jobs. ERP systems can change a company in several ways, including:

- Job changes – ERP systems may make some jobs unnecessary, which could mean that affected employees may be reassigned to new departments or terminated. For employees whose roles change, it is helpful to encourage them to see this as an opportunity to obtain a new skill set to help move them and the company in a new strategic direction.

- A switch in focus – Implementing an ERP system transforms a business from a functional orientation to a process orientation. This change can be worrisome for some task-oriented employees.

- Changes in employee relationships – ERP systems often change the way employees interact with each other. The people in charge may shift departments, merge, or separate, and employees may move throughout the company.

All of these changes affect employees, who may feel that the system is invasive, unnecessary, and inconvenient. In frustration, end users may intentionally or unintentionally undermine an ERP project by spreading negativity, adhering to time-consuming workarounds, or simply refusing to learn how to use the new system. This hesitancy or resistance must be anticipated and managed through change management techniques that include training, communication, and education. As changes take place, employees should be coached on why the change is important to the company and the employee. Understanding the "why" behind the ERP project should foster feelings of ownership and enthusiasm for the change, not fear and uncertainty. Change should be managed in such a way that, even if employees are not 100 percent positive about what's to come, they are at least accepting of the change and understand its objectives. Employees should also be encouraged to provide input into the implementation process and be assured that their input will be considered. Figure 6-1 lists 10 best practices for change management.

Figure 6-1: 10 Principles of Change Management

Address the "human side"	People are innately resistant to change. Employees should feel comfortable sharing their concerns.
Start at the top	Top management behavior must model what they say. They need to take ownership of the change and lead it.
Involve every layer	Leaders should be identified in every level of the company so change cascades through the organization.
Make the formal case	A business case should be formally outlined and communicated throughout the organization so employees see the "big picture."
Create ownership	Ownership is often best created by involving people in identifying problems and developing solutions. It is reinforced by incentives and rewards, both tangible and psychological.
Communicate the message	Besides the obvious, management should communicate the more subtle aspects that employees really care about, such as how jobs will change and what the organizational impact will be.
Assess the cultural landscape	The organization's readiness for change should be assessed. Doing so will bring problems to the surface, identify conflicts, and recognize sources of leadership and resistance.
Address culture explicitly	Leaders should be explicit about the culture and underlying behaviors that will best support the new way of doing business, and find opportunities to model and reward those behaviors.
Prepare for the unexpected	Management should continually reassess the impact of the change and employees' willingness and ability to adapt to the new way of work.
Speak to the individual	Management should let each employee know what is expected by providing clarity and defining rewards for achieving attainable changes.

Source: J. Jones, D. Aguirre, & M. Calderone

The degree to which leaders are able to manage change, develop consensus, and sustain commitment will determine the success or failure of any change initiative. Often, someone is designated to lead change in the organization. This person, known as a **change agent**, should have the clout, conviction, and charisma to make things happen and to keep employees engaged. In essence, they must create order out of chaos. A change agent can be either a consultant or someone designated within the company to serve in this role. Either way this person should be able to:

- Guide, nurture, and shepherd employees to ensure organizational change is accepted enthusiastically, rather than with distrust and fear

- Know how to navigate organizational politics to influence positive results

- Take apart a process and put it back together in original, innovative ways

- Speak many organizational languages, such as sales, accounting, and IT

- Understand the financial impacts of change

An effective change management program includes good communication. Communication with employees should be creative, consistent, and frequent; it should reiterate what change is coming, reinforce the compelling business reasons that make ERP necessary to support the company's strategic direction, and elicit the response from employees that is needed to make the project a success. Listening to employee concerns is key, as is being candid about the change that is to come. It is best practice to put up a website on the corporate intranet where employees can get status updates on the implementation. Another best practice is to identify employees who  are natural opinion leaders and make sure they are on board. These people can use their personal and professional credibility to persuade other employees of the importance of the ERP project.

Training

Training is the cornerstone of any good change management strategy, but research has suggested that it is often the most overlooked and under-budgeted ERP cost component. Furthermore, many organizations wait too long to begin training their employees—often right before go-live. Having prepared and knowledgeable employees before the system goes live lessens the risk that productivity will plummet after go-live.

Training expenses can be high because employees almost invariably have to learn a new set of processes, not just new software. Professional training companies may not always be the best resource as they typically focus on the vanilla workflow as opposed to the way that a company has customized and configured its software. As an alternative to using external resources for training, many companies employ the **train-the-trainer** method, in which "super users" in various functional areas attend in-depth training conducted by the vendor, integration partner, or project team members and then train their coworkers on the software and specific workflow. This approach minimizes the stress on the implementation budget while developing highly trained users who tend to claim ownership of the process. One important point to remember is that training should not end once the system is live. Refresher courses should be scheduled post-go-live to make sure that employees are using the system in the most efficient manner possible. Figure 6-2 presents ways to effectively train employees in using the ERP system.

Figure 6-2: Keys to Effective ERP Training

Allocate plenty of time for training	Rushing the training process will jeopardize the success of the ERP system implementation. Begin training at least 60 days before ERP go-live.
Focus on business processes, not just transactions	End users should be trained in both the technical use of the system and new business processes.
Leverage a multitude of training tools	Different people learn in different ways, so consider how classroom training could be augmented or replaced by web-based tutorials, hands-on simulations, and other effective learning tools.
Reinforce training with more comprehensive organizational change management activities	Discussions about change, targeted departmental communications, well-defined roles and responsibilities, and other key organizational change activities can reinforce training.

Source: Panorama Consulting Group

Super Users

Every ERP project needs a team of super users, especially if the project is being managed internally and not handed off to consultants. **Super users**, also known as **power users**, become part of the extended project team because they comprise a powerful combination of technical knowledge and business process knowledge. This combination makes super users valuable for conducting training for others in their department and providing user support before and post-go-live. When employees need help executing a transaction, identifying the source of a problem, or understanding integration points, they turn first to the super users in their functional area. Thus, super users need a solid understanding of the ERP system, knowledge of business processes, and a great deal of patience. The patience becomes imperative when asked the same question for the tenth time!

Good communication is a requisite skill for super users because they often have to liaise between end users, consultants, and IT in solving problems. Super users are also often the people who write functional specifications for customizations. Once a programmer writes the code, the super user should be able to thoroughly test the customization and understand how the customization impacts other data or processes. The collection of skills needed is broad, as the super user does so many things. It is a difficult and demanding role, but it offers great challenge and satisfaction to those that pursue this opportunity.

Consultants

Throughout the ERP life cycle, consultants are needed for various activities. A recent study found that companies use consultants mainly for implementation, training, and change management. Other areas in which consultants can provide guidance include process documentation, system implementation assurance, and package selection. Hiring consultants significantly adds to the project's cost, but they can bring a skill set to the project that is not available in-house. However, the more a company uses consultants, the more costly the implementation becomes. Figure 6-3 shows various approaches to using consultants. Each approach affects implementation time and internal and external resource costs.

Figure 6-3: Approaches for Using Consultants During an ERP Implementation

Approaches for Using Consultants		Implementation Time	Internal Cost	External Cost
Balanced approach	A cooperative approach between the company and consultants, providing a shared effort for all implementation aspects	Medium	Medium	Medium
Risk: Internal resource capacity				
Turnkey approach	An accelerated, delivered solution, reducing internal investment by minimizing customer contribution and maximizing consultant contribution	Low	Low	High
Risks: User acceptance, change management, organizational learning				
Customer-driven approach	An approach that maximizes the customer's involvement and minimizes consultant involvement	Medium-High	High	Low
Risks: Missed opportunities, maintaining momentum over time, internal resource capacity				
A la carte approach	Customer completely owns the process, with the consultants involved only as requested	High	High	Low
Risks: Lack of guidance, missed opportunities, maintaining momentum over time, internal resource capacity				

Source: Adapted from mcaConnect.net

Consultants should be knowledgeable, experienced professionals who can provide top-level guidance and project team support for important decisions with clear articulation of the associated issues, relevant evidence, and a candid discussion of alternatives. As outsiders, their unbiased recommendations can be invaluable in an ERP implementation. Yet, while its expertise may be substantial, the project team should vigilantly guard against "handing over" all decision-making authority to consultants. Ultimate responsibility, authority, and decision-making should belong to the steering committee and project team. Good consultants empower their clients to make the best decisions by effectively transferring knowledge throughout the implementation to the project team. Figure 6-4 summarizes the benefits and risks of using consultants during an ERP implementation.

Figure 6-4: Benefits and Risks of Using Consultants During ERP Implementations

Benefits	Risks
Vendor independence – Consultants that are unbiased and objective help ensure the best package is chosen	Vendor dependence – Their association with particular software vendors may result in bias toward their favorite packages
Temporary – Consultants are, by definition, temporary. They represent no long-term investment, no health or unemployment benefits, and no 401K	Expensive – Consultants with proven track records command market premiums
Implementation experience – Familiarity with software implementation methodologies minimizes failure and allows for a big picture focus	Lack of knowledge of the client's business processes and culture – Consultants may have to get up to speed and learn on customer time
Knowledge – Consultants bring knowledge to the organization about what ERP features are necessary and which are bells and whistles	Knowledge transfer – Must not "hand over" project ownership to consultants; this means that turnkey implementations are risky
Better ROI – Using a consultant may prevent the organization from wasting time and heading down blind alleys, such as investing in modules and features that aren't needed	Getting stuck with a loser – It's possible to get locked into an unsatisfactory contract with an arrogant, ignorant, or lazy partner. And, terminating the deal may be too costly

Source: strategy+business.com

Before choosing a consultant, the project team should consider these questions:

- Does the consultant have experience with implementations in the company's particular industry?

- How many successful implementations has the consultant completed? What size are those companies? Does the firm have references to similar customer implementations?

- How many years of experience implementing ERP systems does the consultant have? How many years of experience in implementing this particular ERP system?

Implementation Strategies

The criteria for choosing an implementation strategy include company size, urgency, risk tolerance level, amount of resources applied to the project, and project scope. The team should start considering the implementation strategy during planning and package selection and should discuss it with prospective vendors and integration partners. The main ERP implementation strategies used by companies are discussed next.

Phased Implementation

The **phased implementation strategy** (also known as the **waved** or **incremental** strategy) is the slowest method of deploying an ERP system. In a phased deployment, the ERP system is rolled out by module, business unit, or geographical area over a multi-year period. A key reason organizations use the phased strategy is that it minimizes risk to the organization. Instead of one go-live date, there are several. By breaking the implementation up into phases, it is easier to manage. In addition, each smaller deployment can be used to encourage users and the project team for the remainder of the project.

However, the luxury of time can be a downside in the phased approach—"change fatigue" can cause the team and employees to become burned out by lingering and constant change. Instead of completing the project in a shorter time period, phased projects involve change over longer periods, which can be draining. This approach can ultimately lead to resentment, complacency, and doubt that the project will ever end. One issue with a phased-by-module approach is that temporary interfaces must be built between the new ERP modules and the old systems until those old systems are replaced by ERP modules in the next phase. If a phased-by-business-unit approach is chosen, one option would be to implement the ERP system first in a relatively easy, but not atypical, business unit and then begin rolling out the system to other units.

Big Bang Implementation Strategy

The **big bang implementation strategy** is the most ambitious and difficult approach to ERP implementation. Also known as the **direct cutover** strategy, this method entails rolling out all modules at the same time, resulting in one go-live date. This strategy focuses the company for a shorter time frame compared to the phased approach, making implementation more intense and requiring substantially more resources. Most of the ERP horror stories from the late 1990s warn us about this strategy. During that decade, companies faced with Y2K felt a sense of urgency and were compelled to deliver the solution as soon as possible. Now, only smaller and less complex companies use this method.

One advantage of the big bang strategy is that companies generally spend less time and less money on the implementation, arriving at a quicker ROI. One cost savings with big bang is that it reduces the need for temporary interfaces to other systems that phased rollout approaches require. However, due to the often rushed nature of big bang, important details can be overlooked. Also, because all modules are being implemented at one time, problems tend to be more pronounced. The main disadvantage of a big bang implementation is that it is risky because it calls for the entire company to mobilize and change all at once.

Parallel Implementation Strategy

In a **parallel implementation strategy**, both the legacy systems and the new ERP system are run simultaneously for a period of time post-go-live—the rationale being that if there are problems with the ERP system, the company can revert to the legacy systems. During the time frame in which the old systems and the ERP system are operating at the same time, users can learn the new ERP system while working on the old.

While this approach is the least risky of all strategies, it is also the most labor intensive, costly, and confusing. Daily transactions must be entered into both legacy and ERP systems and be reconciled at periodic intervals to make sure that the ERP system is working properly. With multiple production systems, there's a risk that none of the systems are accurate, and there could be confusion as to which is the system of record. In addition, this approach can stunt change management progress because the legacy systems are still available, which slows the urgency among users to learn the ERP system. For these reasons, parallel implementations have largely been replaced by rigorous testing prior to go-live. In other words, the parallel approach to implementation is best done in a test mode (rather than running multiple production systems simultaneously). Testing of the ERP system output against the output of the old systems that are being sunset is a critical exercise to perform prior to go-live.

Which Implementation Strategy is Right for You?

Each implementation strategy has its pros and cons and works best in certain types of companies and contexts. In some situations, the choice is obvious. In cases where the choice is not so obvious, other issues need to be considered, such as executive leadership, change management skills, and centralized versus decentralized operations. Companies with weak executive support for the project, no internal change management skills, and decentralized operations will find it difficult, if not impossible, to use the big bang strategy. Additionally, large, global enterprises with multiple business models, languages, currencies, and subsidiaries, not to mention differing rules and regulations, will find big bang simply too difficult to pull off.

Risk Management

An ERP system implementation is an enormous organizational transformation encompassing an inherent amount of risk. One study found that 54 percent of ERP projects take longer than expected and 56 percent go over budget. Some ERP projects have even become completely derailed, resulting in bitter lawsuits involving the customer, vendor, and integration partner. For instance:

- Waste Management sued SAP for $100 million – Waste Management claimed SAP gave a "rigged" product demo, which tricked them into purchasing the software when it wasn't the best fit for them. SAP alleged that the customer did not provide timely and accurate business requirements and did not have sufficient and knowledgeable internal resources to help with the implementation.

- Marin County, California, sued Deloitte Consulting for $30 million – Marin County claimed Deloitte Consulting provided inexperienced consultants who used the project as "a trial-and-error training ground," resulting in a solution "far worse than the legacy systems it was intended to replace." Deloitte's rebuttal was that Marin County lacked organizational and governance maturity and could not absorb business process changes necessary during implementation.

- Major Brands sued Epicor – The beverage distributor contended that Epicor delivered "absolutely useless" software to them after years of effort and spending $500,000 on software, $670,000 on integration services, and $100,000 on hardware upgrades. Major Brands contended that problems with implementation and training occurred and that the software ran too slow. The two companies settled the lawsuit and terms were not disclosed.

What these horror stories tell us is that failed ERP projects come in all shapes and sizes and are not specific to any one vendor, system integrator, geography, or company size. Each failure has its own set of circumstances that together create the perfect storm. Earlier we discussed that an ERP system is often the most expensive investment a company may ever make, costing in many cases millions of dollars. The scale of this effort and the intricate nature of these systems introduce a myriad of risks that must be carefully managed.

Risk management is an enterprise-wide process put in place by the board of directors, management, and other personnel to identify potential events that can negatively affect the company and to proactively manage these risks within the bounds of the company's risk appetite so that business objectives can be achieved. Risk management should comprise processes for managing IT risks, including those inherent to an ERP implementation. The first step in managing risk for an ERP implementation is identifying all potential risks that could occur. These should be listed and discussed among the members of the project team and steering committee, and steps should be taken to aggressively manage these risks throughout the project. It might also be prudent to have third-party assurance on the project to ensure that risks are being addressed. Systems implementation assurance is discussed in depth in Chapter 11.

Many studies have been conducted on why ERP system implementations fail (see Figure 6-5 for causes of ERP failures). While some people may think that technical issues "hard stuff" are the main reason ERP projects fail or are not entirely successful, the real reason is because of people, or the "soft stuff." For example, top management may not have successfully shared the vision and "rallied the troops." End users may not have been involved early on in the project and now feel ambivalent or even hostile toward the new system. This low morale can result in employees using workarounds, sabotaging the system, or delaying the acceptance of the ERP system and new processes. Dissention in the ranks might cause the project to lurch to a halt, or even worse, signal the start of a slow and steady demise. Consultants can contribute to a failed implementation if, for example, part of their job is to enable change management or project management, and both efforts are subpar.

Figure 6-5: Causes of ERP Failures

Failure	Description
Resource failure	Insufficient personnel and budget were assigned to the ERP implementation. Resources required were under-estimated.
Requirements failure	Requirements gathering was poor or incomplete. Poor process fit to the ERP system, which will entail many customizations downstream.
Goal failure	A failure to describe specific and achievable goals for the ERP system. Incomplete or non-existent business case.
User contact failure	Failure to communicate with and train system users. End users were not involved, and change management was insufficient.
Governance failure	Lack of leadership from top management and steering committee.
Project management failure	The right people were not selected for the project, including the project team members and the project manager. Project plan not realistic or detailed enough.
Size failure	The ERP project was too large and too complex given the organization's abilities.
People management failure	Lack of effort, stifled creativity, antagonistic attitudes, and people clashes.
Methodology failure	Failure to perform necessary activities while spending too much time on unnecessary or unimportant activities.
Consultant failure	Consultants did not give proper advice or did not successfully complete their part of the implementation. Company over-relied on consultants.

Source: Adapted from R. Block

An ERP implementation has been compared to a "three-legged stool," with the legs representing the customer, integration partner, and vendor. If each leg does not hold up, the project can get ugly. The customer must plan well, budget enough money, and be willing to change its business processes. The vendor must deliver software that functions properly and provide ongoing support for its product. The integration partner must set the right expectations, meet project milestones, deliver expertise, and avoid waste.

Not every ERP failure is abysmal—there are varying degrees. The following list categorizes ERP failures in terms of severity. Keep in mind that failure can be avoided by laying out a solid project plan and taking the necessary steps to avoid potential risks.

- The Unmitigated Disaster – The worst type of failure, the unmitigated disaster, occurs when a company spends millions of dollars trying to implement the ERP system but is unable to. Deadlines are repeatedly missed, the relationship between the company and the consultant or vendor is severed, and lawsuits are filed. The company either junks the system and reverts to the legacy systems or tries to implement another system with different consultants.

- The Big Failure – This type of failure is more common and less severe than the unmitigated disaster. The failure is categorized as "big" because the implementation goes grossly over budget and over time and the company gets far less functionality than initially anticipated.

- The Mild Failure – The mild failure is a less severe version of the big failure. The company might go over budget and/or over time by 10 percent or so and receive slightly less functionality than expected.

- The Forthcoming Failure – The forthcoming failure may not be obvious because it appears that the implementation was successful. However, the team has made key mistakes that will come back to haunt the company later on. These mistakes might include insufficient knowledge transfer to the rest of the organization, inadequate system security, and deficient end-user documentation, which will be a problem if key users leave the organization.

ERP Life Cycle – Operation and Maintenance

Go-Live and Stabilization

A successful ERP implementation does not end at go-live. However, too many companies focus solely on the go-live date rather than the years they will be using their system. Planning for go-live is akin to planning for the wedding but not the marriage, and an ERP marriage is about 10-13 years. If anything, the time immediately after implementation can make or break the ERP system's success. Immediately post-go-live, companies will enter into a period of **stabilization**. According to Deloitte Consulting, stabilization normally lasts between three and nine months. During this time, companies will often experience a dip in performance due to continued training needs, the fine-tuning of "to be" processes, and the resolution of issues remaining from the implementation and arising from the user community after go-live. It is critical that support is on hand from key members of the project team and super users to help efficiently resolve any problems that may surface. Once the ERP system has reached a stable state, action should be taken to improve the performance.

One item worth mentioning is that project team members who complete a successful go-live are going to receive their share of external job offers. It's important to reward team members so they don't leave. Financial bonuses are not always used to reward high performance ERP talent, although they are used. Often, in lieu of bonuses, companies may elect to send team members to an all-expense paid trade show of their choosing or offer to pay for their next training or certification.

Center of Excellence

Most likely, members of the project team will not return to their regular jobs full-time even after go-live because there is still so much to do. Best practice is to immediately establish a **Center of Excellence (COE)** to effectively sustain the system. The COE comprises many people from the original project team. They will be tasked with the responsibility to continually improve the ERP system and business processes in order to realize the entire value of the company's investment, not just the obvious and immediate benefits. The COE is generally given the responsibility of conducting **post-go-live audits** at regular intervals (for example, one month, three months, and six months). These audits should focus on three key areas:

- ROI measurement – Most ERP systems do not reveal their value immediately. The COE should return to the initial business case and measure progress against baseline performance metrics to show an ROI from the ERP implementation. This process should be done after the system stabilizes.

- Ongoing training – The COE should seek out areas where employees may not have been thoroughly or properly trained at go-live. Additionally, because updates to the ERP system happen regularly after go-live, ongoing training is a necessity. Best practices recommend refresher training for all system users on a recurring basis.

- Ongoing business process improvement – The ERP system causes massive reengineering, but that doesn't mean that business processes are 100 percent effective and efficient. The COE should seek to further fine tune business processes post-go-live.

Maintenance

Typical ERP maintenance activities include:

- Preventive maintenance – Regularly scheduled tasks must be performed to keep the system functioning properly. Maintenance activities should be developed in the DEV instance and tested in the QA instance to minimize the chance of problems in the live system.

- Software updates – ERP vendors are regularly updating their software with new best practices and bug fixes. Since many customers do not run vanilla implementations and few, if any, run the same versions of each module with the same fixes and updates applied, it is impossible for the ERP vendors to exhaustively test every combination of update in every module against every possible combination of operating system, database, and application server. Responsibility falls to the COE to decide what updates to apply and when to apply them.

- Emergency maintenance – Certain maintenance tasks must be performed immediately. For example, if a software bug is discovered that has potentially damaging effects to the business, then that bug needs to be fixed as soon as possible, even if it may affect regularly scheduled operations. When emergency maintenance is required, the project team must carefully ascertain the urgency of the situation and balance it against the impact to the business.

Figure 6-6: Ways to Reduce ERP Maintenance and Support Costs

Way to Reduce Costs	Description
Negotiate lower software license fees	Ongoing maintenance fees are typically tied to the software contract value, so negotiating lower license fees reduces ongoing maintenance and support.
Limit software customization	Customization leads to escalating long-term maintenance costs.
Explore third-party support and maintenance options	Third-party options may provide support at far less cost than the ERP vendor. Consider researching other options.
Negotiate lower ongoing professional service rates	Upgrades and other changes to the software over time will typically require additional vendor services, so upfront negotiation of service rates is smart.
Quantify total direct and indirect maintenance and support costs	Companies should quantify how much they are paying for support directly from the software vendor and indirectly through third-party consultants and internal resources required to support the ERP system.

Source: E. Kimberling

During planning, the project team should have budgeted for annual maintenance costs when developing the total cost of ownership (TCO). While estimates vary, one source states that annually, ERP buyers are asked to pay between 18 and 25 percent of software license fees for maintenance and support. Figure 6-6 presents ways to reduce ERP maintenance and support costs.

Research has found that many companies fail to see the value in maintenance services even though they are paying for them. Indeed, a Forrester Research survey of SAP users confirms this lack of perceived value. In that survey, 85 percent of respondents said they barely use SAP's Basic Support services. Statistics like these are used to complain about vendors, but the reality is that many companies are not taking advantage of all they could gain from maintenance and are leaving significant ERP value, both technical and business, on the table. These include updates such as improved information flow, new reporting functionality, revised documentation, and updated hardware compatibility. Even though many companies are not getting the full value out of their ERP maintenance plans, without a maintenance plan in place, companies lose the ability to upgrade their ERP software, which results in business operations becoming frozen in time. If this happens, users will become frustrated with the system and start adopting their own workarounds outside the ERP package, ultimately undermining business benefits.

Many companies have nearsighted vision when it comes to ERP because they implement without a view to the future. They are implementing to meet today's needs, but not tomorrow's. Organizations should treat the ERP system as a plant that has to be constantly fed and watered (and pruned if necessary!) in order to squeeze every possible ounce of value out. A commitment to post-go-live audits at frequent intervals can help maximize the ERP investment, while extending its capabilities to achieve even greater success.

Upgrades

According to Oracle, an ERP system has an upgrade cycle of every five to seven years. Upgrading ERP systems requires special diligence, as it can be a double-edged sword. On the one hand, a company will benefit from the vendor's research and development, which can yield improved functionality. However, the downside is that employees can grow tired of constantly adapting their operations to new functionalities and processes. Upgrading is like rolling out the ERP system all over again, and the costs can run as much as 25 to 33 percent of the initial ERP implementation. CEOs and CFOs are going to want to know what the incremental cash outflow will be versus the incremental cash inflow for benefits such as increased efficiencies, higher sales, improved margins, and decreased expenses. The business benefits of the upgrade should be demonstrated just as ardently as when the initial implementation was planned. Despite the potential benefits of upgrading to newer versions of the software, there are many pragmatic reasons why a company may choose to delay or even defer it. However, at some point, the pressure to upgrade the software becomes so great that the company has no choice—they are forced to do so if they want to continue to have annual maintenance and support.

Summary

The ERP life cycle consists of four stages. This chapter discussed the last two stages: implementation and operation and maintenance. Implementation is the stage in which the real work begins. Activities in implementation include installation, customization, configuration, change management, data migration, testing, and training. Within each of these activities, there are many issues to consider. For instance, there are various types of tests that must be performed on the ERP system prior to go-live, including tests on the data, interfaces, security, and functionality. The training budget should contain a combination of techniques, including train-the-trainer, but users must be trained early enough so that this critical part of the implementation is not rushed. Change management is also an important activity, since many users' jobs will change. Change management encompasses training, communication, and education aspects. Consultants are often brought in to lend expertise in critical areas, such as project management and configuration. However, care must be exercised by the company to not "hand over" the implementation to consultants. No one knows your business the way you do! The various strategies used to implement ERP include big bang, phased, and parallel.

The size of the company, risk tolerance level, and amount of resources applied to the project are criteria that dictate which approach should be used. Post-go-live is, in some respects, the most critical part of the implementation. Companies should provide continual training, business process improvement, and upgrades to get the most out of their ERP investments. Establishing a Center of Excellence to manage these functions is best practice.

Keywords

A la carte approach	Data loading
Authorization testing	Data mapping testing
Balanced approach	Data migration
Big bang implementation strategy	Data migration testing
Bolt-on	Data owner
Center of Excellence (COE)	Data scrubbing
Change agent	Direct cutover implementation strategy
Change management	Enhancement
Conference room pilot (CRP)	ETL (Extract, transform, load)
Configuration	Form
Configuration table	Incremental implementation strategy
Conversion	Integration testing
Customer-driven approach	Interface
Customer exit	Modification
Customization	Parallel implementation strategy
Data cleansing	Performance load testing
Data collection	Phased implementation strategy
Data extraction	Post-go-live audit
Data harmonization	Power user

Report	Train-the-trainer
Retro-fit	Turnkey approach
Risk management	Unit testing
Software implementation	User acceptance testing
Software installation	Vanilla implementation
Stabilization	Waved implementation strategy
Super user	

Quick Review

1. True/False: Configuration tailors the ERP system to fit the business by allowing the project team to choose from a limited set of alternatives available in the software.

2. True/False: Data scrubbing is standardizing data, often from different sources, into a common company-wide format.

3. A _____ implementation eliminates all customization requirements and relies only on the ERP vendor's best practices.

4. _____ testing involves testing end-to-end business processes including any customizations, enhancements, or interfaces to external systems.

5. A _____ approach to implementation is a cooperative approach between the company and vendor providing a shared effort for implementation.

Questions to Consider

1. What are the different types of testing performed during ERP implementations?

2. What are the pros and cons of each ERP implementation strategy?

3. What does change management mean and why is it important in an ERP implementation?

4. What are the various types of customizations that are performed during an ERP system implementation? Hint: RICEF

5. What factors can help ensure a successful ERP implementation?

References

Aldrich, J. (2013, January 21). ERP training strategies. [blog post]. Retrieved from http://panorama-consulting.com/erp-training-strategies/

Block, R. (1983). *The politics of projects.* Englewood Cliffs: Yourdon Press.

BSM. (2010). *Data migration in ERP projects: A BSM white paper.* [white paper]. Retrieved from http://www.slideshare.net/BSMConsulting/data-migration-in-erp-projects-white-paper

Committee of Sponsoring Organizations of the Treadway Commission. (2004). Enterprise risk management – Integrated framework executive summary. Retrieved from http://www.coso.org/documents/coso_erm_executivesummary.pdf

Deloitte Consulting LLP. (2010). Realizing value through an ERP center of excellence. Retrieved from http://www.deloitte.com/assets/Dcom-UnitedStates/Local%20Assets/Documents/us_alliances_RealizingvaluethroughaCoE_090910.pdf

Dollries, J. (2009, June 12). SAP super user – What does it take to be one? The Official intelligence U.S. Blog. [blog post]. Retrieved from http://blog.itelligencegroup.com/?p=222

Downing, D. (2006). *Managing quality in your ERP project: 12 mistakes to avoid & best practices to adopt.* Mentora Group. [white paper]. Retrieved from http://www.mentora.com/documents/ManagingERPQualityWP.pdf

Hewlett-Packard Development Company (2007). Enterprise resource planning (ERP) functional testing best practices: Ten steps to ERP systems reliability. Retrieved From http://static.ziftsolutions.com/files/8a7c9fef21c24ec60121c777a41617d0

ITC Infotech (n.d.). ERP testing. Retrieved from http://www.itcinfotech.com/erp/ERP-Testing.aspx

Jones, J., Aguirre, D., & Calderone, M. (2004, April 15). 10 principles of change management. Boaz & Company. [blog post]. Retrieved from http://www.strategy-business.com/article/rr00006?gko=643d0

Jrliem. (2011, May 13). The four major types of ERP system failures. Retrieved from http://whatiserp.net/erp-implementation/the-four-major-types-of-erp-system-failures/

Kanaracus, C. (2010, December 17). Biggest ERP failures of 2010. Retrieved from http://www.computerworld.com/s/article/9201562/Biggest_ERP_failures_of_2010?taxonomyId=10&pageNumber=3

Kanaracus, C. (2012, January 13). Lawsuit claims Epicor's two-year effort delivered "useless" software. *PCWorld*. Retrieved from http://www.pcworld.com/article/248168/lawsuit_claims_epicors_twoyear_effort_delivered_useless_software.html

Kimberling, E. (2006, September 6). ERP's big bang theory. [blog post]. Retrieved from http://panorama-consulting.com/erps-big-bang-theory/

Kimberling, E. (2007, March 8). The importance of ERP post-implementation audits. [blog post]. Retrieved from http://it.toolbox.com/blogs/erp-roi/the-importance-of-erp-postimplementation-audits-14971

Kimberling, E. (2009, June 1). Four reasons why ERP projects take longer than expected. [blog post]. Retrieved from http://it.toolbox.com/blogs/erp-roi/four-reasons-why-erp-projects-take-longer-than-expected-31967

Kimberling, E. (2009). Five ways to reduce ERP maintenance and support costs. Retrieved from http://searchmanufacturingerp.techtarget.com/news/1363832/Five-ways-to-reduce-ERP-maintenance-and-support-costs

Kimberling, E. (2012, June 13). The real reasons to upgrade your ERP system. [blog post]. Retrieved from http://panorama-consulting.com/the-real-reasons-to-upgrade-your-erp-system/

Kimberling, E. (2012, December 5). The case for—and against—ERP customization. [blog post]. Retrieved from http://panorama-consulting.com/the-case-for-and-against-erp-customization/

Kimberling, E. (2013, July 31). The high price of poor communication in ERP implementations. [blog post]. Retrieved from http://panorama-consulting.com/the-high-price-of-poor-communication-in-erp-implementations/

Krigsman, Michael (2011, July 20). Oracle battles Montclair State over failed IT project. [blog post]. Retrieved from http://www.zdnet.com/blog/projectfailures/oracle-battles-montclair-state-over-failed-it-project/13786

Management Study Guide (2013). Configuration control and setting up of base in ERP system. Retrieved from http://www.managementstudyguide.com/configuration-control-and-base-setting-in-erp-system.htm

mcaConnect. (n.d.). Strategies for Consultant Use. mcaConnect.net.

Neely, B. (2011, October 17). Key objectives of conference room pilots. [blog post]. Retrieved from http://panorama-consulting.com/key-objectives-of-conference-room-pilots/

Panorama Consulting Solutions (2013). 2013 ERP report. Retrieved from http://panorama-consulting.com/resource-center/2013-erp-report/

Phillips, S. (2013, January 7). ERP software: Beware of "bolt-ons." [blog post]. Retrieved from http://it.toolbox.com/blogs/street-smart-erp/erp-software-beware-of-boltons-54432

Reed, Jon (2010, July 20). The new rules of ERP: 10 keys to ERP go live in an agile era. *ERP Executive*. Retrieved from http://www.erpexecutive.com/2010/07/10-keys-to-erp-go-live-in-an-agile-era/

SmartDog Services, LLP. *The need for an ERP software upgrade roadmap.* [white paper]. Retrieved from http://www.smartdogservices.com/pdf/Roadmap_ERP_Upgrade_SmartDog.pdf

Strategy+Business. (n.d.). Advantages and Disadvantages of Using Consultants. Strategy-business.com.

Ultra Consultants (2013). Data conversion. Retrieved from http://www.ultraconsultants.com/services/erp-implementation/data-conversion/

Ventana Research. (2010). *A strategic approach to establishing two-tier ERP: A single system may not be the right choice for your company.* [white paper]. Retrieved from http://www.ventanaresearch.com

Welch, J., & Kordysh, D. (2007, September). *Seven keys to ERP (enterprise resource planning) success. Strategic Finance, 89*, 41–48.

Chapter 7

ERP Financial Management

Objectives

- Differentiate between financial and management accounting

- Become familiar with functionality in the Financial Accounting and Management Accounting modules of an ERP system

- Understand functionality in the Asset Management module of an ERP system

- Recognize functionality in the Travel and Expense Management module of an ERP system

Introduction

In today's information economy, accounting and finance professionals must manage an increasingly wide array of complex business processes and synthesize and interpret data from a variety of sources. Modern ERP systems include modules for both financial accounting and management accounting. Financial accounting is geared toward producing financial information, in the form of periodic financial statements, for external decision-makers. The Financial Accounting module includes components for general ledger, accounts receivable, credit management, accounts payable, and cash management. Taken together, these components allow financial and accounting professionals to analyze global financial activity in real time across subsidiaries, business units, and departments.

Modern ERP systems also include functionality for management accounting, which provides accounting information to internal decision-makers so that they can make more informed business decisions as they plan, evaluate, and control the company and assure appropriate use of and accountability for its resources. Management accounting delivers financial and statistical information needed by managers to make both operational and strategic decisions. The ERP Management Accounting module includes components for product costing, profitability analysis, overhead costing, activity-based costing, and cost and profit center accounting. Also included in ERP Financial Management is a Fixed Asset module to keep track of long-term, capital assets such as equipment, computers, buildings, real estate, and vehicles, as well as a Travel and Expense Management module, which controls and manages the planned-trip-to-payment process. The many benefits to implementing ERP Financial Management are described in Figure 7-1.

Figure 7-1: Benefits of ERP Financial Management

Quickly and strategically measure, evaluate, and respond to changing business conditions and enable real-time insight into overall performance
Speed the time needed to generate financial statements by streamlining consolidation across companies, charts of accounts, and currencies
Simplify financial operations while complying with regulations
Increase accounts receivable turnover through automation of credit and collections management
Optimize global cash management by reporting, analyzing, and allocating cash in real time
Improve financial and managerial reporting by enabling reports of performance by company, business unit, department, and cost center
Integrate processes from various applications for a "single version of financial truth"
Operate in multiple geographies, industries, and languages

Source: SAP

Financial Accounting

Financial accounting is the reporting of the financial position and performance of an organization through financial statements issued to external users on a periodic basis. These external decision-makers include stockholders, tax authorities, regulators, financial analysts, creditors, and the general investing public. Financial statements are prepared at least yearly, but are often created monthly for internal users and quarterly for external users. This is accomplished through the Financial Accounting module of an ERP system.

Financial statements must conform to **generally accepted accounting principles (GAAP)**, which are the standards and conventions that U.S.-based companies follow in recording financial transactions and preparing financial statements. If a company operates outside the U.S, it most likely complies with **International Financial Reporting Standards (IFRS)**, which is designed to be a global framework for how public companies prepare and disclose their financial statements. Financial statements consist of the following (in order of preparation):

1. **Income statement** – also known as the statement of earnings or the profit and loss (P&L) statement. This report summarizes the income and expenses during the accounting period to derive the net income or net loss.

2. **Statement of retained earnings** – also known as the statement of changes in equity. This reports details the changes in owners' equity during the accounting period. It is calculated by taking beginning retained earnings (stockholders' equity) and adding net income or subtracting net loss. Any additions to stock are added and payments of dividends are subtracted.

3. **Balance sheet** – also known as the statement of financial position. This report lists the assets, liabilities, and stockholders' equity at the end of the accounting period, usually the last day of a month, quarter, or year.

4. **Statement of cash flows** – this report presents the cash receipts and cash payments during the accounting period.

Financial accounting begins with a well-designed **chart of accounts (COA)**, which is a classification and listing of every asset, liability, equity, revenue, and expense that the organization uses to record transactions. Considered master data in the ERP system, the COA must be entered before any transactions can be processed. When setting up the COA, the unique account numbers, descriptions, and account type (whether it is an income statement or balance sheet account) must be entered into the ERP system. In a corporate group, each company can have its own COA classification or use the same COA classification as the other companies. The latter is optimal, as the related companies can communicate more easily regarding financial transactions in the system. When consolidating, there also may be a consolidation COA that is different than company's operating COAs. Additionally, companies may also be required to use a country-specific COA that includes additional accounts mandated by a country in which they operate.

The next few sections describe typical financial accounting functionality in ERP systems. Figure 7-2 shows a screenshot of the accounting modules and components in SAP. Some of these components are discussed next.

Figure 7-2: SAP Financial Accounting and Management Accounting Menu

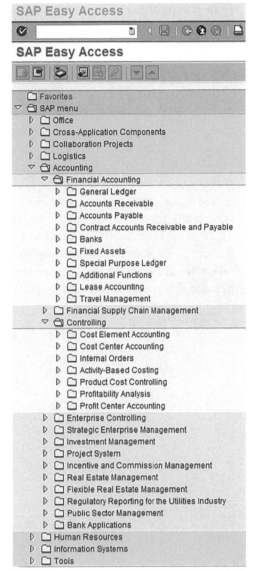

Source: SAP

General Ledger

Modern ERP systems are designed to collect transactional data from all modules and summarize the results in the **general ledger (GL)**, which is the single integrating element in financial accounting. In ERP systems, **transactions** are a type of activity or event that creates journal entries that impact the general ledger (GL). The GL is very important because it keeps balances of all the accounts in the COA and facilitates the **accounting cycle** (see Figure 7-3). The accounting cycle refers to a collective process of recording and processing the accounting events of a company. The **time period principle** in accounting states that a company should prepare its financial statements on a periodic basis (monthly, quarterly, and/or yearly). Therefore, the accounting cycle is performed each period, and at the end of the period, financial statements are prepared.

The accounting cycle is basically the same for every company. First, a transaction takes place, for which the company has an electronic or paper **source document**. This document describes the key facts about a transaction, such as the party involved, date, purpose, items, unit of measure, currency, and amount. The transaction is then recorded in one of the ERP modules. For example, an invoice is sent to a customer. This invoice also becomes an electronic source document created in the Sales module. Since ERP systems are integrated, this transaction creates an accounting document that posts to the GL. From the GL, a **trial balance**, or listing of all the end of period balances of the GL accounts, is prepared. The trial balance is listed in order of the COA, and if all of the accounting entries are recorded correctly, and all the GL balances are correctly extracted, the total of all debit balances in the trial balance will be equal to the total of all credit balances. The trial balance is the first step towards preparation of the financial statements. There are several steps that take place between the trial balance and the financial statements, but for the sake of simplicity (and because this is not an accounting text) we will not elaborate on these steps.

Figure 7-3: Accounting Cycle

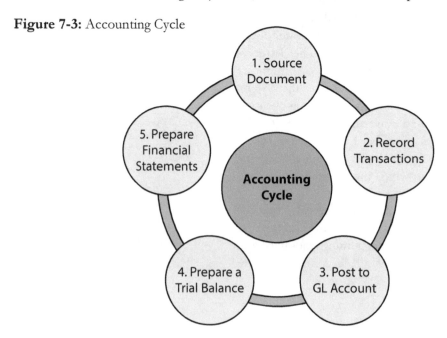

Many ERP systems allow global companies to maintain their GLs in multiple currencies and to comply with country-specific regulations for taxes, reporting, and payment transactions. Many ERP systems also enable companies to conduct **parallel accounting**, which enables them to keep several GLs simultaneously according to different accounting principles and country-specific regulations to ensure that international and local reporting requirements are met. Consolidation is also often performed in the Financial Accounting module; this enables the financial statements of multiple companies within a corporate group (parent company) to be combined. In financial accounting, consolidated financial statements give a comprehensive view of the financial position of the entire corporate group and its subsidiaries, rather than one company's stand-alone position.

Accounts Receivable

The accounts receivable (AR) component in the Financial Accounting module controls all postings to customer accounts and the GL. **Accounts receivable** represents money owed to the company by a customer for products or services provided to the customer on credit. This GL account is treated as a current asset on the balance sheet because the amount is expected to be collected from the customer within a year (usually within 30 to 60 days). Invoicing the customer through the Sales module of an ERP system or a CRM system (see Chapter 8) creates an entry in the customer's AR account.

Accounts receivable is known as a **control account** in the GL because it summarizes or "controls" the details in a **subsidiary ledger**, which is a detailed ledger outside the GL. The purpose of using a control account is to keep the GL free of details while still maintaining the correct balance for the financial statements. Accounts receivable controls the **accounts receivable (AR) subsidiary ledger**, which shows the transaction and payment history separately for each customer to whom the business extends credit.

Figure 7-4 provides an illustration of this concept. The balance of the GL AR control account is $3,145, but to determine which customers owe this money, we have to look to the AR subsidiary ledger to see the details. The AR subsidiary ledger shows that three customers' balances comprise the AR total in the GL. Transactions that affect AR flow from the Sales module through sales invoices and from the Financial Accounting module through cash collections, returns and allowances, and debit and credit memos. ERP systems make sure that the balances in the AR subsidiary ledger always equal the balance in the AR control account in the GL.

Figure 7-4: Accounts Receivable Subsidiary Ledger

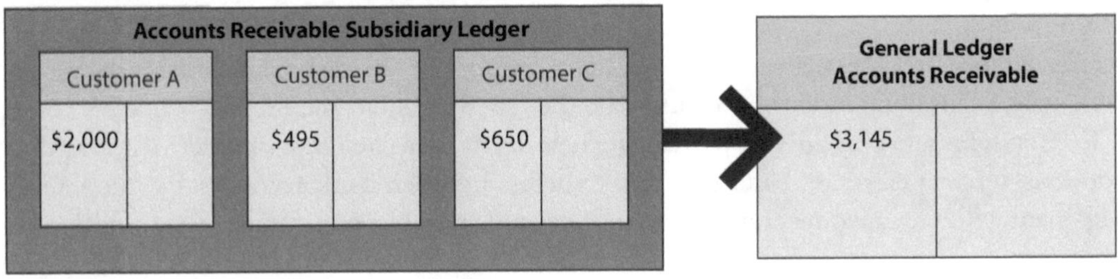

Credit Management

The AR function is controlled by the **credit management** component, which is used to minimize financial risks for the organization by performing a credit check when creating a sales document. Customers' credit limits are recorded in credit management as is their credit risk rating. Using this information, credit management can provide a real-time analysis of the company's credit exposure. Credit management can be configured to place holds on or disallow transactions when customers exceed their credit limit or when there is late payment or non-payment. The main purpose of credit management is to prevent shipping goods to a customer who exceed their credit limit or don't fulfill other credit-relevant criteria.

Accounts Payable

The accounts payable (AP) component in the Financial Accounting module controls all postings to the supplier accounts and the GL. Money that a company owes to suppliers for products and services purchased on credit is called **accounts payable**. This GL account appears on the company's balance sheet as a current liability, since the expectation is that it will be paid in less than a year (generally within 30 to 60 days). Similar to accounts receivable, AP is a control account. The **accounts payable (AP) subsidiary ledger** serves as an important source of information regarding supplier invoicing and payments. The total amount of every supplier's balance at any point in time must equal the balance in the GL AP account. Figure 7-5 shows that the balance of AP in the GL is $2,700, but to determine which suppliers the company owes this money to, we have to look to the AP subsidiary ledger to see the details. Transactions that affect AP flow from the Purchasing module and through the Financial Accounting module through cash payments, returns and allowances, and debit and credit memos.

Figure 7-5: Accounts Payable Subsidiary Ledger

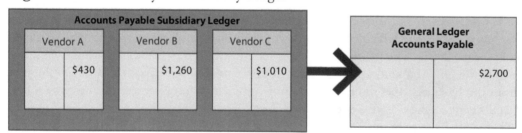

Cash Management

Also referred to as treasury management, the main purpose of the cash management component of the Financial Accounting module is to automate the repetitive steps required to manage a company's cash. ERP systems allow businesses to manage their day-to-day bank transactions including deposits, withdrawals, interest earnings, bank fees, and transfers between bank accounts. By integrating cash management with GL, accounts receivable, and accounts payable, companies can access deposit and payment information by bank account, confirm transactions, and import cleared transactions from their banks for automatic reconciliation. By using the multicurrency feature, bank accounts can be managed in currencies other than the local currency.

In addition to the short-term cash position in bank accounts, finance personnel will use a **liquidity forecast** to project cash flows in the near term. From a business point of view, this means a detailed evaluation of the AR and AP subsidiary ledgers for incoming receipts and outgoing payments.

Cash management provides information to enable payment issues such as:

- Payment delay – If a payment can be delayed for 30 days, the cash used to make that payment can be used for other needs or left in interest-bearing accounts until the payment becomes due.

- Early payments – There is often a savings associated with taking advantage of early payment discounts. Firms should consider paying within the discount period if they are confident that future cash inflows are sufficient to meet other short-term cash requirements.

- Non-routine and long-term cash planning – Organizations can use cash management to plan for cash needs associated with debt repayments, dividend payouts, and fixed asset projects.

An important feature of cash management is that it enables the audit trail of all cash-related transactions. When a cash transaction is posted, it cannot be deleted or voided. To correct mistakes, you must enter an adjusting transaction to reverse the incorrect entry. The ERP system maintains details of all entered or imported transactions, including the user who entered the transaction or adjusting transaction and the user who modified the record. The audit process is streamlined by linking supporting electronic source documents directly to transactions.

Management Accounting

Unlike financial accounting, which primarily involves the preparation of financial statements for external decision-makers, **management accounting** supports the information needs of internal decision-makers. Also called managerial accounting, management accounting involves identifying, measuring, analyzing, interpreting, and communicating information to internal constituents for the purpose of pursuing the company's goals.

While financial accounting must comply with accounting rules and regulations, management accounting does not have to. And, while financial accounting generally communicates historical information of past transactional activity, management accounting produces more forward-looking information. Much of the focus is on "slicing and dicing" financial data to provide more explanation for management. The Management Accounting module is used for a variety of purposes, including risk management; performance management; designing, evaluating and optimizing business processes; budgeting and forecasting; and implementing and monitoring internal controls. One of its main activities is **cost accounting**, which is that part of management accounting that establishes the budget and the actual costs of operations, processes, departments, or products and analyzes variances and profitability.

Product Costing

Determining the internal cost of products manufactured or services provided is the goal of the product costing component of the Management Accounting module. **Product costing** is accomplished by examining every resource that is consumed in producing the product or delivering the service. Some costs, such as wages of factory workers or materials used in production, are treated as **direct costs** because they can be easily traced. Other costs are not so easily traceable and are known as **indirect costs**. Examples of indirect costs include rent and utilities for the manufacturing facility, salary of the manufacturing supervisor, and depreciation on plant equipment. These costs must be applied to the product or service in some manner, which is discussed in the next section.

Direct material costs for a finished product can be determined using the **bill of material (BOM)**. The BOM is master data that lists all the raw materials and sub-components (and their quantities) necessary to make a finished product. Product costing will use the BOM and roll up the individual costs for each item to determine a final material cost for a finished product. Product costing will also use the **routing**, which is a list of the operations required to make a product, to determine the necessary production steps and their related costs. Management can use these costs to determine the standard costs for a finished good, which becomes part of the finished product's master data. Product costing allows managers to see the cost composition of every product made and the cost of every manufacturing step, as well as the cost added in each overhead process. Besides determining how much a product or service costs to make or deliver, product costing can answer the following additional questions:

- Do variances occur when producing a given product? What type of variances are there (price, quantity, scrap)?

- How can an organization arrive at more favorable variances?

- Can the company reduce the cost of making a particular product?

- What is the total cost of goods manufactured by sales order or plant?

Overhead Costing

The Management Accounting module may include an overhead costing component, which provides functionality for planning, allocating, and controlling indirect costs to cost objects. A **cost object** is any product, service, contract, job, project, work center, or other unit for which a discrete cost measurement is desired. Although indirect, overhead must be allocated to cost objects so that management can make accurate and educated product costing decisions. Indirect costs are normally assigned to cost objects using **cost allocation**, which is the process of dividing a total cost into parts and assigning the parts to relevant objects. One method to allocate overhead is to assign the same amount of overhead to each cost object type. However, this technique is generally not very accurate because some cost objects consume more overhead than others.

Traditional methods for allocating overhead costs to cost objects are machine-hours or direct labor hours. These activities are called **cost drivers**, because they "drive" costs to the cost object. In essence, they are the root causes of the incurrence of costs. For instance, suppose a machine ran 1,500 hours this month at a total cost of $105,000 (or $70 per machine-hour). If a manufacturing job consumed 15 hours, that job would incur total overhead of $1,050.

However, in many cases, using machine-hours or direct labor hours as the allocation base for cost allocation is less than accurate because these calculations don't capture the true reason for costs being incurred; they are merely estimates of overhead costs. Other activities can drive costs, such as number of machine setups, number of inspections, and number of purchase orders issued. Many companies will broaden their use of cost drivers when allocating overhead and use activity-based costing for cost allocation refinement.

Activity-Based Costing

Traditional overhead allocation methods that use one or two cost drivers to assign overhead costs to products (cost objects) can provide misleading product-cost information. Another more detailed method of cost allocation is therefore used by many companies. This method, known as **activity-based costing (ABC)**, assigns costs based on activities that drive costs rather than traditional methods such machine–hours or labor–hours only. This approach to allocation of overhead expenses has become even more critical as the direct labor portion of product costs decreases, while overhead and administrative costs increase.

In ABC, costs are allocated to **activities**, which are procedures or processes that cause work to be accomplished. Activities consume various resources, and products consume activities. The first step in the ABC methodology is to identify activities that drive costs. For example, machine setups or quality control activities could drive production overhead. The second step is to identify the cost driver for each activity. For machine setups, the number of setups could be the cost driver. For quality control, the number of inspections could be the cost driver. Once costs of the necessary activities are identified, a proportion of the cost is attributed to cost object based on the extent to which the cost object uses the activity. For example, if there were 227 inspections a month on finished products at a total estimated cost of $8,000, a job that consumes five inspections would be charged $176.

The ABC component of the Management Accounting module supports strategic and operational decision-making by identifying the true reasons for costs. Oftentimes ABC will identify high costs per unit, directing attention towards finding ways to reduce the cost or to charge more for the product. A by-product of ABC is that it can assist in pinpointing non-value-added steps so they can be reduced or eliminated. Thus, ABC is a helpful exercise in process redesign. Activity-based costing is especially useful in allocating indirect costs to items that are difficult to track and assign with the benefit being more accurate overhead costing. However, one drawback to ABC is the time it takes to analyze and define activities and resources and then to implement this approach.

ABC can be used for a variety of activities. For instance, ABC can be used for many service-oriented activities, such as product warranty and claims, engineering and design support, and customer service operations. Companies use ABC to provide more relevant information to managers and answers to questions such as:

- Are activities being conducted efficiently?

- Are certain activities even necessary, or do their costs outweigh the benefits?

- Are certain groups within the organization performing activities better than others?

- Do specific materials or tools help the company complete certain activities more efficiently?

Profitability Analysis

The profitability analysis component considers specific segments of the company and determines the profit they generate. A **profitability segment** can be any number of entities, including products, companies, customers, geographic regions, or the intersection of these. Managers will analyze data such as unit sales prices, costs, profit margins, and units sold to answer questions such as:

- Who are our most profitable customers in the Southwest region? Least profitable?

- How can we change the product mix to maximize our profits?

- What are our profit margins for each distribution channel, for instance, wholesale vs. retail?

Accurate and effective profitability analysis allows management to embrace a philosophy that transfers more responsibly to individual employees because they can see the impact of their efforts on profitability in their geographical region, customer base, and product mix. Using profitability analysis users can generate reports for any dimension of the company—whether by region, industry, business unit, or geographical location.

Cost Center Accounting

In order to trace the origin of costs, managers may designate certain areas in the company as cost centers. **Cost centers**, also called **cost pools**, are distinctly identifiable departments, units, or divisions in a company that are deemed to be accountable for incurring or influencing costs. Examples of cost centers are the accounting, maintenance, inventory control, and human resources departments. In a manufacturing facility, a cost center could be a defined area, machine, or person to whom direct and indirect costs are incurred. Managers of cost centers are usually only responsible for cost containment, not revenue generation or capital investment (long-term purchasing) decisions. As a general rule, cost centers are not demonstrably profitable. They typically only add to revenue indirectly or fulfill some other corporate directive. Cost center performance is often measured by comparing actual costs with budgeted costs over a period of time using variance analysis.

Often, costs from one cost center are allocated to other cost centers if those centers consume some of its costs. For example, an IT help desk may be designated as a cost center in a company because it does not directly generate revenue but instead consumes labor, supplies, and overhead. However, other cost centers, such as the accounting department, may use the services of the IT help desk, and thus part of the help desk's costs should be allocated to the accounting department. A reasonable cost driver for allocation of the IT help desk costs may be number of employees. The more employees in a department, the more IT help desk costs are assigned to it. Another example of reallocation of costs might be if rent is charged to an administrative department and then reallocated to the other departments in the building. In this case, a cost driver of square footage may be used to reallocate part of the rent expense to other departments. Figure 7-6 illustrates the allocation of rent expense to the accounting department.

Figure 7-6: Cost Centers and Cost Drivers

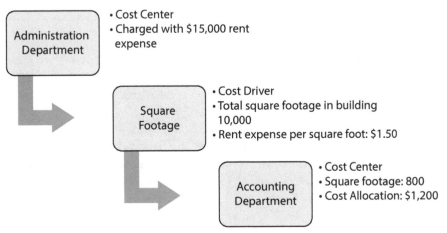

Profit Center Accounting

A **profit center** is an organizational unit in a company that is expected to turn a profit through the sale of goods or services. Various units can be designated as profit centers for internal reporting purposes. For example, a hardware store could make each department its own profit center, such as lawn and garden or tools. Profit centers could also represent divisions. For instance, an equipment dealer could have profit centers for sales and service divisions. Managers of profit centers are responsible for both cost containment and revenue generation, and thus have decision-making authority related to product pricing and operating expenses Dividing the company into profit centers allows for the decentralization of responsibility, as these units are treated as "companies within the company."

When unit managers also have responsibility for the efficient use of fixed assets assigned to them and also oversee all facets including research and development, production, marketing, and customer service, the unit is considered an **investment center**. An investment center is essentially a separate business with its own value chain and ratios, such as return on investment and residual income. In ERP systems, an investment center is represented by a profit center that has fixed assets assigned to it.

Many companies have cost and profit centers but choose not to employ the managerial functionality in ERP systems to organize their accounting practices around these centers. Rather, they operate in the time-honored way of analyzing costs and profits for the company as a whole. However, using cost and profit center features in an ERP system can be helpful in clarifying the source of all costs and profits throughout the company, which is an important source of management information.

Asset Management

The Asset Management module is designed to handle the life cycle of a company's fixed assets, also known as property, plant, and equipment (PP&E) or capital assets. A fixed asset's life cycle includes steps such as planning and approval, procurement, deployment, and disposal at the end of the asset's useful life. During the fixed asset's use, depreciation is calculated and maintenance or upgrade activities may be performed on the asset.

The GL account "fixed assets" is a long-term asset, and the balance of all fixed assets in the GL must equal the detail supporting it in the Asset Management module. Thus, this module can also be thought of as a subsidiary ledger. Companies will implement Asset Management to give them global visibility and control over their fixed assets. Certain information on fixed assets is captured, managed, and shared with other modules, including:

- Date of acquisition and description of the asset, possibly including manufacturer, serial number, and model

- Cost of asset, useful life, accumulated depreciation, and book value

- Depreciation method and calculations for tax and financial statement preparation

- Where the asset is located and who has control over the asset

- Amount asset is insured for and related deductibles and premiums

- The current fair market value of each asset for valuation under IFRS

The Asset Management module will track data and support internal decision-making throughout the fixed asset life cycle shown in Figure 7-7. An explanation of each of the activities in the fixed asset life cycle follows.

Figure 7-7: Fixed Asset Life Cycle

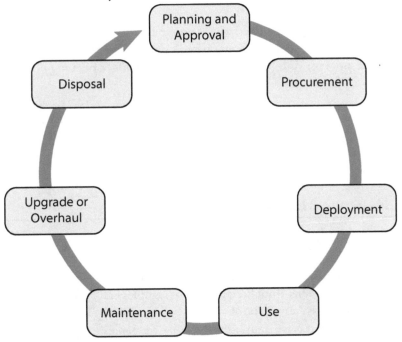

- Planning and Approval – Complete and accurate cost information forms the basis for a fixed asset request. Fixed asset purchases should be aligned with corporate strategy.

- Procurement – Fixed asset purchasing is generally accomplished through the Purchasing module. Requisitions for fixed assets require approvals, and a suitable supplier must be identified.

- Deployment – When a fixed asset is deployed, master data such as asset number, description, location, cost, salvage value, useful life, depreciation method, department responsible for the asset, and warranty information should be entered into the Asset Management module.

- Use – Once deployed, the fixed asset begins to provide value to the organization by serving its intended function. Throughout its useful life, the fixed asset is depreciated, which is an expense onto the company.

- Maintenance – The fixed asset will likely need maintenance to ensure its good working condition. These activities consist of preventive maintenance and repairs when the asset breaks down. See Chapter 9 on information about the Plant Maintenance module.

- Upgrade or Overhaul – If the fixed asset is upgraded with additional features or undergoes a major overhaul to extend its life, certain asset data is affected moving forward. Depending on the type of upgrade, the fixed asset's value, useful life, operating cost, or efficiency may increase.

- Disposal – Upon disposing of the asset, certain information is needed such as its accumulated depreciation, cost basis, and salvage value. The asset may be disposed of through retirement, trade-in, or sale.

Travel and Expense Management

In this global business environment, employee travel is both necessary and expensive. High-performing companies use a Travel and Expense Management module in an ERP system to automate and streamline the **planned trip-to-payment process**. This functionality helps employees submit requests for business travel, book travel online, create travel expense reports, and receive reimbursement. Companies can take advantage of economies of scale by centralizing their travel planning, thus reducing travel costs, while at the same time ensuring compliance with corporate travel policies. Using self-service, employees can connect to low-cost carriers and book hotel reservations. The time and effort required to submit, approve,

process, and pay expense reports is greatly reduced and accuracy is improved. Generally, there are built-in user interfaces for various roles, including travelers, travel planners, travel managers, and expense administrators. Payment of travel expenses is done through integration with the Financial Accounting module or payroll component of the Human Capital Management module, and all supporting attachments are electronically stored. Expense data is automatically transferred to various organizational areas, which can be maintained as cost, profit, or investment centers.

Summary

Financial and Management Accounting modules are core modules in an ERP system. They work together but have different purposes and stakeholders. Financial accounting is concerned with recording transactions and preparing the financial statements for external decision-makers. The Financial Accounting module includes components such as general ledger, accounts receivable, credit management, accounts payable, and cash management. Management Accounting supports internal decision-makers and includes functionality for product costing, profitability analysis, activity-based costing, and cost and profit center accounting. The management of fixed assets is also integral to financials, and the Asset Management module includes functionality to acquire, track, depreciate, and dispose of property, plant, and equipment. Finally, the Travel and Expense Management module is a financial management module that helps to streamline the planned trip-to-payment process by providing integrated, policy-compliant travel bookings and reimbursements for employee business travel.

Keywords

Accounting cycle

Accounts payable (AP)

Accounts payable (AP) subsidiary ledger

Accounts receivable (AR)

Accounts receivable (AR) subsidiary ledger

Activity

Activity-based costing (ABC)

Balance sheet

Bill of material (BOM)

Chart of accounts (COA)

Control account

Cost accounting

Cost allocation

Cost center

Cost driver

Cost object

Cost pool

Credit management

Direct cost

Financial accounting

General ledger (GL)

Generally accepted accounting principles (GAAP)

Income statement

Indirect cost

International Financial Reporting Standards (IFRS)

Investment center

Liquidity forecast

Management accounting

Parallel accounting

Planned trip-to-payment process

Product costing

Profit center

Profitability segment

Routing

Source document

Statement of cash flows

Statement of retained earnings

Subsidiary ledger

Time period principle

Transaction

Trial balance

Quick Review

1. True/False: The chart of accounts (COA) includes the balance owed to every supplier calculated from purchases, returns, allowances, and purchase discounts.

2. True/False: A cost driver is any activity that is the root cause of the incurrence of a cost.

3. True/False: Overhead costs are direct costs that are assigned to a specific cost object.

4. Financial statements are generated from the _____.

5. The _____ component of management accounting takes certain segments of the organization and determines the profit from those segments.

Questions to Consider

1. List three benefits of implementing ERP Financial Management.

2. What are three ERP financial accounting components and what functionality do they provide?

3. What are three ERP management accounting components and what functionality do they provide?

4. List in order the steps of the asset management life cycle.

5. Explain the difference between a cost center, a profit center, and an investment center.

References

Acumatica. (n.d.). Cash management. Retrieved from http://www.acumatica.com/products/cash-management/

Guan, L., Hansen, D., & Mowen, M. (2007). Cost management: Accounting and control (6th ed.). Mason, OH: South-Western Cengage Learning.

Oracle. (2014). Overview of activity-based costing. Retrieved from http://docs.oracle.com/cd/A60725_05/html/ comnls/us/cst/abc.htm

Sage Software, Inc. (n.d.). Cash management. Retrieved from http://na.sage.com/~/media/site/sage-500-erp/assets/datasheets/Sage_500_ERP_Cash_Management_spec.pdf

SAP. (n.d.). Credit management. Retrieved from https://help.sap.com/saphelp_erp60_sp/helpdata/en/4d/ 4653b0cfd70692e10000000a42189b/content.htm

SAP. (n.d.). Ensure financial compliance and growth with integrated Core Finance ERP processes enabled by SAP. Retrieved from http://www.sap.com/pc/bp/erp/software/financials/index.html

SAP. (n.d.) Travel management (FI-TV). Retrieved from https://help.sap.com/saphelp_erp60_sp/ helpdata/en/6e/6bf037f1d6b302e10000009b38f889/content.htm

SAPTOPJOBS. (2011). SAP project costing configuration. Retrieved from http://www.slideshare.net/ AbhishekMittal16/co-product-costing-config-ecc6

Sawyers, R., Jenkins, G., & Jackson, S. (2008). Managerial accounting: A focus on ethical decision making. 5th ed. Mason, OH: South-Western Cengage Learning.

Warren, C., Reeve, J., and Duchac, J. Financial and managerial accounting (12th ed.). Mason, OH: South-Western Cengage Learning.

ERP Sales, Customer Relationship Management, and Knowledge Management

Objectives

- Know the steps in the sales process

- Become familiar with functionality in the Sales module of an ERP system

- Understand the marketing, sales, and service and support functionality in a CRM system

- Be aware of various types of CRM analytics

- Compare traditional CRM with social CRM

- Recognize how knowledge management and CRM work together

Introduction

Generating revenue is critical to every organization. Whether derived from selling products, providing services, or accepting charitable donations, revenue is essential to an organization's survival. ERP systems are adept at processing revenue-related transactions such as taking customer orders, picking inventory, packing, shipping, and billing. However, there is more to the revenue process than simply executing transactions. Smart companies know that building customer relationships is critical to their sustainability, and they take great efforts to know their customers, build strong relationships with them, and anticipate and respond to their needs. Successful companies augment their transactional-based ERP systems with customer relationship management (CRM) systems that enable them to learn more about their customers' behaviors and needs so they can keep them coming back. A

CRM system can efficiently manage customer life cycle events as well as provide key analytics for the marketing, sales, and service departments, making it an integral part of an extended ERP environment. Social CRM can further enhance the customer experience and benefit the company through lead generation, marketing, reputation management, and product management. Finally, this chapter introduces knowledge management (KM) systems, which can be used to reduce customer service costs by helping customers easily get answers to questions and solve problems themselves.

Sales Process

A core module of ERP systems is the Sales module, which supports many of the steps in the sales process, the goal of which is to capture and fulfill the customer order. Often, the sales process is referred to as the **contact-to-contract-to-cash process**, which begins with the first interaction with a potential customer, continues through the contract (sales order), and ends with collecting the cash from the customer. The sales process is also referred to as the **quote-to-cash** or **order-to-cash process**, which begins with a quotation or sales order and ends with collecting payment from the customer. Following is a discussion of each of the steps in the sales process (see Figure 8-1).

Figure 8-1: Steps in the Sales Process

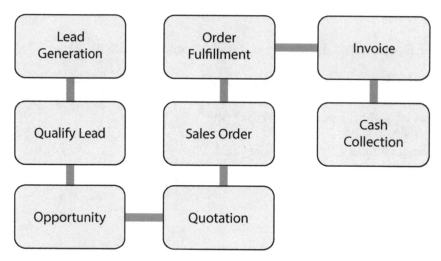

The first step in the sales process is lead generation. A **lead** refers to an individual or organization for whom contact information has yet to be obtained and whose potential has not yet been determined. A lead can be garnered from practically any source, including a purchased marketing list, a casual meeting, or an entry into a web form. Leads are generally kept separate from active contacts and accounts until a sales representative has had a chance to have an initial conversation with the person or someone at the organization and obtain certain information that would help to qualify the lead. A sale representative **qualifies** a lead by obtaining information including:

- Applicability – Does the lead have an immediate or near-term need to purchase the company's products or services? Are they able to switch to a new product or service?

- Authority – Is the salesperson talking to the ultimate decision-maker for the sale? If not, who does the salesperson need to talk to? This person or persons would be the **contact**.

- Affordability – Does the lead have the money to purchase from the company? People who have the money are way easier to sell to!

Oftentimes, companies may also want to add their own criteria into a lead-qualifying evaluation. But, once the lead becomes qualified, it is a **prospect**. However, the lead could become "dead," which means the likelihood of a sale is close to nil. This process of managing the lead process is referred to as **lead management**.

From the newly established prospect company and contact, the sales representative will try to ascertain a potential sales deal, or **opportunity**. For instance, after several phone calls to an organization, a salesperson at a company that sells hardware finally talks to the right person—the IT manager. The salesperson finds out from the IT manager that his company is looking to purchase several new servers. This represents an opportunity, which the salesperson would enter into the system. This opportunity might include whether a specific product is in stock, how much it will cost, and whether the product will be available on a certain date.

Given a valid opportunity, the sales representative can present a quotation to the prospect for products or services identified. A **quotation** is a legally binding offer to deliver certain products or services in a specified timeframe at a pre-defined price. If the prospect accepts the quote, it will be converted into a sales order in the ERP system contingent on a credit check (discussed in Chapter 7) if the customer is purchasing on credit. The **sales order** is a document that specifies products or services ordered by a specific customer at a certain price and includes information such as shipping details, payment terms, and required delivery date. In order to confirm a delivery date, an availability check called **available to promise (ATP)** is conducted to make sure the required delivery quantity can be met on a required delivery date. ERP systems help provide this information by integrating sales, inventory management, and production. At this point, the potential customer is now a customer or **account**, which is a legal entity that is responsible for receipt of goods and services and payment.

Figure 8-2 shows an SAP sales order to Philly Bikes for three items to be sold free on board from the Miami plant with payment terms of "pay immediately" at a total price of $11,750. Once the sales order has been entered in the system, an **order acknowledgement** is sent to the customer as confirmation that the order is booked.

Figure 8-2: Sales Order

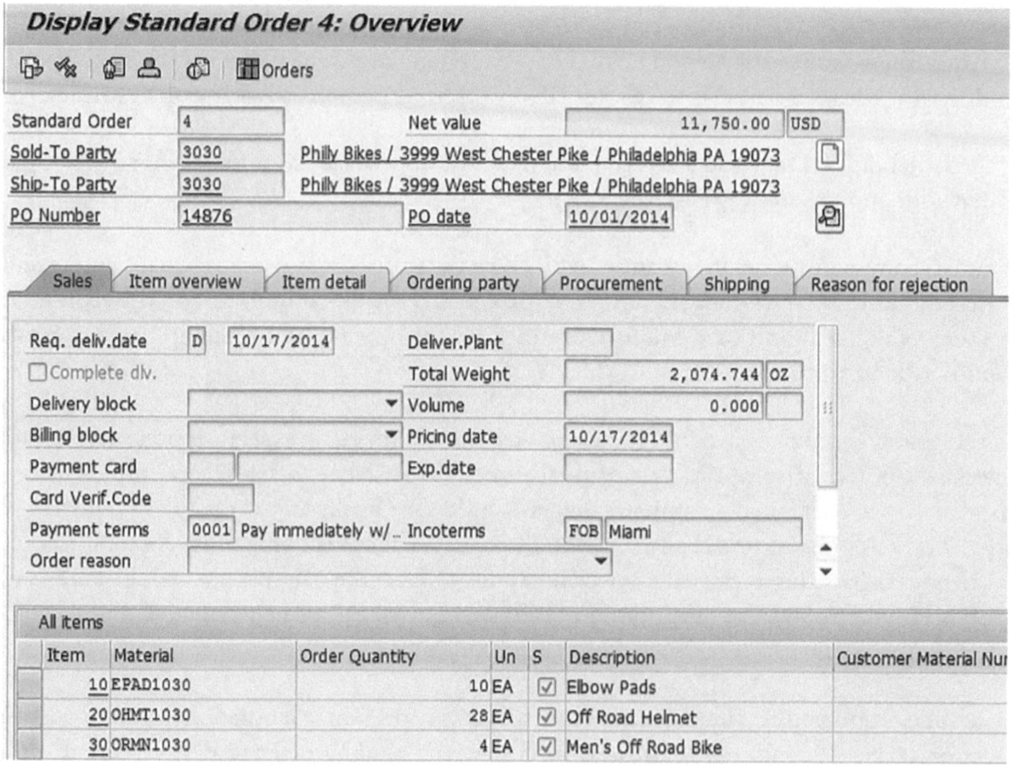

The next step in the sales process is **order fulfillment**, which includes all the activities from the point at which a customer places an order until it is delivered in full (see Figure 8-3 for the order fulfillment process). Once the sales order is released for order fulfillment, a picking date is generated for items in stock, and warehouse employees are directed when to pick the goods from the warehouse. This communication between sales and warehouse personnel is possible because the data is integrated in the ERP system such that picking quantities are available to warehouse personnel.

The next step in order fulfillment is packing, in which ordered items are prepared for shipping. Packaging materials must be identified, weight and volume restrictions enforced, and the delivery assigned to a means of transportation. A **packing slip** will be included with the shipment, either inside the box or affixed to the exterior of the box, describing each item shipped and quantities of each. The packing slip is designed to assist the customer in confirming that all items ordered have actually arrived. A **bill of lading** may also accompany the shipment. This is a legal document between the shipper of the goods and the carrier, serving as a contract to transport the goods to a certain location.

When goods are shipped, title of ownership transfers, and warehouse stock is reduced. An accounting entry is also made to simultaneously decrease the inventory balance in the general ledger (GL) and increase cost of goods sold.

Figure 8-3: Order Fulfillment Process

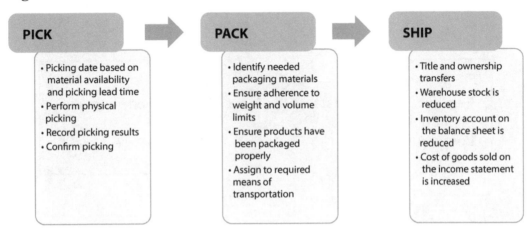

The next step in the sales process is to invoice the customer. An **invoice** is an itemized bill for goods sold or services provided to a customer. The invoice will create an accounting entry to simultaneously increase both accounts receivable (AR) and sales revenue in the GL. The customer's balance is also increased in the AR subsidiary ledger. The final step in the sales process is cash collection. If the goods or services were sold on credit, the accounting department (specifically AR personnel) handles posting of receipts against invoices and reconciling any differences. The posting is made from the **remittance advice**, which is sent in with the cash payment. This entry will clear the customer's AR balance and increase cash in the GL.

Point of Sale (POS) Systems

In the retail industry, ERP systems interface with **point of sale (POS) systems**. At their most basic level, POS systems are electronic cash registers that manage sales-related transactions, but modern POS systems have many bundled add-ons, including credit card verification, inventory management, time clocks, and other accounting features. POS systems must interface with the ERP system where the inventory master data resides and where sales-related transactions must ultimately post. Data transferred from the ERP system to the POS system includes item and pricing data; retail promotional data, such as start and end times for a special price; and bonus buy data, such as "buy 2 get 1 free." Data transferred from the POS system to the ERP system includes POS transactional data such as sales and payments, returns, item exchanges, and gift cards.

Figure 8-4: ERP and POS Systems Data Flow

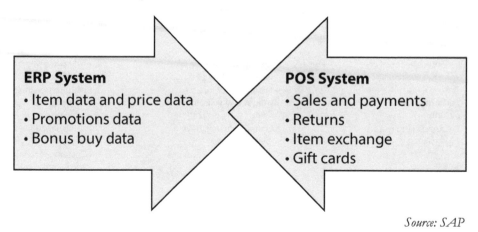

Source: SAP

Customer Relationship Management

In today's business environment—where the cost of switching vendors is relatively low due to the internet and competition—it is important for companies to deliver products, services, and information to their customers that are immediate, tailored to their needs, and reinforced by their social network. Customers have several key demands:

- Know me and know my business

- Help me solve my business problems

- Make it easy for me to do business with you

Customer relationship management (CRM) systems enable businesses to manage relationships with their customers as well as the data and information associated with them. CRM systems help coordinate the efforts of the marketing, sales, and customer service and support departments by integrating customer-facing processes. This integration allows employees in these departments to obtain a 360-degree view of each customer so they can make quickly make intelligent decisions on everything from cross-selling and upselling opportunities to marketing campaigns and competitive positioning tactics. Figure 8-5 highlights the main reasons companies implement CRM systems.

Figure 8-5: Why Implement CRM Systems?

Keep current customers
Attract and acquire new customers
Close deals faster and grow revenue
Gain insight into customers in order to make better business decisions
Interact with customers across all touch points
Build long-lasting relationships with customers
Deliver superior customer service
Achieve a sustainable competitive advantage

Source: SAP

The History of CRM

Before CRM systems, customer data and history were spread out all over the business in spreadsheets, emails, databases, Rolodex entries, and paper notes. Additionally, companies did very little to try to retain customers after they made a purchase. Many companies, especially larger ones, didn't feel the need to cater to their customers—they had the mindset that customers could easily be replaced. However, the modern customer finds information about countless alternatives from any number of sources, increasing the likelihood of losing that customer to a competitor. As well, companies need to integrate sales-related data to enable real-time collaboration among departments.

The Beginning of CRM

In the 1980s, businesses began using database marketing to track existing and potential customers. This method was not nearly as intricate and well developed as the CRM systems used today. It mainly involved the marketing staff interacting with the company's customers through surveys and focus groups. The information obtained tended to be unorganized, and interpreting it was a difficult and time-consuming task.

The Growth of CRM

The term "CRM" first emerged in the mid-1990s to describe how marketing, sales, and customer service departments should work together so that interactions with customers changed from isolated "events" to durable "relationships." Database marketing evolved from a simple database into CRM strategy and software. Unlike in the past, companies began seeing the benefit of giving back to the customer. For example, credit card and airline companies began exchanging reward points or frequent flier miles for customer information. These programs were designed not only to earn new customers, but also to reward customer loyalty.

Fully-Developed CRM

Since the mid-2000s, CRM systems have demonstrated phenomenal growth as organizations have embraced the opportunity to actively manage customer relationships to generate substantial market advantage. The internet boom fueled much of this growth, as it allowed companies to implement CRM without supporting a full database at their own sites. The proliferation of cloud-based CRM systems allows companies to implement faster with less upfront expense. CRM vendors also now offer mobile apps, which enable easy access to customer data on demand. Today, CRM systems are part of the extended ERP environment (see Figure 1-4) and have become fully developed, including a social component (discussed later in this chapter). From customer acquisition to solidifying customer loyalty and encouraging customer social networks, CRM systems are here to stay and the growth rate is one of the highest among enterprise systems.

CRM vs. ERP

Although they are similar in their results, CRM and ERP systems approach the goal of increasing profits differently. The focus of ERP systems is to cut costs and reduce overhead. In creating more efficient business processes, ERP systems allow organizations to invest less capital in those business processes. CRM systems, on the other hand, seek increases in profit through higher sales volume. Everyone in an organization, from sales representatives to executives, has the ability to improve relationships with customers using standardized customer data. As a result of these improved relationships, both profits and brand loyalty increase. These differing focuses are the reason why ERP systems have traditionally been referred to as **back-office systems**. This term implies that they primarily support business processes not necessarily visible to the customer, such as purchasing, production planning, order tracking, and inventory management. CRM systems, on the other hand, are referred to as **front-office systems**, meaning they support activities that interface with the customer.

Integrating CRM and ERP can provide dramatic return on investment. At a minimum, integrating these two systems can eliminate "swivel chair" data entry, which means entering data such as contact information into both systems. One of the main areas of integration is contact and account information, with ERP focusing on the billing and shipping information and CRM emphasizing the leads, prospects, and sales and support. Another area of integration is product catalogs. The CRM system might provide access to the many items the company sells, whereas opportunities and quotes are tracked on an order level in the ERP system. Finally, sales and customer service representatives (CSRs) would have access to the status of sales orders as well as the ability to make and track changes.

Figure 8-6 shows a typical intersection between CRM and ERP for the sales cycle. As the figure shows, certain activities can take place in either ERP or CRM. One example is the pre-sales activity of managing contacts, which can be entered in either system. Various integrations between the systems as discussed can provide transparency and efficiencies in the process.

Figure 8-6: Where ERP and CRM Overlap

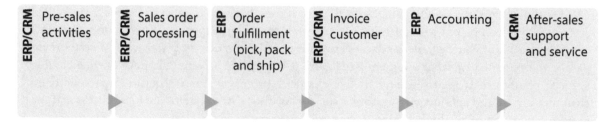

CRM Functionality

Customer relationship management systems organize, automate and synchronize marketing, sales, and customer service and technical support. Each of these CRM components will be discussed next.

Marketing

Marketing begins with targeting various audiences and delivering personalized and relevant messages that they will find valuable and that will generate the greatest response. The top three marketing goals for companies are: generating demand, creating brand awareness, and building long-term profitable relationships with customers. Key marketing functions of a CRM solution include:

- Engaging audiences seamlessly across all interaction channels: websites, e-mail, social media, and point of service

- Designing, executing, coordinating, optimizing, and monitoring the marketing campaign process

- Gathering and qualifying leads

- Segmenting the market to allow for better targeting of groups and to use marketing resources more efficiently

- Personalizing product proposals for each website visitor

- Understanding which channels, messages, campaigns, and leads result in the highest conversions and opportunity wins

Sales

CRM systems help boost sales performance management by enabling more effective cross-selling and upselling processes, closing deals faster thereby shortening the sales cycle, retaining current customers, and understanding existing customers better. These solutions are also instrumental in reducing loss of revenue due to unmanaged sales opportunities by keeping sales staff aware of active opportunities and helping them identify new ones. Other key CRM sales functions include:

- Planning and forecasting revenues and product quantities

- Optimizing the assignment of leads, opportunities, and prospects to specific sales representatives or sales groups based on product knowledge, history of success, or geographic location.

- Tracking the execution of sales-related tasks by sales representatives

- Generating and managing long-term agreements with customers

- Developing, implementing, and managing incentives and commission programs for sales representatives

- Staying on top of opportunities so they turn into sales

This last bullet refers to a key area of reporting in CRM systems, the **sales pipeline**. This report projects the estimated revenue that will be generated in upcoming months and is a good indicator of the health of a company. The closer a company is to landing a certain deal, the higher the percent allocated to the opportunity. For instance, opportunities are included in the sales pipeline, multiplied by the likelihood that a sale will be consummated. If the opportunity is $10,000 but the sales representative is only 25 percent confident the potential deal will become a sale (perhaps because it is in the very early stages), $2,500 shows in the sales pipeline.

Service and Support

Good customer service and support is directly related to retaining customers and increasing lifetime customer value. The three main goals of CRM service and support are to:

- Efficiently assign, manage, and resolve customer support incidents with automated routing, queuing, and service request escalation

- Help identify common support problems, assess customer needs, track processes, and measure service performance

- Share sales and support information and use it to identify top customers and prioritize service needs

CRM service also encompasses **field service**, which is used to manage installations, service, or repairs of systems or equipment previously sold to customers. Field service includes scheduling and dispatching technicians and other staff into the "field" to support service activities, such as equipment installations, break/fix, planned maintenance, and meter reading. Field service also includes an optimization facet that entails dispatching technicians to different locations based on skills, available hours, equipment constraints, and service delivery windows to ensure good use of paid hours while minimizing overtime. The goal is to make technicians more prepared when making service calls, so productivity, service revenue, and customer satisfaction is increased. Also, theoretically, service parts inventory levels are decreased.

CRM Interaction Channels

Today's customers are demanding more and better service, delivered through every conceivable interaction channel. An effective CRM strategy in any organization will have multiple interaction channels, that is, ways to support marketing, sales, and service efforts. This is valuable in both B2B and B2C models. In the B2B model, this process is referred to as **partner channel management**.

- Call center – For many companies, the call center provides the first line of contact with a customer; as such, it offers a unique opportunity to increase customer satisfaction and develop profitable long-term relationships. It is therefore critical that the call center is integrated with CRM so the CSRs can offer the correct information to customers at the right time. Using CRM service, when a call comes in, the customer's case automatically appears, showing everything from contact information and products purchased to billing information. The CSR has access to service entitlements, suggested solutions (see knowledge management later in the chapter), and, if the case needs to be escalated, other CSRs or experts with the requisite knowledge to help. Acquiring new customers is much more expensive than selling to existing ones. Therefore, excellent customer service is essential for businesses to retain their customers. Call centers should be equipped with the essential information to handle customer support cases quickly and effectively, thereby boosting customer satisfaction and loyalty while turning service into a competitive differentiator.

- Mobile – Whether it is used to make offers to customers, give location information, or enable field service teams to update service tickets immediately, mobile CRM is the fastest-growing CRM interaction channel due to rapid acceptance by the user community in recent years. Through the use of mobile apps on various tablet and phone platforms, companies are connecting with both customer and employee for better CRM.

- E-commerce – The e-commerce channel sells to the customer across a company's internet presence through a username/password gateway. Corporate stores and personalized marketing are the key components in an e-commerce channel. Most companies use this functionality primarily to reduce marketing costs and provide customers with an exclusive sales experience.

- Social media – With the emergence of social media-savvy customers, companies are now taking advantage of the many social media networks for marketing with personalized offers, sales offers, and up-to-the-minute customer service response. The use of social media also allows companies to gather metrics that will help them know their customers better and, subsequently, serve them better. Social CRM is discussed next.

Social CRM

The next generation of CRM is **social CRM**. This evolution of CRM involves managing customer relationships through **social media**, which includes the many types of online communications channels dedicated to community-based input, content sharing, collaboration, and interaction. Types of social media include forums, social networking, media sharing, wikis, and microblogging. Some examples of this media are Facebook, LinkedIn, Pinterest, and Twitter.

By leveraging a social element, companies are able to monitor what is being done on their sites, listen to what is being said, and respond accordingly. Companies use **social media monitoring** to track online conversations about a specific phrase, word, brand, or their organization as a whole. By monitoring and listening to this information, companies can gain insight into what is being said, respond to customers' comments and criticisms, and make strategic changes based on feedback. The conversations then become a 24/7 focus group, test market discussion, and comment box rolled into one.

Traditional CRM systems are concerned with customer data and information, but social CRM involves customer engagement and interactions, with transactions as the byproduct. It is the connection of social data with existing customer data stored in the CRM system that provides new forms of customer intelligence. Some examples of using social CRM include:

- Lead generation – A business sets up a Facebook page and consumers who like the company, brand, or products "like" the page. Top leads can be identified, routed to sales personnel, and prioritized.

- Reputation management – Using social media monitoring software such as Facebook Insights, a company can capture what is being said about its products and services and react accordingly by honing in on relevant information while filtering out the "noise." Companies can take a close look at what customers don't like via customer complaint logs and use this information to make changes to products, services, or processes.

- Marketing – Customers often "tell" their social network about their experiences with various companies, whether good or bad. A social profile can be obtained on those customers who are interacting and relevant insights can be mapped to existing customer records.

- Product management – A customer can use social networking to solve a problem regarding a company's product. The company can then capture this information and publish the solution, thereby creating organizational knowledge.

Elements for CRM Success

It is important to note that a successful CRM strategy is not just about buying "magic software" that will do it all for you. The key is having people, process, and technology aligned so the CRM system will be successful. Figure 8-7 shows a model incorporating these three elements, which are described as follows:

- People – Everyone in the organization who will be using the CRM system or be affected by the system must accept the new way of doing work. Often, when implementing CRM, the sales team is the most difficult to get on board because of the extra work it takes for them in the short term and the temporary pull from their commission-generating activities. As discussed in Chapter 6, change management plays a role here. Users must be properly trained on the system. If they are not, then it becomes just another expensive digital address book!

- Process – Once everyone is committed to the project, a company's current marketing, sales, and service business processes must be evaluated. Redesign of current processes should reinforce the CRM strategy from the viewpoint of understanding how the customer can be best served. Most companies begin with a "best practice" approach to CRM. That is to say, "How are the most successful companies in my industry accomplishing the same work?" From that point, they begin to rethink their processes in line with the new technology, specifically focusing on how that technology will help them meet their objectives.

- Technology – A firm should select a CRM system that is user friendly, drives the redesigned processes, and provides high-quality data to employees. The selected CRM solution should enable faster and more accurate decision-making by providing employees with complete customer intelligence. Many companies are choosing a **hybrid approach** to CRM deployment, meaning that a company will have an on-premise ERP implementation but will use a cloud-based system, such as SugarCRM or Salesforce, for CRM. The main challenge to a hybrid approach is data and process integration. Before choosing this option, companies should carefully assess whether the two systems can be tied together smoothly.

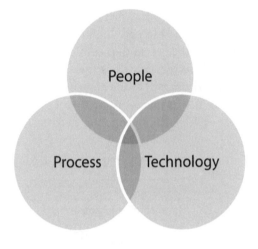

Figure 8-7: The Relationship between People, Process, and Technology

If any of these strategic elements is unsound, the CRM strategy will never reach its greatest potential. Organizations that understand the strategic value of CRM technology to achieve dramatic increases in revenue, productivity, and customer satisfaction will have a significant advantage over their competitors.

CRM Metrics

Chapter 5 discussed the importance of putting in place a solid business case to justify an ERP implementation. The same is true of a CRM system implementation. Part of developing a business case involves estimating the total cost of ownership for the system as well as determining the business benefits and estimated return on investment. A sound business case begins with establishing metrics well in advance so that employees that use the system will know what "success" looks like and will be able to regularly track their performance against goals and expectations. Metrics should be clearly defined and tied to the company's CRM strategy. When metrics aren't clearly defined, often the root cause is that there is no real overarching strategy. Figure 8-8 presents examples of key CRM metrics for each of the stakeholder departments.

Figure 8-8: CRM Metrics for Marketing, Sales, and Service

Marketing	Sales	Service
Number of new campaigns	Number of new prospects	Service cases closed same day
Revenue generated by campaign	Number of new customers	Number of cases handled by agent
Number of responses by campaign	Amount of new revenue	Complaint time-to-resolution
Number of new customers acquired by campaign	Number of open opportunities	Customer satisfaction level
Customer retention rate	Sales cycle duration	Average number of service calls per day

Source: Mycustomer.com

CRM Analytics

A CRM system provides a holistic view of customer operations and relationships. What companies do with that information varies from organization to organization. This is where CRM analytics come into play. CRM analytics are instrumental to gaining a 360-degree view of the customer life cycle and helping companies to make more informed business decisions. Basic types of CRM analytics include tracking and analyzing sales performance by region, marketing campaign, customer, product, or sales unit, including margins, commissions, or sales representative. Listed below are typical analytics found in CRM systems.

- **Event monitoring** – notifying users when specific, defined events happen. For instance, when a customer's purchases reach a certain amount, gift cards are mailed to the customer as a reward.

- **Profiling** – capturing characteristics about the most typical customers that are needed to target sales and marketing campaigns. These attributes can include such things as age, location, life stage, income band, and lifestyle choices.

- **Segmentation** – gathering intelligence about how profiling attributes interrelate to one another to form patterns and groupings. A segment includes people or organizations that have one or more characteristics in common that cause them to demand similar products or services. Sometimes the characteristic is as simple as different age groups. Sometimes, however, these characteristics are not visible to the naked eye.

- **Personalization** – marketing to the individual, or "market-of-one," typically to enhance e-commerce sales. A web page or pages are tailored to specifically target an individual consumer so as to meet the customer's needs more effectively and efficiently, thereby increasing customer satisfaction and repeat visits. For example, when a customer logs into Amazon.com, a personalized webpage appears displaying products that are specifically geared toward that customer.

- **Pricing** – facilitating more aggressive pricing or better pricing policies with various models based on logistics, expected consumer disposable income, or short-term fluctuations in production volumes, labor costs, or raw material costs. Initial prices for goods and services are stored in CRM, but then discounts can be applied based on information specific to an inventory item or to customer attractiveness.

- **Predictive modeling** – using historical and current data to generate a model to forecast future outcomes. This type of analytic, discussed more in depth in Chapter 12, can help determine the likely success of certain events; for instance, models can be generated to compare various product development plans in terms of likely future success given knowledge about current customers.

- **Association** – analyzing events that occur frequently together. For example, a grocery store learns that its customers purchase Cheerios or Wheaties with bananas. So, they position bananas near the cereal so customers will not forget to pick them up as well.

Knowledge Management

Knowledge is information gained through experience, association, or familiarity. Organizations encompass two types of knowledge:

- **Explicit knowledge** – knowledge that is easily documented and codified, including a company's aggregation of documents about its business processes, customers, research results, legal agreements, and other information that might have value to a competitor and is not common knowledge.

- **Tacit knowledge** – knowledge that is contained in people's heads gleaned from years of working in a particular industry and/or for a particular company. This type of knowledge is also called **intellectual capital**, which is the brainpower of humans that can be leveraged internally and externally to create more power than if it was only used by its owner. Tacit knowledge is key to competitive advantage because it is difficult for competitors to replicate.

Both types, when captured, become **organizational knowledge**, or knowledge that has accumulated since the inception of the organization. Companies must be careful that organizational knowledge is not ignored or lost; instead, they should employ knowledge management to improve internal productivity, customer satisfaction, and competitive advantage.

Knowledge management (KM) is a directed process of figuring out what knowledge a company has that could benefit others internal or external to the company, then devising ways of making it easily available. A KM strategy is about finding solutions to problems and then sharing and reusing these solutions many times. A **knowledge management (KM) system** refers to any kind of system that captures and stores knowledge, improves collaboration by sharing knowledge, locates knowledge sources, mines repositories for hidden knowledge, or in some other way enriches the KM strategy. Without a KM system, knowledge may never be discovered or passed along, and employees, suppliers, and customers must constantly reinvent the wheel. A KM system revolves around the **knowledge base**, a dynamic, searchable database of organizational knowledge that pertains to a specific subject.

CRM and Knowledge Management

In recent years, companies have integrated their CRM and KM systems because they realize that knowledge plays a key role in CRM success. The coupling of CRM and KM enables CSRs to accomplish more in less time, which equates to increased productivity, greater cost savings, and higher levels of customer satisfaction. CRM and KM were once considered very different disciplines, but now it is clear that they work together for the same goals: to improve business efficiency, enhance customer satisfaction, and enable the company to "speak with a single voice." The goal for integrating CRM and KM is to answer as many problems as possible quickly, easily, and correctly. Many customers prefer to solve their own problems without having to call for support or come into a store. KM can be integrated into web interfaces so that customers can find answers to their own problems using a search engine instead of submitting emails or calling the call center, thereby reducing overhead. Companies use KM systems to deliver consistent information to customers. The "best answers" to solutions for customer problems are captured, organized, and then published in a knowledge base repository so CSRs and customers can quickly find answers to important questions. The knowledge base helps the sales representative to efficiently identify the proper product, pricing, and even sales strategy when approaching a new or existing customer. Figure 8-9 presents more reasons to implement a KM system.

Figure 8-9: Reasons to Implement a Knowledge Management System

Sharing best practices	Companies can save millions by taking the knowledge from their best performers and applying it to similar situations in their organizations.
Downsizing and outsourcing	Without effective mechanisms in place to capture knowledge, companies may have to pay again for knowledge they once had on tap. Retaining knowledge makes a company more sustainable.
Knowledge commands a premium price in the market	Applied "know-how" can enhance the value and price of a company's products and services.
Globalization and competition	Many organizations rely on knowledge to create their strategic advantage.
Innovation	Companies have found that through knowledge networking they can create new products and services faster and better.

Source: David Skyrme Associates

Implementing a Knowledge Management System

Implementing a KM system should be a strategic business initiative, complementing existing organizational objectives. Various factors such as organizational size, company culture, and employee turnover should be considered when determining the need for KM. Generally, the larger the company and the more geographically disbursed, the more difficult it is to determine who holds what expertise and thus the more necessary a KM system becomes. A KM system would also greatly benefit those organizations that have high turnover because as soon as employees leave, valuable knowledge can be lost. In addition, some companies have a culture that supports knowledge sharing more than others. Sometimes a KM system is not needed if the company has a strong informal network of individuals who readily share information with others. A KM system implementation involves the following steps:

1. Confirm the purpose – It is easier to determine what information should go into a system when you understand its purpose. With any enterprise system, the organization must document the "pain points" that a KM system should solve and analyze the current state of knowledge sharing.

2. Form a team that will be responsible for the process – If the objective of the KM system is to support sales and customer service, key employees in those areas should be involved.

Oftentimes when KM systems are being used throughout the enterprise, a top management position will be created to lead the effort. Often referred to as the **chief knowledge officer (CKO)**, this person oversees the content, strategy, and structure of the KM system.

3. Create a knowledge base – This repository should include best practices, expertise directories, and market intelligence. It should be noted that the information in the repository will not be finite or static; it will continue to evolve with the introduction of new products and services and the needs of customers.

4. Create formal procedures to implement the system – Develop a process for managing change and make sure the organizational culture is supportive of knowledge sharing.

5. Create an efficient process by which information is shared from experts to CSRs to customers – Use multiple communication modes such as frequently asked questions (FAQ), email, live chat, document management, wikis, and other collaboration tools.

By following these steps and overcoming obstacles to implementing a KM system as shown in Figure 8-10, an organization should have a successful KM implementation.

Figure 8-10: Obstacles to Implementing a Knowledge Management System

Starting too big	Companies should start small. Piloting a knowledge-sharing initiative in a department or small business unit minimizes risk.
Relying on technological shortcuts	A KM system should not merely entail storing data in a knowledge base. The information that is retained should be useful. Technology can offer many advantages to KM. But, if misused, it can sabotage the KM process.
Not modeling the behavior	Managers must incorporate KM into their own behavior and create a safe climate for employees to share information. They should understand how existing knowledge is leveraged and how to share knowledge gained on past projects.
Treating KM as a one-off project or quick win	KM is a long-term commitment to the organization's future prosperity. Companies should establish metrics that define what they want to achieve from KM and when.
Ignoring the power of rewards	Knowledge sharing is an unnatural act. Managers should link KM directly to performance and recognize employees who contribute to it. The culture of the organization must be changed from "knowledge is power" to "knowledge sharing is power."
Maintaining the system	A KM system must be continually maintained to ensure that only relevant knowledge is retained. Companies need to avoid knowledge obsolescence by constantly amending, updating, and deleting information.

Source: CIO.com

Knowledge Management Metrics

The objectives for implementing a KM system are to reduce the time and costs associated with solving customer problems (efficiency) by providing proven, consistent, and accurate answers (effectiveness). Efficiency has to do with leveraging knowledge-based assets to improve processes. An example metric for efficiency is diagnostic resource use, or the percentage of time that customers and support representatives leverage existing tools and knowledge resources to diagnose and resolve issues. Talk time, or the time it takes a CSR to convey an answer by phone, is another efficiency metric.

KM effectiveness metrics are used to measure the impact the KM system has on providing accurate, timely, and complete information to internal or external users. One metric may be topic coverage, or the rate at which sought topics are available within the knowledge base. Another KM effectiveness metric may include solution rate, or the rate at which customers indicate they were successful in finding useful information through the KM tool on the company's website. Solution adoption also measures effectiveness. For instance, search engine logs can be analyzed to produce a range of reports showing adoption and use and a breakdown of search terms. A more direct measure for effectiveness is whether the information is being used in practice. As usage actually happens outside the system, it must be reported by the staff and a rewards mechanism put into place to encourage timely reporting.

These objectives of efficiency and effectiveness are the "low-hanging fruit," and the KM team and CKO should develop goals and measures during planning for KM and then monitor them post-go-live to make sure the system is a success. Once efficiency and effectiveness measures are improved, more opportunities for productivity and revenue generation may become obvious. For example, the KM system may result in freeing up CSRs to provide high-touch services for key accounts. More time could be spent on enhancing the knowledge base content to cover more difficult and time-consuming topics. Adding to the knowledge base with new information and proven solutions will further increase the savings associated with the system. Finally, the KM system can help focus resources on service contract renewals and proactively identify potential issues before they become service requests.

Summary

This chapter began with outlining the key activities in the order-to-cash process and how these activities are performed in an ERP system. Next, CRM was introduced as a company-wide business strategy and technology intended to increase firm profitability by solidifying customer satisfaction, loyalty, and advocacy. As part of today's extended ERP environment, CRM systems are used to manage interactions with current and future customers by automating and synchronizing marketing, sales, and customer service. They enable companies to capture key data about their customers so they can respond to their current needs as well as help to predict their future needs. CRM analytics include predictive modeling and also segmentation, personalization, and association. CRM systems now include a social component in which unstructured data is captured and coded so that inferences can be made from it. Many companies interface their CRM systems with KM systems so that customers can obtain answers to issues and questions faster and with less expense. A KM system, although not a transaction-processing system, is an integral part of business because it stores and disseminates organizational knowledge that is helpful to customers and customer-facing employees. In this modern business environment, companies have turned to KM to convert the knowledge obtained internally and externally to knowledge that is accessible throughout the enterprise and to business partners.

Keywords

Account

Association

Available to promise (ATP)

Back-office system

Bill of lading

Chief knowledge officer (CKO)

Contact

Contact-to-contract-to-cash process

Customer relationship management system (CRM)

Event monitoring

Explicit knowledge

Field service

Front-office system

Hybrid approach

Intellectual capital

Invoice

Knowledge

Knowledge base

Knowledge management (KM)

Knowledge management (KM) system

Lead

Lead management

Opportunity

Order acknowledgement

Order fulfillment

Order-to-cash process

Organizational knowledge

Packing slip

Partner channel management

Personalization

Point of sale (POS) system

Predictive modeling

Pricing

Profiling

Prospect

Qualify

Quotation

Quote-to-cash process

Remittance advice

Sales order

Sales pipeline

Segmentation

Social CRM

Social media

Social media monitoring

Tacit knowledge

Quick Review

1. True/False: The sales pipeline is an estimation of sales revenue that will be generated in upcoming months.

2. True/False: CRM software is known as a back-office enterprise software.

3. True/False: Personalization refers to the ability to sell to the "market-of-one."

4. _____ is the practice of identifying and assessing what is being said about a company, product, or brand and looking at it over time through lenses that are relevant for the company.

5. People glean _____ knowledge from years of working in a particular industry and/or for a particular company.

Questions to Consider

1. Define CRM and discuss how it evolved.

2. List the steps in the order-to-cash process.

3. Explain how CRM and ERP overlap.

4. What activities are involved in order fulfillment?

5. What are the steps for creating a knowledge management system?

References

Bland, W. (2010, April 20). *38 CRM metrics to keep your organization on track. CustomerThink. [blog post]*. Retrieved from http://www.customerthink.com/blog/38_crm_metrics_keep_organization_track

CRM Switch Staff. (2013). CRM and ERP: What's the difference? *[blog post]*. Retrieved from http://www.crmswitch.com/crm-value/understanding-crm-erp/

DestinationCRM. (2010, February 19). *What is CRM?* Retrieved from http://www.destinationcrm.com/ Articles/CRM-News/Daily-News/What-Is-CRM-46033.aspx

David Skyrme Associates. (2003). *Knowledge management: Making sense of an oxymoron.* Retrieved from http://www.skyrme.com/insights/22km.htm

Frost, A. (2014, January). Knowledge management. KMT. Retrieved from http://www.knowledge-management-tools.net/

InformationWeek. (2011, August 11). 10 cool social media monitoring tools. Retrieved from http://www.informationweek.com/software/social/10-cool-social-media-monitoring-tools/d/d-id/1099504?page_number=1

Insideview.com (n.d.). Enhance sales relationships with social CRM. Retrieved from http://www.insideview.com/enhance-sales-relationships-social-crm

Jitterbit. (n.d.). Keys to CRM and ERP integration success. Retrieved from http://www.jitterbit.com/blog/4-keys-crm-and-erp-integration-success-02-10-12/

Kimberling, E. (2013, December 11). Integrating ERP with CRM systems. Retrieved from http://panorama-consulting.com/integrating-erp-with-crm-systems/

Levinson, M. (2007, March 7). Knowledge management definition and solutions. Retrieved from http://www.cio.com/article/40343/Knowledge_Management_Definition_and_Solutions?page=4&taxonomyId=3011

Marshall, P. (2013, August 29). How to stop wasting time with tire kickers and qualify prospects in 5 easy steps. Retrieved from http://www.entrepreneur.com/article/227899

Matrix Solutions. (n.d.). Profiling and segmentation. Retrieved from https://www.matrixsolutions.co.uk/ products/inside-intelligence/profiling-and-segmentation/

MJC2. (n.d.). Field service management software. Retrieved from http://www.mjc2.com/field-service.htm

Mycustomer.com. (2014, January 23). CRM metrics: What should you monitor and measure? Retrieved from http://www.mycustomer.com/feature/data-technology/crm-metrics-what-should-you-monitor-and-measure/166328

Rouse, M. (2013, January 28). Social media listening. Retrieved from http://searchcrm.techtarget.com/definition/Social-media-monitoring

Salesforce.com (n.d.). What is CRM? Retrieved from http://www.salesforce.com/eu/crm/what-is-crm.jsp

SAP. (2007). *CRM without compromise: A strategy for profitable growth.* Retrieved from http://www.inst-informatica.pt/servicos/informacao-e-documentacao/biblioteca-digital/areas-aplicacionais/crm/CRM_Without_Compromise.pdf

SAP. (2013, November 13) CRM marketing. Retrieved from http://wiki.scn.sap.com/wiki/display/CRM/Marketing

SAP. (2014). POS integration. Retrieved from http://wiki.scn.sap.com/wiki/display/CK/Integration+Scenario+POS

SAP Global. (2007). *SAP customer relationship management solution overview brochure.* Retrieved from http://www.sap.com/solutions/business-suite/crm/brochures/index.epx

SearchCRM. (2010, August 31). *Social CRM.* Retrieved from http://searchcrm.techtarget.com/definition/social-CRM

Wailgum, T. (2007, March 6). CRM definition and solutions. CIO.com. Retrieved from http://www.cio.com/article/2439505/customer-relationship-management/crm-definition-and-solutions.html

Wingard, N. (n.d.). CRM history: The evolution of customer service. Retrieved from http://www.streetdirectory.com/travel_guide/124130/enterprise_information_systems/crm_history_the_evolution_of_better_customer_service.html

ERP Supply Chain Management

Objectives

- Understand the concept of supply chain management (SCM)

- Become familiar with the ERP modules that enable operations and supply chain

- Be acquainted with the ERP modules that support manufacturing and related processes

- Understand how material requirements planning (MRP) facilitates the purchasing and production plan

- Know important technologies and methodologies that make SCM more efficient

Introduction

The supply chain is the network among various connected companies producing, handling and/or distributing a specific product. In particular, the supply chain encompasses the steps it takes to get a good or service from the supplier to the customer. ERP systems enable a company's supply chain by helping to coordinate inventory, information, and financial flows between a company and its business partners. This coordination facilitates the SCM activities of plan, source, make, and deliver. This chapter discusses the various supply chain modules in an ERP system, such as the Purchasing module, which enables the purchase-to-pay process. Other supply chain modules include Warehouse Management, Supplier Relationship Management, and Transportation Management. Order fulfillment, an integral part of the order-to-cash process discussed in Chapter 8, is also technically part of the supply chain supporting the "deliver" aspect. The Manufacturing module of an ERP system supports the "make" part of the supply chain.

The "engine" of the Manufacturing module is material requirements planning (MRP), which supports the material purchasing and production planning activities so that more accurate finished goods commitments can be made to customers. Other modules that assist with manufacturing include Quality Assurance, which ensures that goods are purchased, produced, and sold at expected quality levels and Plant Maintenance, which ensures that equipment in the plant is properly maintained so that it remains in workable condition and can keep up with expected capacity targets. The chapter concludes with a discussion of several supply chain methodologies and technologies that work with ERP systems to permit the efficient and smooth flow of inventory, information, and finances in and out of the enterprise.

What Is Supply Chain Management?

The art and science that goes into making sure that the right product or service gets into the right customer's hands in the right quantity and at the right time is known as **supply chain management (SCM)**. SCM is based on two key concepts. The first is that nearly every product that reaches a consumer represents the cumulative work of more than one company. These companies are collectively referred to as the **supply chain**. The second idea is that while supply chains have been around for many years, most companies have only focused on what happens within their own four walls. Few businesses understood, much less managed, the whole chain of activities that culminate in delivery to the final customer. The result was fragmented and inefficient supply chain processes.

Supply chain management focuses on product development, planning and forecasting, purchasing, sourcing, supplier relationships, manufacturing, warehousing, and distribution. The physical product and financial flows are the most visible part of the supply chain; however, the information flows allow the various business partners in the supply chain to coordinate their long-term plans and collaborate to maximize customer value and achieve a competitive advantage. Figure 9-1 presents the four main activities in the supply chain, which are also explained below.

Figure 9-1: The Supply Chain

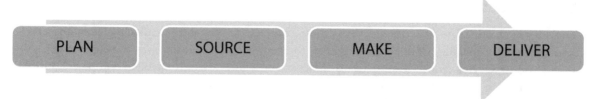

Source: Supply Chain Council

- Plan – Companies should have a strategic plan in place to manage the resources that go into meeting customer demand for their products and services.

- Source – Companies should streamline processes that procure goods and services to meet planned or actual demand.

- Make – Manufacturing activities should be properly scheduled and executed and products should be tested, packaged, and prepared for delivery. Production output, quality, and worker productivity should be measured.

- Deliver – Logistics activities include retrieving inventory from the warehouse per customer orders, choosing the modes of transportation, scheduling deliveries, and transporting the goods to the customer.

Implementing ERP SCM modules has several benefits. The main benefit is increased visibility in the supply chain, which allows for more responsiveness to changes in supply and demand and better forecasting. This information transparency, combined with real-time business analytics can shorten the time between when a party in the supply chain pays for goods and services and when it gets paid for them (called the **cash-to-cash cycle**). SCM partners should be able to decrease their inventory levels and increase their inventory turnover due to this greater information transparency— the manufacturer will make only what is needed and the distributor will ship only product that is forecast to be sold. These reductions in inventory, a major expense in manufacturing, distribution, and retail, lower overall costs. Delays in shipments, on production lines, and in distribution channels can result in poor relationships and lost business. These delays are reduced due to tighter integration and seamless coordination among business partners in a supply chain. Finally, a greater awareness of customer trends allows for more flexibility and responsiveness to customers' needs.

In companies with ERP systems, supply chains are a unified set of processes working in concert to support the plan, source, make, and deliver activities. These companies' ERP systems not only share data and information internally, but they also share data and information with business partners up and down their supply chains, allowing for better visibility and decision- making. Additionally, integrating CRM with SCM allows for better sales forecasting accuracy. The CRM system captures customer orders and uses them to analyze trends and buying habits. These sales inputs and intelligence assist in making better make and buy decisions. Discussed below are core modules that are considered part of SCM in ERP systems.

Purchasing and Sourcing

The Purchasing module supports the **purchase-to-pay process**, the main objective of which is to order goods and services when needed, receive them in satisfactory condition, and pay only for what is ordered and received (see Figure 9-2 for steps in the purchase-to-pay process).

Figure 9-2: Steps in the Purchase-to-Pay Process

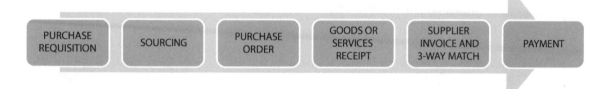

The first step in the purchase-to-pay process (also known as the **procure-to-pay process**) is the **purchase requisition**, which is an internal document generated by a user or department requesting goods or services. This document can be manually entered into the ERP system, or it can be automated, such as when the material requirements planning system requests raw materials based on production plans. Generally, purchase requisitions are subject to approval and budgeting constraints.

Sourcing is a strategy in which a company seeks to find the most cost-efficient location for manufacturing a product or purchasing a product or service. The process of sourcing includes understanding the company's internal requirements and the external market, identifying and evaluating potential suppliers, conducting negotiations with them, and then agreeing to supply contracts with the suppliers. If no supplier exists for a requested item, the sourcing department will identify potential sources and may ask them to submit quotes in response to a **request for quote (RFQ)**. An RFQ is a business document that solicits price and delivery quotes for a specific quantity of a type of goods and/or services. Suppliers respond to the RFQ with quotations, which are entered into the ERP system. The sourcing department will use multiple criteria, such as price, quality, and service, to evaluate which suppliers will be awarded business. Accepted quotations become purchase orders in the ERP system.

A **purchase order (PO)** is a binding contract between the buyer and seller setting forth quantities, prices, discounts, payment terms, date of shipment or performance of a service, and other associated terms and conditions. Figure 9-3 shows an SAP purchase order to Olympic Protective Gear for 60 off road and 150 road bike helmets at $25 each for a total of $5,250. The supplier may send a **purchase order acknowledgment** upon receipt of the purchase order.

The next step in the purchase-to-pay process is the **goods/services receipt**. In Chapter 7 we learned the difference between a transaction and an event. Up to this point in the purchase-to-pay process, each of the activities corresponds to an event because no journal entry is made. However, when the company receives goods, a transaction is recorded. Depending on the type of receipt, either an asset or an expense is increased in the general ledger (GL) and a liability recorded. The Purchasing module's inventory management functionality will now keep track of the movement of inventory in and out of the warehouse and the physical count and dollar value of those items.

Figure 9-3: Purchase Order

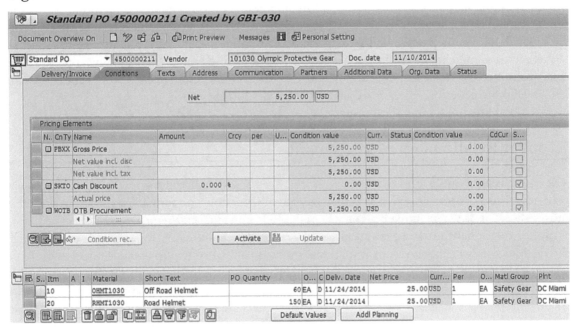

Source: SAP

Next, the supplier invoice is received, which triggers accounts payable, a liability, to be recorded to offset the liability generated with the inventory receipt. The invoice receipt is also a transaction since it affects the GL.

During the inventory/service receipt and the supplier invoice transactions, the ERP system performs a check to compare the contents of three documents. This check is known as the **three-way match** and is a configured control in the ERP system that will attempt to "match" three documents together—the purchase order, goods receipt, and supplier invoice—before either accepting goods or paying a supplier. Many companies will not consider a supplier invoice to be payable until they have a purchase order with a price that matches the price on the invoice and a goods receipt document indicating that the correct quantities were received (or services rendered) and are in good order. The three-way match is the most commonly used method for recognizing a valid financial obligation in the purchase-to-pay process. ERP systems allow companies to configure **tolerance limits**, which allow for slight differences between quantities received and quantities ordered and actual purchase price versus purchase price on the PO, so that an inordinate amount of time is not spent "chasing" immaterial differences. These small differences will be posted to a quantity or price variance GL expense account.

After the invoice is verified, the company owes the supplier for the goods or services and must pay according to the terms set forth in the PO. The final transaction in the purchase-to-pay process is the settlement of the accounts payable. The payment, often an electronic funds transfer (EFT), will clear out the accounts payable and reduce the bank account. Later in the chapter we will discuss electronic data interchange, radio frequency identification, and vendor managed inventory, which can speed up the purchase-to-pay process, reduce errors, and help suppliers and buyers communicate and collaborate better regarding forecasts and inventory levels.

Supplier Relationship Management

The Purchasing module automates many of the events and transactions in the purchase-to-pay process; however, it does not effectively manage the collaboration with suppliers in order to derive the most value. This is where implementing a Supplier Relationship Management (SRM) module helps. **Supplier relationship management** refers to a company's comprehensive approach to managing interactions with its suppliers, similar to how it may use a CRM system to manage interactions with customers. It takes traditional sourcing to another level by addressing both the buyer and seller sides, which can provide mutual benefits for each organization through an appropriate investment of time, resources, and executive support. SRM personnel are responsible for maintaining regular contact with suppliers, determining their needs, and letting them know what their own needs are. They will use SRM to define replenishment strategies with suppliers, manage contracts, and establish strategic sourcing relationships with them. Suppliers are treated more as partners rather than just commodity brokers. The SRM module also includes RFQ functionality with competitive bidding features and contract negotiation tools. This feature gives the purchasing and sourcing personnel a view of the demand for goods or services across the company so it can negotiate better prices with key suppliers.

Typically, SRM will include a web-based portal so that sourcing personnel can communicate with suppliers in real time. Buyers can check the status of shipments, while suppliers can monitor stock levels to determine when the buyer's inventory should be replenished. Collaborative tools allow for the sharing of data such as buyers' sales forecasts. One aspect of SRM is **supplier performance management (SPM)**, in which buyers can assess supplier performance using a host of metrics, including quality, delivery, cost, and responsiveness, in an effort to cut costs, reduce risks, and drive continuous improvement. Suppliers are also evaluated these days of their "green initiatives."

Another feature of the SRM module is that it allows companies to collect, categorize, and evaluate their expenditures in order to identify any wasteful spending and contracts that need to be renegotiated. This is referred to as **spend analysis**. Other issues that spend analysis can bring to the forefront are categories of spend where there may be too many suppliers and/or no contracts in place. SRM also helps companies manage best-in-class contracts with choice suppliers. These centralized contracts enable companies to consolidate their total spend across business units in order to negotiate better prices. This process is referred to as **contract management**.

Catalog management functionality in SRM makes available supplier catalogs to procurement and other staff so they can easily purchase items. This functionality empowers end users to find and purchase policy-compliant products and services across multiple catalogs using a familiar shopping cart experience. A set of business rules controls the amount and type of spend. SRM can also be used to facilitate self-service procurement for employees in the company via an internet portal. Figure 9-4 shows key functionality in an SRM module.

Figure 9-4: Supplier Relationship Management Functionality

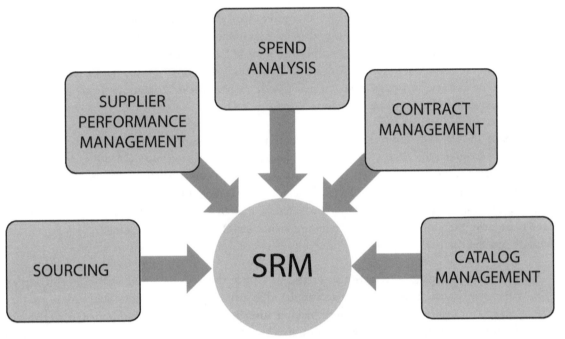

Source: Deloitte

Warehouse Management System

A Warehouse Management System (WMS) supports the day-to-day operations in a warehouse. It includes logic to control the movement of inventory into, out of, and through the warehouse and provides the exact location of inventory in the warehouse. Standard WMS processes include receiving, putaway, order picking, and shipping. The WMS also includes optimization of these processes. For example, suppose a warehouse worker is putting away recently received material instructed by a hand-held mobile device. After putaway, the worker is then directed to count additional items at a nearby location, and while at that location, pick an item for delivery to the shipping area. The worker, therefore, is in a continuous loop of activity directed by the WMS module via the mobile device.

In addition to the optimization of worker activities, the WMS can optimize the storage of items. For example, it can direct the placement of faster-moving items toward the front of the warehouse and slower-moving items toward the back. This storage logic minimizes putaway and retrieval times, while increasing warehouse throughput, reducing labor costs, and improving customer service.

The WMS module uses certain master data to optimize activities and provide a safe environment. For instance, weights and dimensions of warehoused material should be stored so the system does not try to exceed a safe load capacity for storage or shipping or try to assign a large item to a small warehouse location. Additionally, indicators for hazardous or perishable material should be checked in the material master record so the material is safely stored in the warehouse and sold before the shelf life expiration. Master data should also be maintained on the warehouse space itself. For instance, every storage location in the warehouse should have a unique address, known as a **bin**, or **coordinate**. A given warehouse can also employ a combination of storage types, including high rack storage or carousel systems. The optimal use of any of these storage methods requires that certain data and characteristics be defined in the module.

The heart of the WMS is the picking and placement strategies employed to intelligently place and pick material to speed the flow of material into and out of the warehouse. On the receiving side, a WMS may offer a number of placement options for newly received material, including putting the item in the next empty bin, adding it to existing stock, or placing it in a fast-moving or slow-moving area. A WMS also may allow for picking strategies such as first in, first out (FIFO), last in, first out (LIFO) or next expiring batch in environments that employ batch management. WMS will also facilitate picking methods such as:

- **Two-step picking** – Warehouse employees pick the required materials for a group of customer orders. The material is accumulated in a staging area and individual orders are then picked from this area. The two-step picking strategy minimizes the number of trips through the warehouse and is particularly useful in a small package shipping environment where the same product may be ordered by a large number of customers.

- **Wave picking** – Customer deliveries are organized into "waves" based upon common characteristics such as route, carrier, or scheduled time of departure. Depending upon the capabilities of the system, this process may be automated, with picking waves "released" throughout the workday for processing and shipment.

- **Serpentine picking** – The system directs warehouse staff up one aisle and down the next in a "snaking" motion, which optimizes the movement of workers through the warehouse.

A WMS can also provide a number of options for maintaining inventory accuracy. The traditional approach for inventory accuracy is a regularly scheduled physical inventory count, which can be employed on an annual or more frequent basis even without the aid of a sophisticated WMS. But wall-to-wall inventory counts can be disruptive, requiring warehouse operations to be stopped until the count has been completed. Thus, **cycle counting** is often employed in which a small subset of inventory, in a particular location, is counted on a specified day. For example, using cycle counting warehouse employees may count one-twelfth of the inventory items each month. By continually counting inventory, every item in the warehouse is counted at least several times over the course of a year. Cycle counting is less disruptive to warehouse operations than a full wall-to-wall inventory, although individual warehouse bins must be blocked for use while being counted. More sophisticated WMS may support **dynamic cycle counting**, which allows normal warehouse operations to continue during bin counts without the requirement for bins to be blocked for placement or removal, resulting in even less business disruption. It should be noted that a good cycle counting program will improve inventory accuracy in the warehouse but may or may not replace the requirement for a complete annual inventory.

Transportation Management System

Companies that transport their own inventory or the inventory of others are under constant pressure to reduce their operational costs and take better ownership and control of their key logistical processes. A Transportation Management System (TMS) manages and optimizes inbound (supplier-to-plant), outbound (plant-to-customer) and internal stock (plant-to-plant) transport. The TMS evaluates the pool of orders, consolidates them into shipments, and determines the optimal transportation mode, carrier, and route to minimize transportation expenses while maintaining customer service expectations. This allows for improved accountability with visibility into the transportation chain. Most TMS encompass functionality to:

- Combine inbound deliveries to form inbound shipments

- Combine outbound deliveries to form outbound shipments

- Assign mode of transportation—road, rail, sea, and air

- Plan and monitor deadlines

- Plan and dispatch transportation orders and monitor transportation with carrier and handling exceptions

- Manage freight cost calculations and settlements

Manufacturing

Historically, systems that enabled manufacturing activities supported a single purpose and were not integrated. Organizations relied on large amounts of materials in the form of raw materials and work in process in order to ensure the smooth flow of operations. In the 1990s came the advent of ERP systems, which helped to plan, manage, and control complex manufacturing operations. ERP systems encompass a number of functionalities that reduce the need to finance materials necessary to maintain efficient production levels. The Manufacturing module, a core module in ERP systems for the manufacturing sector, manages production and procurement planning as well as shop floor control (production execution) activities. This module enables the production planner to create realistic production plans across the company's manufacturing plants in order to fulfill customer demand in a timely manner and according to standards expected by the customer. This advanced functionality enables goods to be manufactured at the right quality and quantity and at the right time in order to fulfill customer demand. A good manufacturing system will answer five questions:

- What are we going to make?

- When are we going to make it?

- What does it take to make it?

- What do we have?

- What do we need?

An integral component of the Manufacturing module is **material requirements planning (MRP),** a software-based production planning and inventory control system initially developed in the 1970s. MRP assists production managers in scheduling and placing orders for items of dependent demand. **Dependent demand** items are components of finished goods—such as raw materials, component parts, and subassemblies—for which the amount of inventory needed depends on the level of production of the final product. The material plan takes into account inventory already on hand, customer orders, forecasts, and capacity to determine what needs to produced. Planning is done in time periods in the future, referred to as time buckets. MRP uses data from various ERP modules to meet four objectives:

- Ensure that materials are available for production

- Make sure that finished goods are available for delivery to customers

- Maintain the lowest possible raw material and finished goods inventory levels

- Plan manufacturing activities, delivery schedules, and purchasing activities

Without an MRP system, manufacturers typically react by purchasing material they *might* need. In contrast, with an MRP system, manufacturers purchase material they *do* need. When properly used, MRP can reduce inventory because the manufacturer should only make or buy what is needed when it is needed. MRP can also improve employee and equipment utilization because it is possible to better plan and control the use of resources. Figure 9-5 presents a visual of the inputs and outputs to an MRP system. The figure also shows the integration with the purchase-to-pay and order-to-cash processes.

Figure 9–5: Manufacturing Process

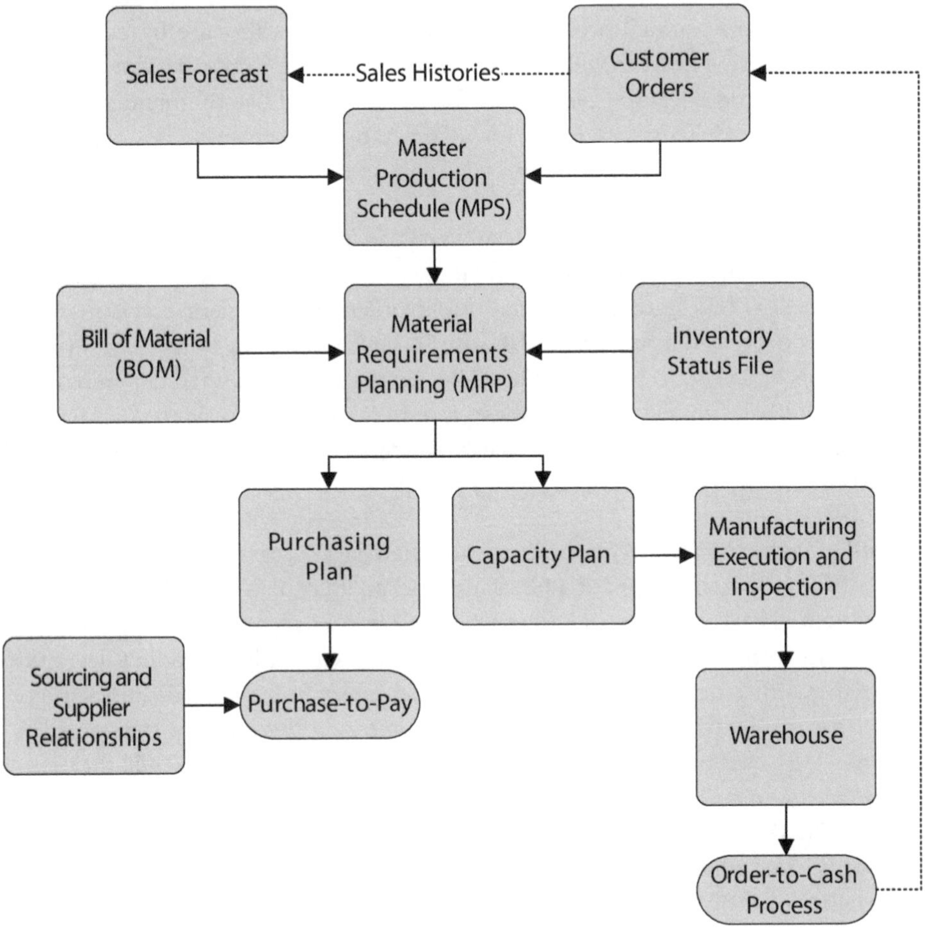

Based on planning data from the sales forecast and actual customer orders, MRP takes information from several sources to meet the objectives above. The inputs to MRP include the master production schedule, the bill of material, and the inventory status report. Each of these inputs is discussed below.

- MRP identifies what parts should be made or bought to meet the **master production schedule (MPS)**, which is a plan detailing what finished goods to produce, in what quantities, and at what dates. Quantities to be produced are specified in a short-range planning horizon for each week, known as a bucket. The MPS starts with an aggregate sales and operations (S&OP) plan and disaggregates it to arrive at a specific schedule for each finished product. The MPS can be considered an agreement between marketing, finance, purchasing, and manufacturing to support demand.

  Demand is made up of two inputs: The first input is actual customer orders, called **customer independent requirements**. The second input, known as **planned independent requirements**, are planned production or sales quantities that are based on some sort of forecast procedure. The MPS will also take into account production cycle times, staffing levels, and capacity. It provides the foundation for making good use of manufacturing resources, making customer delivery promises, resolving tradeoffs between sales and manufacturing, and reaching strategic objectives in the sales and operational plan.

  To illustrate the difference between these two types of requirements, imagine that a company plans to sell 200 bikes in the month of January 2016 based on sales in the same month of 2015. These 200 bikes are the planned independent requirement for January 2016. Since every bike is produced using two pedals, the 200 bikes you plan to sell in January 2016 result in 400 pedals you need to procure. These 400 pedals are the planned dependent requirement for January 2016. On the basis of these numbers, MRP can calculate—including current stock levels—how much bikes and pedals you actually need to produce/procure. The pedals are part of the BOM explained next.

- The **bill of material (BOM)** is the list of the materials necessary to make a finished product. Since a BOM rarely changes for a particular end product, it is considered master data in the ERP system. The BOM contains the part number, part name, description, unit of measure and quantity needed of every material that comprises a finished product. In anticipation of a desired quantity of finished products, the necessary raw materials and sub-components needed for production can be calculated to determine the amount that must be on hand when needed—this process is known as "exploding the BOM." MRP will then communicate the purchasing plan to the purchasing staff so they can order the materials. In essence, the MPS and the BOM indicate what goods should be ordered; the MPS, production cycle times, and supplier lead times then jointly determine when POs should be placed. Figure 9-6 shows a screenshot of a BOM for a Deluxe Touring Bike (red) in SAP.

Figure 9-6: Bill of Material

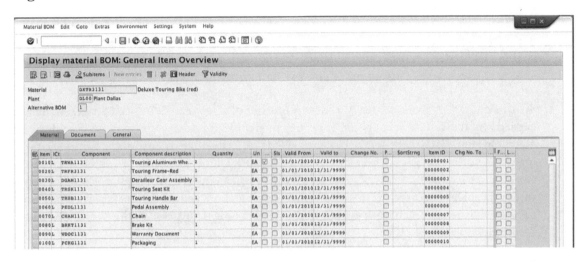

- A third input to MRP is the **inventory status report**. This report contains information about the on-hand balance of inventory including raw materials, subassemblies, and even finished goods. In addition, this report describes inventory on order and the lead time for each item. Knowing what is on order and when it will arrive is important information for production and gives a better picture of net requirements.

MRP generates two basic outputs: the purchasing plan and the capacity plan. The **purchasing plan** details what needs to be purchased and when POs should be released so that the materials will be received in time to support production. The **capacity plan** will detail the start and completion dates for planned orders while taking into consideration the availability of production personnel and machines. These planned orders are then released, which authorizes their execution on the shop floor. Both purchase orders and factory orders result in an increase in inventory: POs cause an increase in raw materials and factory orders result in an increase in work in process and, ultimately, finished goods.

The Manufacturing module is integrated with cost accounting to track the cost of goods manufactured and to relate these costs to established cost standards. Costs are tracked as they move from raw materials through the manufacturing process. Cost accountants and production managers analyze variances on raw material, direct labor, and factory overhead. Once the finished product is manufactured, costs will move from cost of goods manufactured to finished goods inventory on the balance sheet.

The Manufacturing module uses various types of master data in order to process transactions such as production orders and purchase orders. Besides the BOM, the Manufacturing module requires master data on inventory, work centers, and routings.

- **Material** – Any inventory item that the company procures, manufactures, stores, and ships must have a record in the material master table. Because inventory is used in so many different ways in the company and can represent a large dollar amount on the balance sheet, it is important to maintain the integrity of this data. Of course, this point applies to all data in the ERP system, but having incorrect data in the material master table can affect sales, shipping, warehousing, inspecting, valuation, and manufacturing.

- **Work center** – A work center is a location in the plant where value-added operations are carried out. It can represent people or groups of people, machines or groups of machines, or assembly lines. Each work center has an available capacity, such as how many labor–hours or machine–hours can be performed in a given amount of time. Formulas are entered into each work center so that the costs of operations can be calculated. A work center is also assigned to a cost center (discussed in Chapter 7). Information about setup and breakdown time needs to be established for each work center, so the correct time is allocated to the overall estimated duration for a factory order.

- **Routing** – The production order cannot be generated until there is information on how the finished item is created; this information can be found in the routing. A routing is a series of sequential operations that are carried out to produce a final product. In essence, the routing should define how to make the product from the BOM. The routing has one or more operations, each of which is assigned to a work center.

Quality Assurance

Maintaining high-quality products is integral to every activity in a company—from purchasing and production to customer delivery. Product quality improves the bottom line by reducing product returns and customer complaints. The Quality Assurance (QA) module of an ERP system helps to ensure that products purchased, made, and sold meet stringent regulatory standards and company product specifications and are safe and uniform.

Figure 9-7 shows a process map for the QA process. One of the first steps in the QA process is to set parameters (rules) into the module that will define what material to inspect and when to inspect it. Inspectors create an **inspection lot**, which is a sample of material chosen according to a sampling plan. It can be based on raw material received from a supplier or finished goods that have been manufactured. It can be an entire receipt or production run or a part of these. If the inspection lot is based on goods produced, it must consist of material produced under the same conditions as the entire lot and using similar materials, workers, and methods. The inspection lot is **restricted stock** for the time being because it cannot be used in production or sold. However, this type of stock is valued on the balance sheet until further notice.

Figure 9-7: Quality Assurance Process

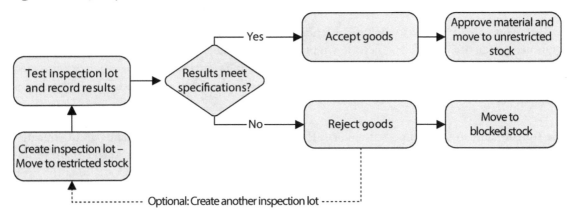

Source: Adapted from SAP Basics

Next, the inspection lot is tested. The type of tests to be conducted on the sample is stored in the QA module and the results are recorded. Information on tolerance limits for acceptance, or how much deviation from the standard can be "tolerated," is also stored in the module. Based on the results of the tests, the inspection lot is either accepted and moved to unrestricted stock or rejected and moved to blocked stock. **Unrestricted stock** is stock that can be accepted from a supplier, used further in the manufacturing process, or sold. This type of stock is valued on the balance sheet. **Blocked stock** cannot be used and is not valued on the balance sheet. This stock may need to be sent back to the supplier or reworked. If nothing can be done to this stock to make it usable, or it cannot be sent back, an inventory write-off may occur.

Implementing a QA module has many benefits, the most obvious one being that it helps alert those responsible when quality deviations occur. The earlier a defect is detected, the better. If a faulty product is detected early in receiving or manufacturing, it may cost a few dollars, but if it is found after the product is in the hands of the consumer, it could cost much more, especially is there ends up being a recall. Some other key benefits of QA include the ability to:

- Record quality tests in a consistent and controlled way

- Build quality into inventory management and production processes

- Minimize time spent inspecting material, collecting data, testing, and retesting

- Reduce scrap, rework, and customer returns

Plant Maintenance

Management should be able to identify potential problems with plant assets, such as manufacturing equipment, facilities, and fleets, before a replace-or-repair decision needs to be made. Likewise, management should be able to quickly fix a plant asset that has malfunctioned—an expensive piece of equipment standing idle waiting for a part can cost a company thousands of dollars in lost productivity!

The functionality in the Plant Maintenance (PM) module of an ERP system helps an organization increase the availability of plant assets, reduce the number of breakdowns through preventive maintenance, coordinate and employ personnel to complete maintenance and malfunction work orders, and reduce the costs of maintenance and inspections. This module also helps to improve sustainability through better environmental performance of plant assets and more efficient asset utilization. There is tight integration between the PM module and the Asset Management module discussed in Chapter 7. For instance, PM uses master data on plant assets, such as asset number, description, and location, which is typically entered into the Asset Management module.

Figure 9-8 presents the workflow for plant maintenance. Maintenance schedules for plant assets are entered in the module so the ERP system notifies the maintenance worker when work needs to be performed. Thus, the first activity involves creating a maintenance work order. If parts are needed, a purchase requisition is generated and then authorized by purchasing, which sends the PO to the supplier through the Purchasing module. The inventory/receiving department receives the part when it arrives, and the part is issued to the maintenance work order. At this point, a maintenance manager might approve the work order, schedule it, and release it so that the worker can complete the job. Once the job is complete, costs of the work order are settled to the appropriate cost center.

Figure 9-8: Plant Maintenance Workflow

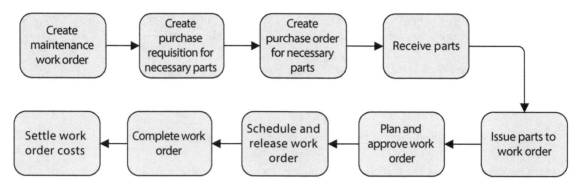

Source: Adapted from SAP Basics

Goals for implementing the PM module are to:

- Extend the useful life of equipment

- Minimize downtime and maximize uptime of equipment

- Improve communication and collaboration between production and maintenance staff

- Monitor equipment performance and utilization

- Lower costs of maintenance, production, and labor costs

- Comply with safety and emission regulations

Environment, Health, and Safety

An increasing number of companies are investing time and effort into producing corporate social responsibility (CSR) reports for their stakeholders, including employees, customers, suppliers, and investors. These reports describe a company's CSR activities in such areas as the environment, health and safety of employees, and product safety. Companies are becoming more concerned

with environmental compliance at their facilities as well as where they do business and with whom they do business. The Environmental, Health, and Safety (EHS) module has been designed to maintain compliance with national and international directives, including the global reduction of greenhouse gases. Companies must also show compliance with health and safety regulations that arise from local, state, and federal agencies. These agencies, including the largest one, the Occupational Safety and Health Administration (OSHA), impose rules and regulations that are becoming increasingly complex, resulting in higher compliance costs and greater business risks. Injuries and unsafe conditions for employees both in the workplace and at suppliers and facilities across their supply chain carry significant risks to companies. Additionally, businesses are expected to exercise due care when designing their products and services to make sure they fit their intended purposes and do not present any hazard to health and safety.

Figure 9-9 provides example CSR activities that companies may report on regarding environmental and occupational and product safety processes. For each activity, there can be considerable complexity and uncertainty in aggregating the data and performing calculations on it. The EHS module can centralize this data from the Supply Chain, Manufacturing, and Human Capital Management modules, providing the necessary information to mitigate those risks. Used as the foundation of a company's CSR initiative, the EHS module can help overcome the inherent problems of disparate systems, regions, and business units.

Figure 9-9: Example Corporate Social Responsibly Activities Collected in the EHS Module

Environmental	• Reduce emissions
	• Conserve energy in facilities
	• Reduce water consumption
	• Treat water before discharging
	• Recycle waste
Product Safety	• Communicate hazards associated with products manufactured and sold
	• Produce "green" products
Occupational Health and Safety	• Educate and train employees on rules and regulations, including handling of hazardous substances
	• Seek to eliminate on-the-job accidents and lost workdays

Supply Chain Technology

Supply chain technology seeks to eliminate much of the guesswork between suppliers, manufacturers, retailers, and customers by enabling more visibility up and down the supply chain. Certain enablers of the supply chain are discussed next. As with any new system or technology, companies must overcome various obstacles in order to fully realize the value. Several of these obstacles include:

- Gaining trust from suppliers and partners – Supply chain partners must agree to collaborate, compromise, and help each other achieve their goals.

- Resistance to change – Traditionally, operations personnel were accustomed to managing the supply chain with phone calls, faxes, and emails. They must be convinced that it is worth their time and expense to use SCM technologies and methodologies.

- Making mistakes at first – In the first few weeks and months after implementation of SCM technologies, forecasters and planners may find that the technologies and the ERP system with which they are interfaced need to be fine-tuned to become effective, and that the first exchanges of information may not be perfect.

Radio Frequency Identification

Radio frequency identification (RFID) systems consist of tiny computer chips called tags that are embedded in products and packaging, allowing them to be tracked via wireless networks by a transceiver. This **transceiver** reads the radio frequency and transfers the data in real time to the ERP system. This technology enables the transceiver (reader) to identify, categorize, and track moveable items without requiring line of sight, making it superior to bar code scanning.

There are two types of tags: active and passive. **Active tags** have an internal battery that constantly transmits data and permits them to be read from up to a few hundred feet away. **Passive tags** do not have a battery and only transmit data when a transceiver activates them by coming within a certain range. These tags only transmit within a range of a few inches. Although active tags are more expensive, they have more potential applications.

Common applications of RFID technology include tracking goods in the supply chain from manufacturing through shipment and customer delivery, tracking plant assets, and tracking parts through a production line. RFID can also prevent the use of counterfeit products in the supply chain and decrease losses due to theft or inaccurate counting of goods.

To interface RFID technology with an ERP system, it is necessary to configure processing rules in the ERP system. For instance, if goods are moved through one door, that might trigger a goods receipt. But, if they are moved through another door, that might signal a shipment. By providing real-time visibility into inventories and supporting a perpetual inventory system, RFID enables companies to maintain and control optimum product levels to save costs and ensure better customer service.

One of the major advantages of using RFID for tracking inventory is that instead of using first in, first out or last in, first out inventory movement assumptions, RFID can track units on an individual basis. Each item can have a tag, and each tag can transmit manufacturer codes, product codes, exact costs, date manufactured, length of time on the shelf, and other useful information. Using RFID in conjunction with a WMS can reduce labor costs, speed up the handling process, and greatly reduce human error. As technological advancements lead to even higher levels of data transmission—in addition to an inevitably lower cost—RFID technology will become ubiquitous within the supply chain industry, increasing overall efficiencies and significantly improving the ROI.

Electronic Data Interchange

Electronic data interchange (EDI) is the computer-to-computer exchange of business event data between business partners, such as between manufacturers and distributors or distributors and retailers. Business event data exchanged between EDI business partners, known as **trading partners**, is data contained on any number of documents, including purchase orders, RFQs, invoices, and advance shipping notices (ASNs). Generally, companies use EDI for high-volume transactions running in batch mode, or in situations where just-in-time information is required. The transmissions can be conducted over the internet or private networks. Figure 9-10 presents a visual for EDI.

EDI documents must be in a structured format so they can be processed by the trading partner's business systems, including ERP. An EDI standard format describes each piece of data and its format, such as whether the field is a date field or an integer. There are currently several EDI standards in use, including a widely used one from the American National Standards Institute (ANSI); further, for each standard, there are multiple versions. When two trading partners decide to exchange EDI documents, they must agree on the specific EDI standard and version of that standard. Companies also use an **EDI translator**—either as in-house software or via an EDI service provider—to translate the EDI format so the data can be used by their ERP system. ERP vendors provide

Figure 9-10: Electronic Data Interchange System

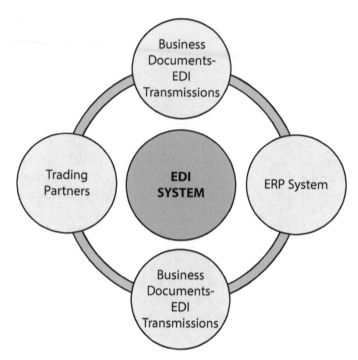

EDI technology or will partner with a third party to provide it. The third party, known as a **value-added network (VAN)**, will act like a "post office" for many different companies conducting EDI. The VAN will receive transmissions and route the right ones to the appropriate trading partner. The VAN will also provide an audit of the transmission, making sure it conforms to the EDI standard being used, and will handle telecommunications support and encryption. The outsourcing of this service to a VAN by trading partners relieves them of the headaches of setting up the security and transmission infrastructure necessary for conducting EDI.

Benefits of EDI include reductions in the amount of data capture and rekeying activities, which allows for quicker processing of business event data and efficiencies such as fewer stock-outs and cancelled orders. Automating paper-based tasks allows employees to concentrate on more value-added work and supports business-critical data being tracked in real time. Additionally, EDI helps reduce data entry errors, which improves data quality. EDI also streamlines the ability to enter new territories and markets because it provides a common business language that facilitates trading partner onboarding anywhere in the world. Finally, EDI promotes corporate social responsibility by replacing paper-based processes with electronic alternatives. This saves money and reduces carbon dioxide emissions.

Vendor Managed Inventory

Vendor managed inventory (VMI) is a process for organizing inventory replenishment in which the buyer of goods sends its supplier information about sales and inventory levels and allows the supplier to make decisions about restocking. In the typical business model, the buyer manages its own inventory levels and decides when to send purchase orders to the supplier. In the VMI model, the buyer sends daily demand information to the supplier, and the supplier generates replenishment orders for the buyer based on this information. The supplier and buyer are bound by an agreement that determines inventory levels, fill rates, and costs.

The information sent by the buyer to the supplier is often transmitted using EDI, while supplier relationship management establishes the process. The trading partners' ERP systems must be configured to handle this data exchange (or to use a VAN to facilitate the exchange). There are various EDI transactions that enable VMI, including an 852, an 855, and an 856. The 852 is a product activity record, which contains sales and inventory information and is sent from the buyer to the supplier on a weekly basis, or even more frequently in high-volume industries. This transaction set includes data such as quantity sold, quantity on hand, and forecast quantity, which helps the supplier make a determination on replenishment based on existing agreements with the buyer. The 855 EDI transaction is a purchase order acknowledgement. However, in this case, the transaction is being used as notification of a supplier-generated order. This usage advises the buyer that the supplier will ship inventory as prearranged in their VMI partnership. This data then becomes the purchase order in the buyer's ERP system. Finally, the 856 transaction is an advanced shipping notice (ASN) that the supplier sends to the buyer when the shipment is made. Figure 9-11 shows a process map of this VMI scenario between vendor and buyer.

Figure 9-11: Vendor Management Inventory (VMI) Process Map

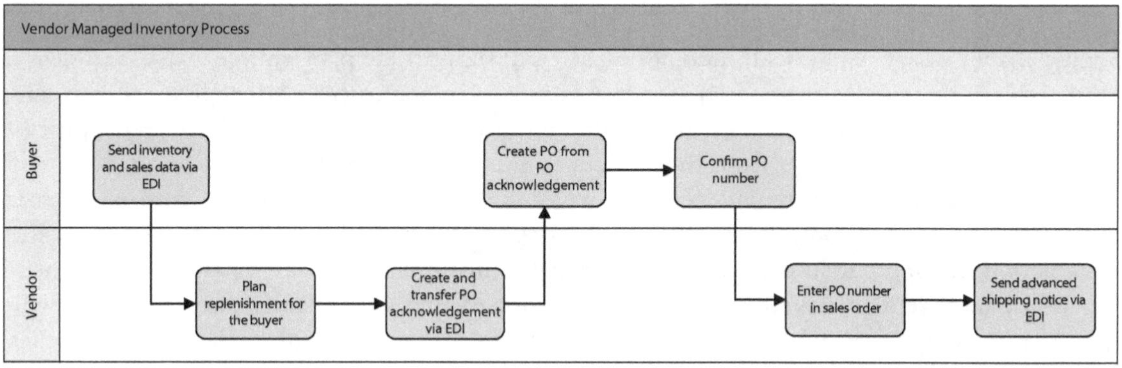

Source: SAP Help

The goal of VMI is to streamline supply chain operations for both parties. The business value is better inventory accuracy, faster inventory turnover, better forecasting ability, and enhanced customer service. Hurdles to overcome include challenges in communication, cultural resistance, and setting clear lines of responsibility between the parties involved. Figure 9-12 shows the individual and collective benefits of VMI for both the vendor and the buyer.

Figure 9-12: Benefits of Vendor Managed Inventory (VMI)

Vendor Benefits	Buyer Benefits	Dual Benefits
Visibility of the buyer's point-of-sale data makes forecasting easier even when buyers are running promotional plans	Planning and ordering costs decrease because these responsibilities are being shifted to the supplier	Data entry errors are reduced and processing speed improved due to computer-to-computer communications
A reduction in buyer's ordering errors, which results in fewer returns	Overall service levels are increased by having the right product available at the right time	Customer satisfaction is improved; having the correct item in stock when the end customer needs it benefits all parties involved
Visibility into buyer's stock levels helps to identify priorities (replenishing for stock vs. a stock-out)	Supplier is responsible for providing goods required so buyer does not need to hold safety stock; lower inventories leads to cost savings	A true partnership is formed between the supplier and buyer

Source: Vendor Managed Inventory.com

Summary

Supply chain management (SCM) modules of an ERP support the plan, source, make, and deliver processes of the supply chain. In particular, the SCM modules help streamline the financial, information, and goods flows, including the movement of raw materials, work-in-process inventory, and finished goods from their origin to their ultimate point of consumption. Robust SCM functionality is a key requirement for many companies and therefore a core concern in ERP software selection projects. ERP systems encompass a variety of modules that are tightly integrated, including purchasing, supplier relationship management, transportation management, warehouse management, manufacturing, quality assurance, and plant maintenance. A new module that supports corporate social reporting helps to capture and report on data related to companies' sustainability activities across the supply chain, in manufacturing operations, and in employee and product safety. Today's ERP systems also work with SCM technologies, such as EDI and RFID, and processes such as VMI, that make it easier to coordinate inventory, information, and financial flows between a company and its suppliers and customers. ERP SCM and manufacturing-related modules help increase quality, speed production, and reduce costs—and extend these benefits to a company's supply network.

Keywords

Active tag

Bill of material (BOM)

Bin

Blocked stock

Capacity plan

Cash-to-cash cycle

Catalog management

Contract management

Coordinate

Customer independent requirements

Cycle counting

Dependent demand

Dynamic cycle counting

EDI translator

Electronic data interchange (EDI)

Goods/services receipt

Inspection lot

Inventory status report

Master production schedule (MPS)

Material

Material requirements planning (MRP)

Passive tag

Planned independent requirements

Procure-to-pay process

Purchase order (PO)

Purchase order acknowledgment

Purchase requisition

Purchase-to-pay process

Purchasing plan

Quotation

Radio frequency identification (RFID)

Request for quote (RFQ)

Restricted stock

Routing

Serpentine picking

Sourcing

Spend analysis

Supplier performance management (SPM)

Supplier relationship management (SRM)

Supply chain

Supply chain management (SCM)

Three-way match

Tolerance limit

Trading partner

Transceiver

Two-step picking

Unrestricted stock

Value-added network (VAN)

Vendor managed inventory (VMI)

Wave picking

Work center

Quick Review

1. True/False: A bill of material is a list of all the raw materials and components needed to produce a finished product.

2. True/False: Unrestricted, restricted, and blocked stock are valued on the balance sheet.

3. The _____ module of an ERP system makes sure that products bought, made, and sold adhere to company standards and are safe and uniform.

4. The technology used to exchange business event data electronically between companies in a standardized format is called _____.

5. The outsourcing of inventory replenishment to suppliers is called _____.

Questions to Consider

1. List three input files to material requirements planning (MRP) and explain why each is important.

2. List the steps in the purchase-to-pay process and note which ones represent financial transactions.

3. Describe basic functionality in an ERP Warehouse Management system.

4. List benefits of electronic data interchange (EDI) to both the supplier and the buyer.

5. Explain why the Plant Maintenance module is useful in a manufacturing environment.

References

Deloitte. (n.d.) Supplier relationship management (SRM) information. Retrieved from http://www.globalspec.com/learnmore/industrial_engineering_software/enterprise_plant_management_software/supplier_relationship_management_software_srm

EDIbasics. (2011). Benefits of EDI. Retrieved from http://www.edibasics.com/benefits-of-edi/

Handfield, R. (2011). What is supply chain management? Retrieved from http://scm.ncsu.edu/scm-articles/article/what-is-supply-chain-management

IHS GlobalSpec. (n.d.). Supplier relationship management. Retrieved from http://www.deloitte. com/view/en_TR/tr/services/consulting/strategy-and-operations/supply-chain-man agement/91814b2e98392410VgnVCM3000003456f70aRCRD.htm

Investopedia. (n.d.). Supply chain management. Retrieved from http://www.investopedia.com/ terms/s/scm.asp

Krotov, V. (2008). RFID: *Thinking outside of the supply chain*. Retrieved from http://www.cio.com/ article/174108/RFID_Thinking_Outside_of_the_Supply_Chain

Kumar, P., & Kumar, M. (2003). *Vendor managed inventory in retail industry*. [White paper.] Retrieved from http://www.tcs.com/resources/white_papers/Pages/ VendorManagedInventoryinRetailIndustry.aspx

Martec International, Inc. (2004). *Smarter supply chain utilization for the retailer*. [White paper.] Retrieved from http://www.handson.com.au/Libraries/White_Papers/Smarter_ Supply_Chain_Utilisation_for_the_retailer.pdf

Murray, M. (n.d.). Vendor managed inventory (VMI). Retrieved from http://logistics.about. com/od/forsmallbusinesses/a/VMI.htm

Murray, M. (n.d.). RFID and SAP. Retrieved from http://logistics.about.com/od/ supplychainsoftware/a/Rfid-And-Sap.htm

Murray, M. (n.d.). Production routing. Retrieved from http://logistics.about.com/od/ tacticalsupplychain/a/Production-Routing.htm

MWPLV International Inc. (n.d.). Transportation management system (TWS) consulting services. Retrieved from http://www.mwpvl.com/html/tms.html

1 EDI Source, Inc. (2003). *EDI 101: A guide to EDI*. [White paper.] Retrieved from http:// www.1edisource.com/

ParCon Consulting. (n.d.). SAP transportation management (SAP TM). Retrieved from http://www.parcon-consulting.com/en/application-consulting/sap-transportation- management-tm.html

SAP. (2011). *Vendor-managed inventory: SAP best practices for chemicals*. *Retrieved from* https://help.sap. com/saap/sap_bp/BBLibrary/Documentation/928_ERP605_Process_Overview_ EN_XX.ppt

SAP Basics. (2012). Plant maintenance. Retrieved from http://www.sapbasics.com/wp-content/ uploads/2012/06/SAP-Plant-Maintenance.png

SAP Basics. (2012). QM Introduction. Retrieved from http://www.sapbasics.com/qm/introduction/

Supply Chain Council, Inc. (2010). *Supply chain operations reference (SCOR®) model.* Retrieved from https://supply-chain.org/f/SCOR-Overview-Web.pdf

Vendor Managed Inventory. (2014). Vendor managed inventory. Retrieved from http://www.vendormanagedinventory.com

Wailgum, T. (2007). Supply chain management definition and solutions. Retrieved from http://www.cio.com/article/40940

ERP Human Capital Management

Objectives

- Understand the meaning of human capital management

- Become familiar with functionality in the ERP Human Capital Management modules

- Identify benefits of employee self-service

- Know the reasons organizations outsource human resources functions

Introduction

Legacy human resource (HR) applications typically specialize in one or more areas such as personnel administration, recruitment and applicant tracking, or payroll and benefits. Like most legacy systems, these HR solutions often contained redundant data, such as employee name and address, and the applications and data models were often not well architected or managed. As we know by now, data integration leads to a number of operational benefits as the stovepipes are deconstructed, the data is shared across the enterprise, and the business processes are reengineered. This chapter discusses the functionality of the Human Capital Management (HCM) suite of ERP systems, which includes multiple modules each working together to provide comprehensive functionality. This core suite comprises the strategy and processes that transform employees into competitive assets who support the company's operational and strategic goals. Modern HCM solutions encompass not only the typical functionality of HR legacy systems, but also advanced features that better enable the management of employees, contractors, and temporary workers. ERP HCM modules also include self-service features that enable employees to interact directly with the system to input and edit their own master data and initiate certain transactions in the workplace that affect them. Since HR is subject to constantly changing governmental regulations and tax laws, many companies choose to outsource some of their HCM functions. Therefore, this chapter will also discuss key HR functions that companies outsource, the main reasons they do so, and issues to consider when hiring a service provider.

Human Capital Management

The set of skills, competencies, knowledge, and intangible attributes that employees acquire in their jobs through training and experience and that create economic value for the organization is known as **human capital**. The methods and strategies embraced to optimize the value of this asset are collectively known as **human capital management (HCM)**. In ERP systems, the HCM suite facilitates a coherent and strategic approach to the way organizations manage and support their people, who individually and collectively both empower the organization with their abilities and burden the organization with their personal agendas, desires, and needs. As part of ERP core functionality, HCM is a complete and integrated solution consisting of a suite of modules that enable companies to effectively manage employees throughout their life cycle with the company. This employee life cycle is also referred to the **recruit-to-retire process**. Figure 10-1 lists the steps in the employee life cycle. Collectively, this process allows companies to recruit and hire the best talent, develop employee skills, align employee goals with business objectives, measure and reward performance, plan for future succession into strategic roles, and transition employees through retirement and exit. The HCM suite automates core HR processes to increase efficiency, reduce costs, and support compliance with related laws and regulations.

Figure 10-1:
Employee Life Cycle

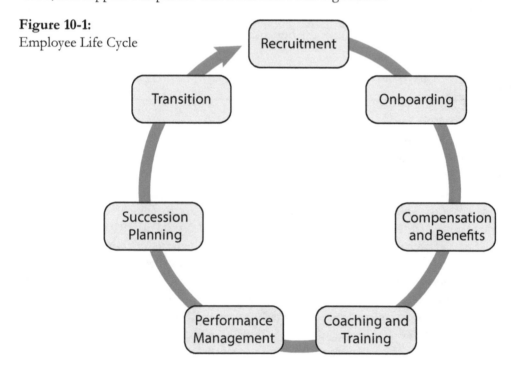

Companies implement the HCM modules because:

- **People matter** – An organization's most important assets are its people and the intellectual capital created through their employment.

- **HR activities are data intensive** – Beginning with job placement advertisements and employment applications and continuing throughout hiring, training, and evaluating, HR actions generate voluminous amounts of data.

- **HR data is extremely sensitive** – HR records are governed by various requirements regarding care, custody, and control. The information contained in HR files must be kept secure and private. As government policies create additional requirements, new risks of fines and penalties can result from error or noncompliance.

- **HR data is valuable to the rest of the organization** – Nearly every ERP module references employee master data. For instance, employee data is needed to assign employees to projects and to give credit to salespeople for sales. Furthermore, every transaction that is written to the database is assigned to a responsible party for audit trail purposes.

Employee master data has become extremely complex since it not only describes a person, but also all the characteristics and relationships that define his or her role, competencies, security privileges, compensation package, and reporting structure. The HR department is the primary data owner for employee master data. As discussed in Chapter 6, **data owners** are the employees who approve access to certain data in the company and are responsible for the data's accuracy, integrity, and timeliness.

The HR department's duties begin with the recruitment process, where employees will focus on screening and interviewing quality applicants with an eye to placing individuals with the right skill sets into the right positions within the company. Along with placement, the HR department may also oversee, or at least be involved in, the creation of entry-level training programs, as well as continuing education opportunities and coaching sessions for existing employees. Determining company policies and procedures as they relate to personnel is another key aspect of HR duties. These policies can include establishing vacation and sick leave guidelines and instituting an employee code of conduct.

The HR department is also responsible for helping the organization stay compliant with the myriad of federal and state laws and regulations that enact reporting requirements. Some of these laws and regulations depend on the employer's industry, size, or its contractual relationships, but the majority of employers must comply with equal employment opportunity (EEO) laws and the Occupational Safety and Health Act (OSHA) law and regulations. The following sections elaborate on the various modules within the HCM suite, ranging from traditional, basic functionality to more advanced functionality. The menu of SAP's HCM modules is presented in Figure 10-2.

Personnel Administration

The Personnel Administration module captures much of the employee master data that is the basis for subsequent processes in HCM. Examples of employee master data include name, address, departmental assignment, bank details, and compensation. As well, each employee is assigned a unique employee number that is used to designate the employee throughout the ERP system. Basic personnel procedures occur in this module, including hiring, organizational assignments and reassignments, salary increases, promotions, leaves, and terminations.

Benefits Administration

The Benefits Administration module involves establishing, maintaining, and managing employee benefits. Employee benefits can include medical insurance, retirement plans, vacation time, flexible spending plans, 401(k) plans, and maternity leave. An enrollment profile for every employee is created and maintained in this module, which requires various master data such as date hired, marital status, number of dependents, total hours worked, part-time or full-time status, and attendance in order to determine eligibility for certain benefits.

Time and Attendance Management

Managing time and attendance can be complex for any company, especially for those that have distributed teams and remote workers spread across time zones and country borders. The

Figure 10-2: HCM Menu in SAP

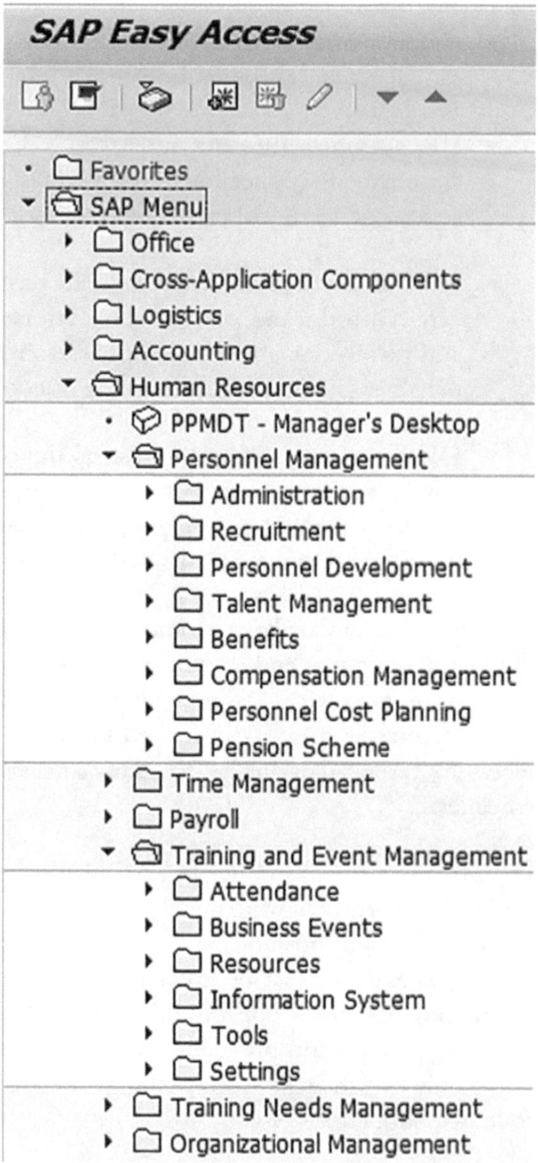

Time and Attendance Management module empowers employees through self-service to enter and review their time and attendance information online using a PC, shared kiosk, electronic time clock, or smart phone. Managers use this module to schedule and approve employee time, absence, and leave time more efficiently, thereby preventing over- or understaffing and overtime issues. Managers can also schedule employees based on skills, certifications, seniority, availability, preference, hours worked, and other criteria. Time and Attendance Management also assists managers in tracking time to specific activities and jobs for cost accounting purposes, for billing employee time to customers, and for analysis of employee abilities. For instance, if employee "Smith" finished a job while maintaining quality in six hours and employee "Jones" completed the job with the same quality in five hours, "Jones" performed better on that job. This information would be an input to employee performance management, which is discussed later.

Recording time and attendance is also an internal control function in organizations. If there were no system in place to track hours worked, employees could take advantage of their employers and claim they worked more than they actually did. To prevent "buddy punching," many companies use bolt-on biometric technology that requires employees to "clock in and out" using an imprint of their index finger.

Overall, using the ERP system for time and attendance helps companies control costs, optimize the productivity of its workforce, provide key information for payroll, and support the forecasting of labor requirements.

Compensation Management

The Compensation Management module involves designing, implementing, and administering salary and wage policies to attract and motivate employees, who will be productive in achieving the company's vision, objectives, and goals. One aspect of compensation is **job pricing**, which helps to answer the question "What should an employee be paid?" With job pricing, jobs in the company are assigned points based on the authority and responsibility that they hold. The higher the points, the more the job's compensation. Job pricing takes into account the job description and the relative industry and regional values of the work and then analyzes the data to decide on the appropriate pay scale for a particular job.

Compensation can include fixed pay and life-event pay such as stock options. Another form of compensation, variable pay, is used to recognize and reward employee contribution toward company productivity, profitability, teamwork, or some other metric.

Payroll

Basic activities of the Payroll module include accounting and preparation of payroll checks for employees, temporary workers, and contractors, including calculation of gross salaries and wages, tax deductions, and benefits (if applicable). To calculate payroll, master data updates are needed from Personnel Administration, time data from Time and Attendance Management, benefits selection information from Benefits Administration, and expense reimbursement amounts from Travel and

Expense Management. Employee payroll results are then posted as expenses and liabilities in the general ledger, as are employer payroll taxes. This module also manages the direct deposit process, which helps minimize security risks associated with issuing paper checks. Many companies will use a separate payroll checking account for internal control purposes. The total amount of the payroll will be deposited into the account, and theoretically the balance should be zero after all employees cash their checks or receive their direct deposits.

Recruitment Management

The Recruitment Management module is used in the very early stages of the employee life cycle to help attract job candidates and convert talented individuals into successful hires. This module also handles the analysis, administration, and storage of electronic recruitment information. Figure 10-3 presents a visual of the recruitment management life cycle, which involves recruiting activities, onboarding, and management information.

Figure 10-3: Recruitment Management Life Cycle

Source: Recruitment Management Software

- Candidate attraction – Communicating career opportunities to broad, qualified applicant pools (both internal and external). One way companies do this is by using data from professional networking sites such as LinkedIn. Here members can ask for "recommendations" from other members based on their professional associations.

- Candidate tracking – Streamlining and organizing the processing of job applications, including the ability to accept data from third-party providers, on-line job services, and candidate self-service.

- Candidate selection – Evaluating an applicant's suitability as an employee by using a set of criteria to qualify the candidate, review job fit and background, and match the candidate with a job description. Experience, education, and expertise can be confirmed in the screening process and compared to the requirements noted in job descriptions.

- Onboarding – **Onboarding** refers to bringing a new employee into the organization and providing information, training, mentoring, and coaching throughout the transition. This strategic process begins when an offer is accepted and continues through the first six to twelve months of employment. One of the first steps in onboarding is orientation.

- Management information – Gaining insight into such questions as how the recruiting results align with overall talent strategy.

Career and Talent Management

In this competitive environment where the war for talent, an aging workforce, and globalization are of great concern, managing a talent pipeline is a top priority. It is important for companies to identify, retain, and grow talent as well as deploy it where it has the most strategic impact. By identifying the competencies and skills employees possess, managers can align them to business objectives and ultimately to business strategy. And, by placing employees in the positions they are most suited for, companies can create a challenging and rewarding work environment by ensuring that employees stay engaged. This, in turn, helps to lower employee turnover and increase **bench strength**, or the capabilities and readiness of employees who are prepared to fill vacant professional and leadership positions in the company. Vacant positions for key managers could arise because the company has grown, restructured, or changed strategy, or because existing managers leave and take their talent and skills with them. Unless companies prepare in advance, either of these scenarios could result in scrambling for new talent—which costs money and time. Identifying key employees that have the capabilities and readiness to be promoted to critical professional and leadership roles in the company is known as **succession planning**.

In the Career and Talent Management module, employees are also empowered and encouraged to play a key part in their own career development plans. Using this module, employees can view new opportunities within the organization and assess their own suitability for certain roles. This empowerment helps motivate and engage employees, as they have a clearer picture of all development activities and opportunities organization-wide. It also improves communications by promoting an open dialogue between managers and their employees, which better supports a continuous review process.

Key master data in this module is the **talent profile**, which allows employees, managers, and talent management specialists to enter all talent information relevant for an employee. The employee can enter some data himself, such as work experience and mobility. The manager or specialist can add other information such as assessments of the performance or potential of a particular employee. The talent profile can be used for side-by-side comparisons of employees up for certain promotions and to organize talent into various groups.

Learning and Event Management

In the past, employees earned the right to receive training as they moved up the corporate ladder. But today, continuing education is necessary throughout every level of the company in order to increase employee intellectual capital and comply with regulated training requirements such as those involving hazardous material handling. Each employee's development should enable both individual goals and larger, organizational goals.

The Learning and Event Management module of an ERP system maintains employee education and training profiles, including what internal or external courses they should take and the progress made towards completion. Employee learning is typically presented in a variety of formats such as face-to-face, computer-based, webinars, and virtual classrooms. This module includes an instructor portal, a learning portal, learning management and testing software, tools for structuring content, and support for content management. Additionally, this module helps to plan and administer other types of business events such as conferences and lectures by managing bookings, pre-bookings, and cancellations. Master data includes available courses, instructors, attendees, and evaluations. Depending on whether the event is internal or external, costs can be billed to attendees or allocated to various cost centers through the Management Accounting module.

Employee Performance Management

The term **employee performance management (EPM)** refers to the process for putting into place a shared understanding among employees about what is to be achieved at the company level and involves aligning organizational objectives with employees' skills, competency requirements, agreed-upon measures, development plans, and the delivery of results. The emphasis is on employee improvement, learning, and development in order to achieve the overall business strategy and to create a high-performing workforce. The Employee Performance Management module provides functionality to:

- Establish performance goals

- Develop performance plans

- Give and receive feedback to employees

- Evaluate performance (performance appraisals)

- Reward performance

- Address performance problems

- Improve performance (development plans)

- Fire employees

From this list of functionalities, you can see that there is a high level of integration between EPM, compensation, talent management, and training. How an employee performs is (or should be) an input to compensation planning. Also, by using the Employee Performance Management module, top employees can be identified early through succession planning tools, and learning and development tools can be used to nurture and encourage talent.

Employee Self-Service

As discussed previously, HCM is highly data intensive and tracks innumerable data points on each employee, including personal information, skills, compensation, performance, and training. Additionally, HR records tend to churn a great deal. Employees come and go. They change their positions, supervisors, and subordinates. Their skills, accomplishments, goals, and benefit choices also change often. Keeping this data current, complete, and accurate creates a substantial administrative burden for the HR staff, distracting them from more strategic activities that provide greater value to the organization. For example, instead of updating employees' benefit plan data, HR staff could be spending their time analyzing current benefit providers and determining if changes are needed.

Employee self-service (ESS) minimizes the toll on HR staff by off-loading some of the maintenance of employee master data onto the employees themselves as well as allowing employees to initiate documents and activities related to themselves. Generally, employee self-service is accessed through a portal or dashboard via the corporate intranet or a data collection device such as an electronic time clock in the case of time recording. Once an employee enters an activity such as a travel request, workflow will direct the manager approval process via notifications in the ERP system and email reminders.

Advantages of self-service include improved service for and communication with employees, streamlined administrative processes, and reduced costs, especially for the HR department. Studies have shown that employees view self-service positively because they gain a sense of ownership of their personal information and a renewed sense of trust in their employer. Also, putting data directly in the hands of the people who know it best generally reduces errors. To get the full benefit of ESS, user interfaces should be easy for employees to navigate without in-depth training or HR or IT staff intervention.

Self-service empowers managers to make better and faster tactical and strategic decisions in areas such as compensation, staffing, and budgeting. Managers can perform any number of activities using self-service, such as initiating recruitment for vacancies, completing annual employee performance reviews, authorizing personnel leave requests, tracking expenses and budget consumption on projects, and analyzing critical labor-related variances.

Outsourcing Human Capital Management Functions

The management of human resources has become more costly, complex, and challenging for a variety of reasons. For one, a greater number of companies have employees and contractors spread all over the world, complicating payroll and compliance issues. When processing payroll, global companies must take into account the myriad of country, state, city, and local employee and employer tax rates. Global compliance with employment-related laws and regulations can be overwhelming. Just in the U.S., companies must comply with the Family and Medical Leave Act (FMLA), the Americans with Disabilities Act (ADA), Occupational Safety and Health Act (OSHA), and the Affordable Care Act (ACA). Because of the headaches involved with managing HR processes, numerous companies of all sizes are choosing to outsource HR-related functions.

Outsourcing refers to contracting out certain business activities previously performed internally to a third party, or **service provider**. For many companies, HR outsourcing makes sense because management can obtain expertise without hiring additional personnel that they can't afford. Also, HR outsourcing can help with compliance issues that can be a tremendous risk and turn into a legal liability. Thus, outsourcing can offer an extra layer of protection.

An estimated 50 percent of large companies outsource all or part of their HR needs to service providers such as ADP or Paychex. While some companies may entrust their HR needs to a single service provider, it's not uncommon to see firms parceling out functions to a range of providers. Top reasons companies outsource HR functions are to:

- Save money

- Focus on strategic functions, not administrative (non-core) tasks

- Gain expertise not available in-house

- Improve compliance to minimize risk of lawsuits, such as wrongful termination

- Improve accuracy

- Take advantage of technological advances, including business analytics

- Improve recruitment

However, outsourcing HR functions, particularly payroll, can also carry real risks. Thus, vetting service providers should be a priority. Similar to hiring an employee, a company should take time to properly review prospective service providers' qualifications and skills. Questions worth finding out the answers to include:

- Is the company nationally recognized?

- Does it have a reputation for high ethical standards?

- Is it publicly traded and so adheres to SEC regulations?

- Does it have liability insurance?

Companies seeking an HR provider should be knowledgeable about the kinds of payroll fraud that exist. Ghost employees is a scheme in which someone with access to do so sets up and pays fictitious employees in the payroll system. Company money is then funneled out of the payroll account and distributed to these falsified employees. This fraud is possible if access into Personnel Administration and Payroll modules is not kept separate. Commission schemes involve paying inflated commissions to employees through fabricated sales records, invoices, and other financial documents. Falsifying hours or salary information happens when the number of hours worked is inflated and therefore take-home pay is increased for certain workers. Companies should keep an eye out for these fraudulent schemes as well as others that look suspicious. Knowledge of the internal controls at the service provider can help ease concerns about these activities. HR service providers handle sensitive company data, including employee information and tax documents. Thus, it is vital that the provider have internal controls surrounding HR information to keep it safe, accurate, and private. Companies should request an internal controls review report from the service provider before signing a contract. These reviews are typically performed by an accounting firm and detail the types of controls in place over customer data in addition to testing these controls.

Besides fraud, companies seeking to outsource HR functions need to be aware that turning over HR functions to an outsider is inherently risky because the two parties likely have different—and sometimes conflicting—goals and agendas. One of the most common problems with outsourcing HR is lower-quality service, especially when the provider lacks sufficient knowledge about the outsourcer and its business practices. Before signing a contract with a provider, companies should assess the competency of internal HR against the service provider, because—especially in large companies—in-house staff may be just as knowledgeable. Finding the right partner is crucial as is reviewing the arrangement on a periodic basis to make sure it continues to be successful.

Even though certain HR functions are being outsourced, it's wise to keep a small staff in the HR department. Local knowledge could be lost if a third party manages all responsibility. Furthermore, when tough decisions on hiring and firing are made, an organization wants in-house expertise to take care of things. Finally, despite moving key processes to a third party, companies should retain responsibility for their overall HR strategy.

Companies can choose to outsource any or all of their HR functions, but most will pick and choose which ones they outsource based on a cost–benefit analysis and the amount of control they are willing to give up. Companies typically consider the five functions listed in Figure 10-4 when choosing which HCM functions to outsource.

Figure 10-4: Top Five HR Functions to Consider Outsourcing

Payroll	Outsourcing payroll can ease concerns about tax compliance and eliminate dealing with changing tax rates, withholdings, and taxes.
Legal compliance	From affirmative action and discrimination polices to safety and medical insurance, outsourcing this HR minefield can greatly reduce a company's compliance burden while lowering risk.
Benefits administration	Handling benefits, including insurance and 401(k) plans, can be a non-stop administrative headache, and the time could be better spent elsewhere.
Background checks and drug screening	Since companies simply need results, outsourcing checks and screens can greatly reduce recruiting and onboarding processes and is well worth the cost of letting these tasks go.
Strategic workforce analytics	Voluminous amounts of data regarding labor usage, retention rates, and performance are available and may be worth tapping into. Outsourcing workforce analytics to a data analytics company can make good business sense.

Source: Nolan

Summary

People are an organization's most valuable assets and are increasingly viewed as a key differentiator in this competitive business environment. The Human Capital Management (HCM) suite of modules comprises the strategy and business processes that transform the organization's human capital into a competitive asset that supports its operating and financial results. Collectively, the HCM suite manages the recruit-to-retire business process, or employee life cycle. Organizations can benefit from HCM to maintain employee master data, track applicants, onboard new employees, manage benefits, compensate, train and educate, and evaluate. Using integrated components for these functions means that one record exists for each employee that is linked to all activities for that employee, from compensation to continuing development. Human capital management costs can be reduced using self-service for various functions, including time and attendance recording and employee master data maintenance. Also, as HR capabilities are not typically a core competence for most companies, outsourcing certain components can save money and free HR staff to work on more strategic tasks. However, the risks to outsourcing should be addressed, including making sure the service provider has proper internal controls surrounding employee and payroll data.

Keywords

Bench strength

Data owner

Employee performance management (EPM)

Employee self-service (ESS)

Human capital

Human capital management (HCM)

Job pricing

Onboarding

Outsourcing

Recruit-to-retire process

Service provider

Succession planning

Talent profile

Quick Review

1. True/False: The set of skills that employees acquire in their jobs through training and experience that increases their value in the marketplace is known as human capital.

2. True/False: Matching an applicant's experience and education with job descriptions is a task performed in talent management.

3. The _____ captures much of the employee master data that is the basis for subsequent processes in HCM.

4. _____ refers to the process for putting into place a shared understanding among employees about what is to be achieved at the company level.

5. Identifying key employees that have the capabilities and readiness to be promoted to important roles is known as _____.

Questions to Consider

1. List key reasons organizations implement the HCM modules.

2. List the steps in the employee life cycle.

3. Explain the functionality in the Career and Talent Management module.

4. What are some advantages of using employee self-service?

5. What are some of the risks to outsourcing HR functions?

References

ADP. (n.d.). Time and attendance. Retrieved from http://www.adp.com/solutions/large-business/ services/time-and-attendance.aspx

Biro, M. (2013, December 1). Top 5 reasons HR is on the move. Retrieved from http://www.forbes. com/sites/meghanbiro/2013/12/01/top-5-reasons-hr-is-on-the-move/

Downing, V. (2012, June 18). Does your company have the bench strength you need? Retrieved from http://www.remodelersadvantage.com/does-your-company-have-the-bench-strength-you-need/

Nakisa. (n.d.). CareerPlanning™. Retrieved from http://www.nakisa.com/solutions/solutions-overviews/career-planning-career-development.htm

Nolan. (2013, April 17). Better business – 5 human resources functions to outsource. Retrieved from http://www.jobscience.com/blog/better-business-5-human-resources-functions-to-outsource/

Park City Consulting Ltd. (n.d.). The potential disadvantages of outsourcing your HR function. Retrieved from http://www.parkcity.co.uk/potential-risks-hr-outsourcing

PAPweb. (n.d.). Why *outsource payroll.* Retrieved from http://www.payweb.ca/payrolloutsourcing. php

Paychex. (2014, May 21). Payroll fraud: How to tell the legitimate companies from scam artists. Retrieved from http://www.paychex.com/articles/payroll-taxes/payroll-fraud-how-to-tell-the-legitimate-companies

Recruitment Management Software. (2012, November 6). Applicant tracking system – Great assessment. Retrieved from https://owl.english.purdue.edu/owl/resource/560/10/

Rouse, M. (2012, March). Benefits administration. Retrieved from http://searchfinancialapplications. techtarget.com/definition/benefits-administration

SAP. (n.d.). HCM, core processes in talent management. Retrieved from https://help.sap.com/ erp2005_ehp_05/helpdata/en/9a/368bbac042457d99118cbadd490a65/frameset.htm

SAP HCM. (2011, April 5). Chapter 1 – SAP HCM – Introduction to compensation management. Retrieved from http://isaphr.blogspot.com/2011/04/sap-hr-enterprise-compensation. html

Simplilearn. (n.d.). SAP time management, its features and advantages. Retrieved from http:// www.simplilearn.com/resources/sap-certification-articles/sap-time-management-its-features-and-advantages-rar115

Chapter 11

ERP Security and Implementation Assurance

Objectives

- Become acquainted with the concept of internal control and its objectives

- Differentiate between IT general and application controls

- Understand the process of ERP systems implementation assurance

- Recognize the various IT certifications for professionals involved in ERP implementation assurance, audit, security, governance, and risk

Introduction

Throughout this book, we've learned that ERP systems are integrated business systems that enable the management, control, and evaluation of operations. At their core, ERP systems process transactions that record journal entries in various modules that ultimately post to the general ledger (GL), from which the financial statements are prepared. Companies provide their financial statements to stakeholders, including investors, financial analysts, governmental agencies, and creditors. The information in these financial statements must be accurate, reliable, and complete. It follows, therefore, that the ERP system and the supporting infrastructure in which it operates must be secure so these goals may be achieved. The security of the ERP system and its underlying technical infrastructure can best be achieved by implementing various policies and procedures, or internal controls, that minimize IT risk.

This chapter introduces the concept of internal control and discusses the various types of controls that need to be present in an ERP environment to minimize IT risk. One category of controls are IT general controls, which include program change controls, logical access controls, and data center controls. Another category of controls is application controls, which are programmed or configured within the ERP software itself, and include checking for invalid input data, configuring the three-way match in the Purchasing module, and controlling employee access in the system. Risks can also occur during the implementation of the ERP system, so many companies will engage a third party to provide an objective assessment of the implementation, known as systems implementation assurance (SIA). Finally, this chapter acquaints the reader with IT certifications that professionals can obtain to demonstrate that they possess the experience and knowledge to meet the challenges of the modern enterprise.

Internal Control

Internal control is the policies and procedures put in place by an organization's board of directors, management, and other personnel to provide "reasonable assurance" regarding achievement in the following objectives:

- Effectiveness and efficiency of operations – includes attaining performance and profitability goals and safeguarding resources

- Reliability of financial reporting – pertains to the preparation of accurate financial statements and other financial data about a firm's performance

- Compliance with applicable laws and regulations – means adhering to those laws and regulations to which the organization is subject

An example of an internal control is having someone other than the person signing checks perform the bank reconciliation. This type of internal control is a manual control. An **IT control** is a procedure or policy that provides reasonable assurance that the IT used by an organization operates as intended, that data is reliable, and that the organization is in compliance with applicable laws and regulations. IT controls are some of the most important internal controls because of the organization's pervasive reliance upon automated transaction processing. Therefore, IT controls must be designed properly and operate effectively.

Because of the inherent limitations in all internal control systems, an internal control, no matter how well designed and operating, cannot guarantee that an entity's objectives will be met. The concept of "reasonable assurance" acknowledges that limitations, uncertainties, and risk, which no one can predict with absolute precision, can exist in all systems.

In the U.S., public companies, government entities, and companies in regulated industries must be audited. If an auditor identifies issues in a client's internal control structure, the client company must take action to remediate the problems and demonstrate how the original business objectives will now be achieved. By doing so, companies are in a better position to receive an **unqualified audit report** of their year-end financial statements. This report reflects a "clean bill of health" denoting that there is "reasonable assurance" the general ledger accounts are properly valued and internal controls are effective, showing compliance with the Sarbanes-Oxley of Act of 2002 (SOX). As a result of SOX Section 404, management at publicly traded companies must:

- Establish internal controls and procedures over financial reporting

- Document, test, and maintain those internal controls and procedures to guarantee their effectiveness

The Public Company Accounting Oversight Board (PCAOB), created as a result of SOX, is a nonprofit corporation established by Congress to oversee the audits of public companies in order to protect the interests of investors and advance the public interest in the preparation of informative, accurate, independent audit reports. The PCAOB issued Auditing Standard No. 5, which states that the objective of an audit of internal controls over financial reporting is "to express an opinion on the effectiveness of the company's internal controls over financial reporting." The auditor must plan and perform the audit to gather "competent evidence that is sufficient to obtain reasonable assurance about whether material weaknesses exist as of the date specified in management's assessment."

While these requirements are specifically targeted at publicly traded companies, many privately held companies, nonprofit organizations, and governmental agencies also make efforts to meet these requirements and undertake similar internal control audits for various reasons. For example, such an auditor's report may help a company as it seeks financing. In addition, taking steps toward being "SOX-compliant" can make a company more attractive as a takeover target by lowering the risk for acquisition-minded companies and their underwriters. One of the main reasons, however, for adhering to SOX requirements is focused inward—becoming a healthier, control-conscious organization.

ERP and Internal Controls

Because ERP systems process transactions that affect the financial statements, a company's year-end audit must include an inspection of IT controls that govern the system. As an independent third party, auditors look for any internal control issue that exposes the ERP system and its data to material misstatements of the entity's financial statements.

Modern ERP systems are designed with internal controls in mind. As the foundation of a firm's transactional processing, the ERP system maintains all data pertaining to business processes from beginning to end. Generally, once data is entered, there is no need to re-verify it. Processes are automated and postings do not require human intervention. **Edit checks** occur at the point of data entry to make sure data adheres to specific data standards—checking, for example, for blank fields, negative numbers, and invalid dates. However, many IT controls must be "turned on" through configuration of the system during implementation—the three-way match discussed in Chapter 9 is an example. ERP systems also ensure process integrity by including a log of transactions, or **audit trail**, that records when the transactions were entered and by whom.

However, security problems still exist in every layer of an ERP system: presentation layer, application layer, and database layer. Following are security issues that can exist in the three-tiered architecture of ERP systems.

- Client tier – The presentation layer contains the code responsible for displaying the user interface of the application. Inaccurate data entry may occur accidentally, such as when a transaction is entered incorrectly by a poorly trained employee, or intentionally, such as when an employee purposely alters data in a nefarious scheme to defraud the company. Mistakes and fraudulent entries can become hard to catch once they are in the system. Companies routinely face both of these risks. Employees need to be trained on what data to enter and where and access controls must be built into this layer to allow user input only where it is appropriate.

- Application tier – The integrated nature of ERP applications means that data entered at one stage in the process is carried forward to later stages. The validity of the data entered earlier is implicit, and there is often no re-verification at later stages. Every data field needs to be accurate at all stages of a process. Again, controls at this layer require clear definitions of who should be allowed to do what in the system. Additionally, many activities and updates (postings) occur without human intervention. These activities and postings are based on the configurations made in the ERP system. Therefore, it is critical that during implementation, configurations are made correctly and are in line with the control requirements of the business.

- Database tier – The database layer especially is a prime target because it comprises highly sensitive data, such as intellectual property; personally identifiable consumer and employee data; and financial information. Using a database that is shared across the company enhances data availability and visibility, but the "dark side" is that it also increases the threat that trusted parties, especially employees, can commit fraud, particularly if their access is not properly controlled and monitored.

Many companies still think information security is only about protecting the physical and network perimeter security, and they overlook security within their systems. They think by having their servers in physically secured rooms and behind network firewalls that the systems are secure. However, this is not the case in today's interconnected world, in which companies share information and processes with their customers, suppliers, and other business partners. As additional modules, legacy systems, and bolt-on technologies are integrated or interfaced with an ERP system, security problems escalate. The next section describes the types of internal controls needed in an ERP environment to reduce IT risk.

IT Application Controls

IT application controls (ITACs) control the input, processing, and output functions of an ERP system by enabling, disabling, or limiting the actions of system users and enforcing business-driven rules and data quality. These controls are either programmed in the system or configured during implementation to facilitate data accuracy, completeness, validity, verifiability, and consistency to help guarantee the confidentiality, integrity, and availability of the ERP application and its associated data. Figure 11-1 describes the three types of ITAC and gives examples of each.

Figure 11-1: Types of Information Technology Application Controls (ITAC)

Description	Control
Input Controls – Ensure that all data input into the system is accurate, complete, and authorized	• Sequence checks to prevent missing transactions • Drop-down menus to only allow valid items • Authorization and approval rights for transactions based on user roles • Override capabilities restricted to only certain users • Edit checks to ensure accurate, valid, and complete input • Standardized input screens • Checks for duplicate entry of data
Processing Controls – Ensure that valid input data is processed accurately and completely	• Automated tracking of changes made to data that associates the change with a specific user; enables the audit trail • Automated checks of data from feeder systems, a process known as an **interface control** • Automated tracking of overrides made during processes • Checks to ensure that automated calculations produce expected results
Output Controls – Ensure that output is complete, accurate, and distributed only to the appropriate personnel	• Distribution of sensitive reports only to appropriate personnel • Adherence to record retention periods • Analysis of error reports and corrective action to rectify issues • All successful transactions posted to subsidiary ledger and summarized in the GL

Segregation of Duties

One of the important ITACs is **segregation of duties (SoD)**, which is the concept of requiring different people to complete different parts of a process. By segregating duties, companies reduce the risk of erroneous and inappropriate actions by their employees. Segregation of duties is a deterrent to fraud because it requires three functions to be kept separate—no one person should (1) approve a transaction, (2) record and reconcile the transaction, and (3) have custody of the assets involving the transaction. When these functions cannot be separated (such as in small companies), other controls must be put in place to compensate for this lack of segregation.

Figure 11-2 presents the SoD in the purchase-to-pay process. Note that Employee A authorizes the payment to the vendor, while Employee B issues the check, or maintains custody of the asset. Presumably, a third employee would keep records by inputting vendor invoices in the ERP system. Another example not shown in the figure is that the person who requisitions the purchase of the service should not be the person who approves the purchase order, and the person who approves the purchase order should not be the person who signs off that the service is complete.

Figure 11-2: Segregation of Duties

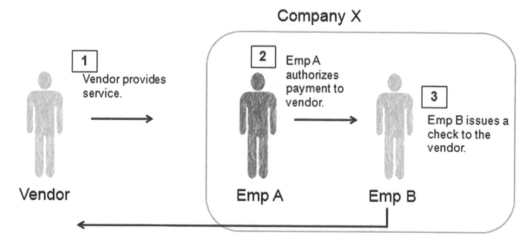

Role-Based Access Control

Authorization refers to the level of access a certain user has in the ERP system. In an ERP system, authorization is accomplished through **role-based access control (RBAC)**, which assigns individuals to organizational roles and those roles to specific access in the system. A **role** is a job assignment or function; examples include data entry clerk, purchasing manager, business analyst, HR manager, and accountant. Authorizations in the ERP system are grouped by role name and restricted only to certain individuals authorized to assume a particular role. A person can be assigned to more than one role, but may be required to act in a single role at any one time. Changing roles may necessitate logging out and then logging in again, or inputting a special role-changing command.

Role-based access control is employed at the company, application, and transaction level. For instance, a certain user may be assigned to the accountant role in Company X within Parent Company A. That user is authorized to work only in Company X, within the Financial and Management Accounting modules, and within those modules, there are certain transactions and master data that this user can **create, read, update, delete** (known as **CRUD**). Role-based access controls help enforce segregation of duties.

Auditing Information Technology Application Controls (ITAC)

It is very important to subject a company's ERP software to a thorough and detailed audit because transactions involving its money, material, and services are recorded in the application. When evaluating ITACs in an ERP system, the auditor would focus on the modules. The first questions the auditor should ask are "What does this module do?" and "What business process or processes does this module support?" This can be accomplished by studying the operating and work procedures of the organization, including process maps, process narratives, and interviewing key personnel in the business process under investigation.

Once the auditors know what the module does, they can identify the potential risks associated with the business processes in question by asking "What could go wrong?" Then they can see how the risk is handled by asking the question "What controls the risk?" To answer these questions, the auditor must have business and technical knowledge. Auditing of application controls is a complex process and is outside the scope of this book. However, several example ITAC audit steps include:

- Inspection of system configurations in the Purchasing module to make sure quantities and prices are being checked in the three-way match

- Inspection of system configurations to ensure that duplicate vendor invoices are disallowed and that duplicate vendors cannot be entered into the system

- Inspection of a user access list for employees who can access payroll data and verification that this list reflects those who truly need this access

- Verification that audit trails and logs exist to ensure that all transactions can be traced to the individuals who entered them

IT General Controls

Controls that apply to all systems components, processes, and data for a given organization or IT environment are called **IT general controls (ITGCs)**. These controls work to both secure and validate the data contained in the systems that process financial transactions. The objectives of ITGCs are to ensure the proper development of and changes to applications, databases, and operating systems; controls over logical access to the network and applications; and controls surrounding the data center. Figure 11-3 shows these three types of ITGC as pillars that support typical application controls in major business processes. They are represented as pillars because, for ITAC to be effective, the auditor must first ascertain that the ITGCs are functioning properly. The rationale is that if the IT environment is not secure, then users cannot feel confident that controls within the applications are functioning properly. The ITGCs are the first line of defense in a secure ERP environment.

Figure 11-3: Relationship between IT General Controls and IT Application Controls

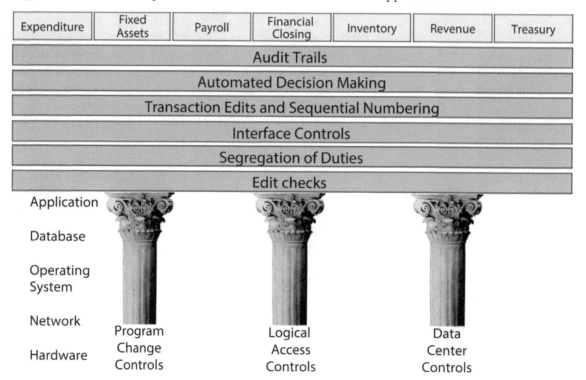

Source: Deloitte

It should be noted that an organization will never have 100 percent assurance that all risks to IT resources are eliminated through IT controls. Because of the costs associated with protecting IT resources, companies must identify the potential risks facing their information systems and perform a cost-benefit analysis to determine the appropriate level of protection. Let's study each of these ITGC pillars in depth.

Program Change Controls

The controls that govern the changes made to programs, including any changes made to the ERP system and underlying database, based upon requests from users or due to general maintenance requirements are called **program change controls**. These controls seek to ensure that the development of and changes to systems are properly designed, tested, validated, and approved prior to migrating the changes to the production environment. Examples of changes include patches, bug fixes, updates, program code changes and enhancements, and minor upgrades. Deficiencies in program change controls increase the potential for fraudulent or unauthorized changes, transaction processing errors, and incorrect and unexpected application behavior and program logic. For example, a programmer who can authorize a change to the Financial Accounting module of an ERP system and move that change into production has the potential to insert malicious code into the module or change the module in such a way that the financial statements contain errors. This lapse in SoD would create an audit red flag and would lead the auditors to expand the scope of the audit by doing additional testing. In addition, the client would have to remediate the SoD problem, even if no fraud or errors had occurred. ITGCs should be tested early in the audit process, so that in the event problems are detected, the audit team can adjust its approach to testing and the client has the opportunity to remediate the issues.

Figure 11-4: ERP System Landscape

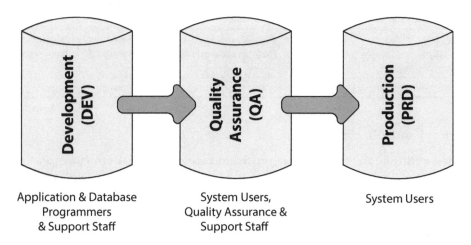

Figure 11-4, also discussed in Chapter 2, depicts the stages through which program changes should progress in an IT environment. The figure also shows the roles that typically have access to each instance. These separate instances serve to control the process of program change. As changes to the database and ERP system are developed and deployed, the transition from one instance to the next indicates that each change meets objective criteria for promotion. In addition, the controls over program changes should be adequately documented to eliminate all doubt, from the auditor's point of view, that they function properly. It is important that all program changes are documented and auditable and that all unauthorized changes are investigated. Examples of program change controls are listed in Figure 11-5.

Figure 11-5: Examples of Program Change Controls

Program changes are only initiated with a valid IT or business justification.
An IT manager or management in the business area requesting the change approves the program change prior to development in the DEV instance.
Application programmers should only make changes in the DEV instance. Once work is completed, application programmers should move the program changes to the QA instance.
Depending on the type of program change, functional users and/or IT staff test to make sure the application works correctly in the QA environment. These staff members are separate from programmers/developers.
Prior to moving changes to PRD, an **impact analysis** is performed to determine the potential effect of the proposed change to other systems and modules as well as to users.
Program changes moved to PRD are scheduled during downtime, and users are notified in advance when the changes will occur.
After testing and sign-off in the QA instance is complete, an IT employee—separate from the employee who developed the change—moves the change to PRD.
Programmers should not have direct access to the PRD instance and should not make changes directly into PRD. Emergency changes into production may be allowed using a temporary firefighter role, which is monitored and logged.
Documentation exists to show proper approvals and procedures in the program change control process.

Source: ISACA

Logical Access Controls

Logical access controls are the policies, procedures, organizational structure, and electronic controls designed to restrict access to information systems and data only to individuals with genuine authority to access the information. These controls are different from **physical access controls**, which refer to a mechanical lock and key or other devices controlling access to a building or room. For instance, a data center would have physical access security mechanisms on the doors, but logical access controls for the ERP system loaded on the servers in the data center.

Logical access is part of a larger concept—that of **identity and access management (IAM)**. IAM refers to the management of individual identities and privileges or permissions within or across system and company boundaries with the goal of increasing security and productivity while reducing costs, downtime, and repetitive administrative tasks. Without a properly functioning IAM, it is very difficult to prove, control, and monitor which users access what information and to determine whether that access is in compliance with internal and external regulations. Privacy concerns, various categories of system users, and multiple information systems compound these issues.

An IAM system performs three main activities. The first is **identification**, which is the process of describing an individual to a system with a unique user ID. The second activity, **authentication**, involves verifying that a user's claim to a particular identity is, in fact, true. This process is commonly carried out through the combination of user IDs and passwords. Authenticated identities then become the foundation for the third activity, authorization, or the level of access a particular authenticated user should have to resources controlled by the system. Authorization was discussed earlier in the chapter.

The process of verifying the identity of users through a user ID and a password is authenticated using a knowledge factor, or "what the user *knows*." However, this can be combined with a possession factor, or "what the user *has*," and an inherence factor, or "what only the user *is*," to add more layers of logical access control. Requiring two forms of authentication factor is called **dual-factor authentication** and requiring more than two forms is called **multi-factor authentication**. An example of "what the user has" is using a security card such as an RSA SecurID, which is an authentication token that uses a built-in clock and factory-encoded random key to restrict access to systems. An example of "what only the user is" is **biometric software**, which enhances security by linking a user's unique physical attributes to the data he or she is allowed to access. The user provides a fingerprint or other biometric characteristic to the system, where it is then authenticated against a stored image. Biometrics can also be used for granting physical access to the data center.

Figure 11-6 presents examples of essential logical access controls. Deficiencies in logical access controls can create the potential for viewing unauthorized data, recording fraudulent transactions, overriding ITACs, making unauthorized changes to program calculations, and creating accidental changes to data and information system resources.

Figure 11-6: Examples of Logical Access Controls

Documentation exists to show proper approvals and procedures to grant logical access.
Use of privileged access in applications such as SYSADMIN is limited only to appropriate personnel.
Procedures are put into place to notify IT security personnel when employees change roles and responsibilities or are terminated. Access privileges of such individuals are immediately changed to reflect their new status.
Roles and responsibilities related to IT security are assigned to appropriate personnel.
Data encryption, firewalls, network segmentation, and other measures are put in place to keep hackers, cyber-criminals, and other outsiders from accessing the ERP system and database.
Effective password management policies, such as periodically changing passwords and requiring passwords that are not easily guessed, are in place and enforced.
Dual-factor or multi-factor authentication is enforced when logging onto the network.
Default passwords are effectively replaced upon first login to the ERP system.
Direct access to the ERP database is closed and programmatically prevented.
Effective use of HTTPS for remote access is enforced.

Source: ISACA

Data Center Controls

Data center controls help protect computer facilities and resources from environmental hazards, espionage, sabotage, damage, and theft. These controls focus on the physical security of the data center where the servers that support the ERP system are kept. The data center should be audited by an IT audit or assurance professional to make sure that proper controls are in place to provide physical security, protection of data, and reliability and availability of operation (see Figure 11-7). **Reliability** is the ability of a system or component to execute its required functions under stated conditions for a specified period of time. **Availability** is the degree to which a system or component is accessible and operational when it is needed. Reliability factors into availability as does recovery time after a failure occurs. In a data center, having a reliable system design is the most critical variable. However, once a failure does occur, the most important consideration becomes getting the IT equipment and business processes up and running as soon as possible, thus keeping downtime to a minimum.

Figure 11-7: Data Center Controls

Physical Security	Protection of Data	Reliability and Availability
Build on the right spot	Employ redundancy by storing copies of data in multiple locations	Use an uninterruptible power supply (UPS)
Use surveillance cameras	Back up critical data	Use emergency backup generators
Limit entry points and avoid windows	Use fire detection and suppression	Use fiber optic cables
Use biometrics for access	Destroy hard drives when retiring them	Have a disaster recovery plan
Employ 24/7 security and use perimeter fencing	Shred paper	Maintain service-level agreements with customers
Keep a roster of those who are allowed access to the data center	Use proper air conditioning and have redundant utilities	Have a data recovery plan

Source: ISACA

System Implementation Assurance

ERP systems, while achieving great economies of scale and employing many advantages, carry unique risks, many of which can be mitigated if the implementation is executed successfully. Often, companies implementing ERP systems will seek out a third party to give an unbiased opinion on the progress of the implementation and the work accomplished by the internal project team and consultants. This third-party opinion is called **systems implementation assurance (SIA)** and is an independent assessment of the health and expected outcome of the ERP implementation and corresponding change initiative.

Various entities can do this type of work, but oftentimes the company's internal audit staff or external auditor is engaged to render this objective assurance. This assurance team will act independently of the system integrators with a "dotted line" to the ERP project sponsor and steering committee and operate in an "assess and recommend" mode. Typically, SIA will focus on three main types of risks throughout the ERP life cycle: control risk, project risk, and business risk. These risks happen at various points in the ERP life cycle as shown in Figure 11-8.

Figure 11-8: Points in the ERP Life Cycle Where Assurance is Beneficial

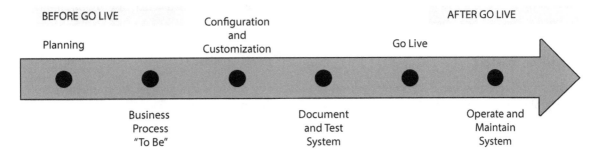

Control Risks

One of the major risks in an implementation is whether the design and implementation of ITGCs and ITACs will satisfy financial reporting, operational, and regulatory requirements. Thus, the organization should take a security mindset from the beginning of the project. Many implementations are not staffed with full-time security and controls experts, and thus these risks are often overlooked. While poor internal controls are not generally the reason ERP projects fail, it could result in a "forthcoming failure" because for a period of time internal controls will be lax. Also, building controls into the system and around the system after the fact can be very costly. Identifying control risks and putting a plan in place to mitigate these risks should therefore start early.

Assurers should review the project plan and recommend how to incorporate security and controls during the implementation. They should ensure that the design of the configurable controls is done during business process design, rather than identifying and correcting weaknesses after go-live. Assurers will look at many types of control risks in the following key areas:

- ITAC – Has management evaluated the best mix of manual versus automated or configured controls necessary to accurately and completely capture and validate data?

- ITGC – Do the IT infrastructure and manual IT processes support the new ERP system?

- Data quality – Has the legacy data been successfully migrated to the ERP system, and is it accurate and in a usable format?

- Interfaces – Do interfaces between the ERP system and other systems transport data properly to ensure data integrity?

During SIA, assurance teams may find that internal controls are not clearly identified during the requirements and design phase, employees have conflicting user access rights (improper SoD) in the ERP system even after go-live, and privileged user access and/or default system user accounts are not properly managed after go-live. Other findings are that training on security is incomplete and security controls are not negative tested. A **negative test** tests software to ascertain if it is doing something it is not supposed to do, like accepting an all-letter password when the requirement is that the password has at least one number.

Business Risks

Some of the risks to the ERP implementation present themselves early on in the implementation during planning. In this phase, the SIA team will want to evaluate the:

- Business case – Is there a solid business case in place for the ERP investment, and is it aligned with corporate strategy?

- Benefits realization plan – Are there appropriate key performance indicators that back up the business case and will they produce measureable outcomes?

- Organizational structure – Is the project properly structured and does it include a high-level sponsor and steering committee that will proactively lead the desired change?

One of the main business issues found during SIA is that the project is being led by IT with minimal involvement from key functional areas or the project is being handed over too much to consultants. Another issue found during SIA is that business benefits have not been measured or evaluated post-go-live.

Project Risks

Another major type of risk involves project management. This risk to the implementation involves whether the ERP system will be delivered on time and on budget, whether the system will meet the stated requirements, and whether the employees are adequately prepared for the new system and processes. Assurance on project risks will take place from the beginning of the project through go-live. The SIA team will want to evaluate:

- Project management – Are timelines and resources being effectively managed?

- Project governance – Is there appropriate management support throughout the implementation?

- Functional readiness – Are mechanisms in place to develop functional requirements?

- Technical readiness – Are mechanisms in place to translate the functional requirements into the ERP software (i.e. configuration and customization)?

- Organizational readiness – Are changes to processes being effectively communicated and understood throughout the organization? Is training being conducted effectively?

An ERP project is a massive undertaking, and many things can go wrong. Key issues found during evaluation of project risks include testing defects that remain at go-live, testing that is performed before all data is migrated, and testing scripts that do not match the real-world scenario (and instead are "canned" test scripts). Also, it has often been found that in some implementations, training on the software is inadequate or incomplete and as a result, users have difficulty using the ERP system at pre- and post-go-live. Sometimes it is found that organizational change management strategies are poorly defined or nonexistent, and the project team is too inexperienced.

ISACA Certifications for IT Professionals

The independent, nonprofit, global association engaged in the development, adoption, and use of globally accepted knowledge and best practices in IT is the **Information Systems Audit and Control Association (ISACA)**. ISACA was founded in 1967 by a group of computer auditors who realized there was a need for a centralized source of information to help them do their jobs better. Today, ISACA is the leading organization that disseminates information for IT governance, control, security, and audit professionals. ISACA's IS auditing and IS control standards are followed by a constituency of more than 115,000 practitioners worldwide in more than 180 countries. ISACA members hold various positions, including IS auditor, consultant, educator, IS security professional, regulator, internal auditor, and chief information officer (CIO). Some ISACA members are early in their careers, while others are in senior-ranking positions. ISACA members also work in many different industries, including manufacturing, public accounting, government and public sector, and financial services.

The market for individuals possessing skills relevant for IT audit, assurance, security, risk, and governance has grown. To emphasize their expertise and differentiate themselves in the marketplace, IT professionals and business professionals have become certified by ISACA in one or more of these growing areas of IT. Choosing the most appropriate certification depends on many factors, including a person's level of technical expertise, business experience, education, and desired career path. Obtaining an IT certification is desirous as it confirms knowledge and experience, quantifies and markets expertise, and demonstrates that the professional has gained and maintained a level of knowledge required to meet the challenges of a modern enterprise. Following is a brief description of ISACA certifications. To obtain and maintain one of these certifications, a candidate must pass an exam, possess the required educational and work experience, undertake continuing professional education, and practice ethical conduct.

CISA

The **Certified Information System Auditor (CISA)** is the flagship certification of ISACA, qualifying an individual as globally proficient in the areas of IS audit, assurance, and security. Established in 1978, the CISA designation showcases a practitioner's information systems (IS) audit experience, skills, and knowledge and demonstrates the capability to manage risks, institute controls, and ensure compliance with laws and regulations. The CISA exam covers five practice areas:

- The process of auditing IS

- Governance and management of IS

- IS acquisition, development, and implementation

- IS operation, maintenance, and support

- Protection of information assets

The largest percentage of the exam, 30 percent, covers protection of information assets, which includes questions regarding ITGC and ITAC. Information regarding the ERP life cycle would be tested in the areas of IS acquisition, development, and implementation and IS operation, maintenance, and support.

CISM

The **Certified Information Security Manager (CISM)** designation uniquely targets the professional who manages, designs, oversees, and assesses an organization's information security program. This certification is for those who understand the relationship between information security and the overarching business objectives, goals, and strategy and is relevant for professionals with management experience. The CISM certification exam covers four practice areas:

- Information security governance

- Information risk management and compliance

- Information security program development and management

- Information security incident management and response

The largest percentage of the exam, 33 percent, covers information risk management and compliance. The exam includes questions on how to integrate risk management throughout the IS life cycle, who to communicate risks to and how, and the role of the IT steering committee. This certification requires a high level of risk and security knowledge and five years of security management experience. Passing the CISA exam prior to taking this exam can substitute for some of the work experience.

CRISC

The **Certified in Risk and Information Systems Control (CRISC)** certification is intended to recognize a wide range of IT and business professionals for their knowledge of enterprise risk management (ERM) and their ability to design, implement, monitor, and maintain systems controls to reduce risk. A deep understanding of risk management is necessary for those considering taking this exam. **Risk management**, discussed in Chapter 6, is the identification, analysis, assessment, control, avoidance, minimization, or elimination of unacceptable risks. **IT risk management** applies this concept to the area of IT and information systems. The CRISC exam includes four practice areas:

- IT risk identification

- IT risk assessment

- Risk response and mitigation

- Risk and control monitoring and reporting

The largest percentage of the exam, 28 percent, tests IT risk assessment. Candidates for the CRISC need specific knowledge of risk standards and frameworks, quantitative and qualitative risk evaluation methods, threats and vulnerabilities related to business processes, the ERP life cycle, and project management. One major part of the exam entails identifying the current state of existing controls and evaluating their effectiveness for IT risk mitigation.

CGEIT

The **Certified in the Governance of Enterprise IT (CGEIT)** designates a professional with the knowledge and application of enterprise IT governance principles and practices. This certification recognizes those professionals who have the necessary level of professional knowledge, skills, and business experience to move to the C-suite if they aren't already there. The core theme of this certification is **IT governance**, which consists of the leadership, organizational structures, and processes that ensure that an organization's technology sustains and extends its strategies and objectives. The CGEIT exam encompasses five practice areas:

- Framework for the governance of enterprise IT

- Strategic management

- Benefits realization

- Risk optimization

- Resource optimization

The main practice area tested, 25 percent of the exam, is the framework for governance of enterprise IT. Examples of specific knowledge needed across job practice areas include developing a business case for an ERP system, value measurement techniques, IT organizational structure including roles and responsibilities, SIA methodologies, and IT business process improvement techniques.

Summary

ERP systems have many advantages, but they also present many risks to organizations if not successfully implemented and maintained. Properly assessing and managing these risks and putting controls into place is essential to an IT risk management program. IT controls are classified as general or application. IT general controls enhance the IT infrastructure surrounding the ERP system. IT application controls are configured or programmed into the ERP system. Three types of IT general controls are controls over program changes, logical access, and the data center where the ERP system is housed. These controls are pervasive, minimizing IT risks across information systems. IT application controls are designed to prevent inaccurate or fraudulent data from being input into the ERP system as well as to ensure that information is properly processed so that the output is reliable. ERP systems can contain key security vulnerabilities that must be addressed and periodically audited. During an implementation, a company may engage an objective party to give an unbiased opinion as to its efficacy. The end goal of systems implementation assurance is to maximize the likelihood of the ERP project's success and address any potential risks as early as possible. Many professionals who engage in this type of work become certified by ISACA to greatly enhance their credibility in the marketplace. This chapter ends with a discussion of certifications offered by ISACA that differentiate professionals as knowledgeable and technically competent in various aspects of IT.

Keywords

Audit trail

Authentication

Authorization

Availability

Biometric software

Certified in Risk and Information Systems Control (CRISC)

Certified in the Governance of Enterprise IT (CGEIT)

Certified Information Security Manager (CISM)

Certified Information System Auditor (CISA)

Create, read, update, delete (CRUD)

Data center control

Dual-factor authentication

Edit check

Identification

Identity and access management (IAM)

Impact analysis

Information Systems Audit and Control Association (ISACA)

Input control

Interface control

Internal control

IT application control (ITAC)

IT control

IT general control (ITGC)

IT governance

IT risk management

Logical access control

Multi-factor authentication

Negative test

Output control

Physical access control

Processing control

Program change control

Reliability

Risk management

Role

Role-based access control (RBAC)

Segregation of duties (SoD)

Systems implementation assurance (SIA)

Unqualified audit report

Quick Review

1. True/False: IT general controls include program change controls, logical access controls, and IT application controls.

2. True/False: Identity and access management (IAM) includes three main functions: identification, authentication, and authorization.

3. _____ controls help protect computer facilities and resources from environmental hazards, espionage, sabotage, damage, and theft.

4. Programmers should make changes to application software in the _____ environment.

5. The _____ certification qualifies an individual as globally proficient in the area of IS audit, control, and security.

Questions to Consider

1. List three examples of program change controls that should be implemented to guard against unauthorized changes to the ERP system and database.

2. Explain the concept of role-based access control and how it relates to logical access.

3. Contrast the differences among the elements of identity access management (IAM).

4. What are the three main risk areas focused on in systems implementation assurance? Give an example of each.

5. List three examples of data center controls that should be implemented to protect computer facilities.

References

Bellino, C., Wells, J., Hunt, S., & Horwath, C. (2007). *Global technology audit guide (GTAG) 8: Auditing application controls*. Institute of Internal Auditors. Retrieved from http://www.theiia.org/ bookstore/downloads/ freetomembers/0_1033.dl_gtag8.pdf

COSO. (n.d.). Internal control – Integrated framework. Retrieved from http://www.coso.org/ documents/ Internal%20Control-Integrated%20Framework.pdf

Fowler, R. (2010, October 20). What are some application controls? Retrieved from http://www.isaca.org/Groups/Professional-English/application-controls/Pages/ ViewDiscussion.aspx?PostID=3

Hartman, S. (2012, October 12). Understanding data center reliability, availability and the cost of downtime. Retrieved from http://blog.schneider-electric.com/datacenter/2012/10/12/understanding-data-center-reliability-availability-and-the-cost-of-downtime/

Herman, B., & Donahue, S. (2012). *The role of internal audit and compliance teams in providing real-time assurance during an SAP implementation, upgrade, or consolidation project.* Dedham, MA: Wellesley Information Services.

ISACA. (2014). CISA glossary. Retrieved from https://www.isaca.org/Knowledge-Center/Documents/ Glossary/cisa_glossary.pdf

ISACA. (2014). ISACA Certification: IT audit, security, governance and risk. Retrieved from http://www.isaca.org/CERTIFICATION/Pages/default.aspx

Magee, K. (2011, June 14). IT auditing and controls – A look at application controls. Retrieved from http://resources.infosecinstitute.com/itac-application-controls/

PCAOB. (n.d.). PCAOB overseas the auditors of companies to protect investors. Retrieved from http://pcaobus.org/Pages/default.aspx

PRLog. (2009, September 17). *How can we keep our ERP database protected at all times?* Retrieved from http://www.prlog.org/10345486-how-can-we-keep-our-erp-database-protected-at-all-times.html

Privaris. (n.d.) *Biometric software security systems.* Retrieved from http://www.privaris.com/biometric_software.html

Rothacker, A. (2011, May 13). ERP vulnerabilities differ from those at the database level. Retrieved from http://www.infosecisland.com/blogview/13716-ERP-Vulnerabilities-Differ-from-Those-at-the-Database-Level.html

Rouse, M. (2010). IT controls. Retrieved from http://searchcompliance.techtarget.com/definition/IT-controls

SAP. (2013). *SAP Solutions for Governance, Risk, and Compliance.* Retrieved from http://www.sap.com/solutions/sapbusinessobjects/governance-risk-compliance/index.epx

Sayana, S. A. (2004). Auditing security and privacy in ERP applications. Retrieved from http://www.isaca.org/Journal/Past-Issues/2004/Volume-4/Pages/Auditing-Security-and-Privacy-in-ERP-Applications.aspx

Sayana, S. A. (2002). Auditing general and application controls. Retrieved from http://www.isaca. org/Journal/Past-Issues/2002/Volume-5/Pages/Auditing-General-and-Application-Controls.aspx

Scalet, S. (2005, November 1). *19 ways to build physical security into a data center.* Retrieved from http:// www.csoonline.com/article/220665/_Ways_to_Build_Physical_ Security_into_a_Data_ Center?contentId=220665&slug=www.csoonline

Sullivan, D. (2009). *The definitive guide to security management.* Channel Partner Realtime Publications. Retrieved from http://www.windowsecurity.com/uplarticle/NetworkSecurity/DGSM-Ch4-Excerpt.pdf

Wikipedia.com. (2014). Identity management systems. Retrieved from http://en.wikipedia.org/ wiki/ Identity_management_systems

Wikipedia.com. (2014). Multi-factor authentication. Retrieved from http://en.wikipedia.org/ wiki/Multi-factor_authentication

Chapter 12

ERP and Business Analytics

Objectives:

- Understand how the discipline of business analytics intersects with ERP systems

- Recognize the various data stores for business analytics

- Become familiar with the types of business analytics

- Learn the role of KPIs and what corporate performance management entails

- Know the essentials of the balanced scorecard as a corporate performance management framework

- Be aware of the importance of data governance in business analytics

Introduction

ERP systems are transaction processing systems, capturing cross-functional data in all areas of the company. While ERP systems are excellent at processing transactions and storing data for retrieval, they can be lacking in data analysis and reporting. ERP data is very granular and the typical user can get bogged down trying to wade through it for knowledge discovery. However, the volume of data stored in ERP systems is a gold mine of knowledge waiting to be discovered. Since ERP systems may not have sufficient data analytic functionality, additional tools are often needed to unlock the gems of information waiting to be discovered.

Because of companies' rapidly expanding information needs, there is a strong demand to turn data into actionable information, and for this reason business analytics has become a key companion to ERP systems. Business analytics allows users to identify valuable trends, risks, and opportunities hidden in the volumes of data gathered by an ERP system. Business analytics includes low-complexity business intelligence techniques such as reports, queries, and corporate performance management for dashboards and scorecards. These methods employ mostly structured historical and current data to see what's happening and why it's happening, as well as what actions can be taken to attain the organization's goals and mission. Business analytics also incorporates more high-level analyses such as data mining, which discovers previously unknown patterns in data, and predictive modeling, which helps forecast the future. Business analytics also can be used to make sense of big data, which are collections of data so large that they are hard to process using traditional database techniques. It is important that data governance processes are put into place so that data stores used for business analytics contain high-quality data.

Business Analytics

Business analytics (BA) can be defined as the comprehensive use of data and quantitative analysis for decision-making. It is how an organization uses modeling (involving extensive computation) to arrive at an optimal or realistic decision based on existing data. BA includes basic analytics such as querying and reporting, but it also encompasses greater levels of mathematical sophistication such as predictive modeling for forecasting. While the term "analytics" may conjure up images of number-crunching "quant" types who aren't necessarily in tune with business issues, business analytics, as a

somewhat newer concept, seeks to bring this stereotype to an end. With BA, statistics are harnessed to meet defined business objectives and empower people in organizations to make better business decisions, improve processes and performance, and attain desired business outcomes. Gone are the days where data is compiled and analyses are performed but never used, or analyses don't fit the way that the decision is framed. Business analytics brings the quantitative analyses to the business and emphasizes making decisions on results of statistical models rather than merely intuition.

An organization's ERP and BA strategies should be an extension of each other. To gain actionable insights, the starting point is collecting transaction and master data, which is what an ERP system does. But BA harnesses this knowledge and sifts through the mounds of ERP data, combined with data from other systems and external data, to make sense of it all. If a company's ERP system is creating valuable data but has failed to help the business make strategic decisions, it is time to contemplate implementing BA. Figure 12-1 presents warning signs that an organization needs business analytics.

Figure 12-1: Warning Signs an Organization Needs Business Analytics

You have to wait longer than a day for someone to make or change a report for you.
Across the organization there are more than 100 pending requests for reporting /dashboard/scorecard changes waiting for a specialist to make them.
At meetings, there are multiple numbers being quoted for the same thing—and no one knows which is correct.
The commentary on a report is larger than the automatically generated report.
The report is not generated automatically, but is a handcrafted labor of love by either yourself or one of your staff.
There are hundreds of reports available to you, but you don't trust them and you spend time trying to manually validate key numbers.

Source: Oz Analytics

Over the last few years, the term business analytics has become more in vogue than the term business intelligence, a term that has been around for decades. **Business intelligence (BI)** refers to the ability to take information resources and convert them into knowledge that is useful in decision-making. At its core, BI simply examines mostly internal, structured, historical data to see what has happened. It is basically a "rear-view mirror" approach to gathering information in order to guide business planning. Business intelligence mainly consists of reports and queries pulled from a database. The discipline of business analytics, on the other hand, not only examines the past, but also develops new insights and predicts likely future scenarios. BA extends the knowledge from "this is what the report says" to "this is what we think will happen next." However, the foundation for both methods is historical data.

While BI uses only structured data, BA uses both structured and unstructured data in its effort to find underlying relationships and build predictive models. **Structured data** is data that is stored in a field within a record or file. This includes data contained in relational databases and spreadsheets. **Unstructured data** refers to information that doesn't reside in a traditional row-column database or spreadsheet. This includes data such as email, documents, social media posts, audio files, machine-to-machine data, and video footage. It also includes the digital data from sensors, which are devices that measure physical quantities. Sensors are always on, capturing data at a low cost and continually fueling the "internet of things." Potential uses of sensors are to monitor machines or infrastructure, such as energy meters, airplane engines, and ventilation equipment.

Figure 12-2 shows how BA capabilities have matured from reactive decision-making and a low degree of intelligence and competitive advantage (historically viewed as business intelligence) to more proactive decision-making yielding higher degrees of intelligence and competitive advantage. Degrees of intelligence have evolved from basic reporting describing what has happened (past results) to more advanced analytics that answer the question, "What can happen given the behavior of a certain community?" The BA market has found traction in solutions for spend analytics, risk and fraud, marketing, and strategy and planning. Many leading ERP vendors, such as Oracle, Infor, and SAP, offer BA solutions to their customers. Additionally, best-of-breed analytics vendors, such as Tableau, SAS, and MicroStrategy, as well as the open source product "R," occupy a major share of the market.

Figure 12-2: Business Analytics versus Business Intelligence

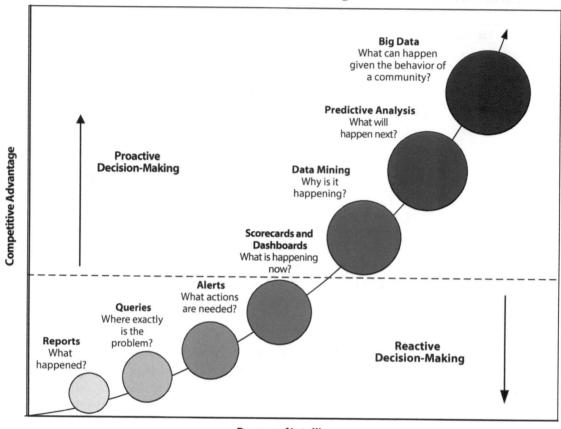

Source: *Adapted from SAS Institute, Inc.*

Types of Business Analytics

Reports

The most basic type of BA (and BI) is a **report**, which is a presentation of data that has been transformed into formatted and organized information per business requirements. A report generally is a multi-page printable document that contains detailed information, but can also include charts and graphs. Reports answer the simple question, "What happened?" They represent a snapshot in time, are static by nature, and tend to look like a document. Many BA solutions allow users to sort, filter, and drill up, down, or through data in reports.

Queries

A **query** is the primary mechanism for retrieving information from a database. It consists of questions in a predefined format presented to the database. Sometimes, structured query language (SQL) is used (discussed in Chapter 2), but BA tools make it easy on the user by providing a simple interface for a the user to enter queries. Instead of writing an entire SQL command, the user can just fill in blanks or select items to define the query. This type of querying from the database is called **query by example (QBE)**. Using QBE, users can generate complex queries to display information from multiple tables from nearly any context, such as by customer, project, or business unit. QBE is offered with analytic packages and most database programs, though the interface is often different between applications.

Alerts

An **alert** is an automated message or notification that indicates when a predefined event or exception on a metric (too much over or under a metric) has occurred and an action is needed. Alerts are programmed so that the responsible party is notified about the exception via email with an embedded link to the relevant BA object in a graph, report, or dashboard. For example, a store manager can be alerted when the stock level of a critical item falls below a certain level. Alerts enable "management by exception" and notify users when something critical occurs, thereby relieving them of the need to continuously monitor results or produce reports in hopes of finding a problem before it negatively impacts the business.

Dashboards and Scorecards

Analytics makes use of **data visualization**, which helps users understand the significance of data by placing it in a visual context. Patterns, trends, and correlations that might be difficult to spot can be recognized more easily with data visualization. The main visualization tool used in BA is the **dashboard**, which displays information in a condensed but efficient manner (see an example SAS dashboard in Figure 12-3). Whereas a report may take time to digest, depending on the level of detail and amount of data, a dashboard typically consists of a single webpage intended to give answers at a quick glance. Dashboards do not typically contain reports, but instead summarize data with color-coded bar charts, graphs, gauges, and other visual indicators that should be monitored because they are important to the user's functional area. Dashboards should be built to have a customizable interface and be able to pull real-time data from multiple sources. Dashboards should also be developed with security in mind so that users only see the charts and graphs that are relevant to their role or area of responsibility. By making mission-critical metrics available in real-time, employees are in a better position to take actions that help the organization accomplish its goals.

Figure 12-3: Sample Dashboard

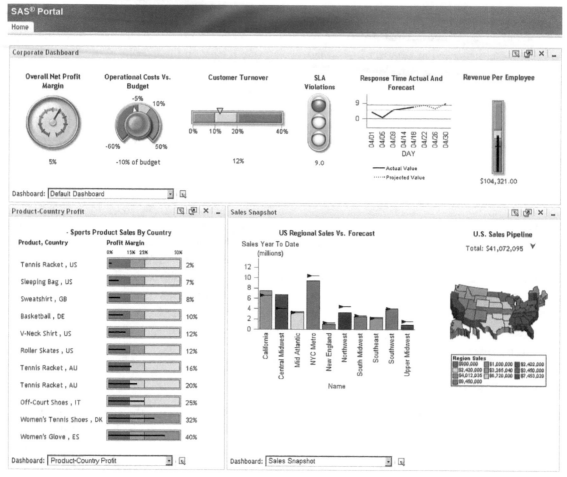

Source: SAS Institute, Inc.

Scorecards are very similar to dashboards, and in fact the lines are blurring between the two. Historically, scorecards were a direct result and visual representation of the theoretical balanced scorecard approach to business strategy developed at Harvard Business School and discussed later in this chapter. Scorecards are generally used within a formal framework for corporate performance and enable executives and management teams to manage strategy effectively and understand the relationships among various business metrics. They also help improve visibility into the ways in which performance in one area, such as research and development, affects outcomes in another area, such as sales. Scorecards often employ "traffic light" visualizations—red, yellow, and green elements that give visual cues about performance. Red means there is a problem, yellow suggests a potential concern, and green indicates that performance is meeting or exceeding a goal. The term "scorecard" is often used in conjunction with corporate performance management, discussed later in the chapter.

Data mining

Data mining is the statistical analysis of large pools of data to find hidden correlations and trends. Also called **knowledge discovery**, this method seeks to find patterns and relationships in data and summarize it into useful information that can be used to increase revenue, cuts costs, or both. Data mining may start with a hypothesis or research question, or users can allow the data to "tell its own story." Because data mining looks for previously unrecognized patterns in data, it is often described as "what you didn't know you didn't know."

Data mining has its roots in marketing and financial services, although many other areas now use the technique. Data mining tools are built into CRM applications discussed in Chapter 8. Marketing and sales employees use data mining to understand customer buying behavior, discover hidden patterns of buying, target marketing efforts more specifically, and identify opportunities that will move the company into a position to gain greater market share. In financial services, data mining can be used to identify anomalies that may point to fraud or other security problems.

Predictive Analytics

Situated at the high end of both degree of intelligence and competitive advantage is **predictive analytics**, which uses data about the past to predict future behavior and probable outcomes. Some of the CRM analytics discussed in Chapter 8 are examples of predictive analytics, such as when an organization looks at customer buying habits to predict what they may purchase next. Predictive analytics has been useful in identifying cases with a high likelihood of fraud, as well.

The key element of predictive analytics is the **predictor**, which is a variable that can be measured for an individual or entity to forecast future behavior. For example, income, gender, and age might be used as predictors for future buying decisions. Multiple predictors are combined into a predictive model, which is used to forecast probabilities. Each response (or non-response) of a customer, purchasing decision, defection to another company, act of fraud, credit default, and complaint provides the enterprise with new experiences from which to learn. Model generation and performance is an act of learning from the experience, both positive and negative, within the data. In other words, data is collected, a model is formulated, predictions are made, and the model is validated or revised as more data becomes available. Thus, the model is a deliverable that has been "learned."

One note about predictions is that they can go terribly wrong if they are divorced from common sense and domain knowledge. So it's important that consultants or users within the organization, who are trained on BA tools, have both common sense and knowledge of the research domain before trying to fit a predictive model.

Big Data

As more and more processes are automated, the amount of data being collected in enterprise servers increases. This deluge in the number of data points to process and interpret has mandated the need to build more sophisticated technology systems. According to SAS, the term **big data** is used to describe the exponential growth and availability of data, both structured and unstructured. The basic idea behind this phrase is that everything we do is increasingly leaving a digital trace. According to Google's executive chairman, Eric Schmidt, from the dawn of civilization until 2003 humankind generated five exabytes of data (that's 5 trillion bytes). Now we produce five exabytes every two days (!), and the pace is accelerating, says Schmidt. Most of this data is user- generated content, including videos, pictures, instant messages, and tweets. With advanced BA solutions, companies can do all sorts of things with this data. However, the big question is, should they? Is it worth it and will the analysis yield anything useful?

There is so much buzz over big data because of the potential for business and society to use this data to lead to more accurate analyses. More accurate analyses should lead to better decisions, and for businesses, greater operational efficiencies, cost reductions, more profit, and reduced risks. In the early 2000s, industry analyst Doug Laney articulated the now-mainstream definition of big data, which consists of the "three Vs"—volume, velocity, and variety. SAS has added two more descriptors—variability and complexity. Figure 12-4 presents these basic descriptors for big data.

Figure 12-4: Basic Tenets of Big Data

Volume	Both structured and unstructured data are increasing at an exorbitant rate. In the past, storage costs were an issue. Now, the issue is how to determine what data is relevant and how to create value from it.
Velocity	Data is streaming at an unparalleled speed and much of it must be dealt with in real time. Reacting quickly enough to handle the vast amounts of data is a challenge for most organizations.
Variety	Organizations must be able to manage, merge, and govern the varied types of data being captured by their systems.
Variability	Data is often produced at certain peak times, such as when a product is trending. Inconsistent data flows can be challenging to manage, especially those involving unstructured data.
Complexity	Data comes from multiple sources, and a company must link, match, cleanse, and transform it across systems. Being able to organize this data is important, or it can spiral out of control.

Source: SAS Institute, Inc.

Data Stores for Business Analytics

Data

The central building block for BA is **data**, which is information in a raw and unorganized format. In order to conduct BA, a data store must be populated with data. The challenge to setting up a BA data store is how to integrate, rearrange, and consolidate large volumes of data from other systems and external sources into a unified information base. Internal sources will most likely include ERP systems, point of sale (POS) systems, and possibly legacy systems. This data needs to be extracted and copied to the data store. Data from external sources may include competitor information, industry information, and economic data. Furthermore, unstructured data can be coded so that it can be used in BA. Of upmost importance in BA is the **data quality**. Quality data means that the data is complete, accurate, available, and timely so that better, more informed, and reliable decisions can be made.

As discussed in Chapter 6, extract, transform and load (ETL) processes and technologies are used to extract data from various systems, transform it, and load it into the data store. As part of the "transform" process, the data may only require reformatting, but depending on the data sources and their integrity, the data might also require cleansing to remove duplicates and enforce consistency. Data cleansing, also introduced in Chapter 6, is the process of detecting and correcting (or removing) corrupt or inaccurate records from a record set, table, or database. Also, ETL software will examine individual data fields and apply rules to consistently convert the contents to the form required by the target repository. For example, the category "female" might be represented in three different systems as "F," "female," and "0." This process is referred to as data harmonization. The ETL software would know that these entries mean the same thing and convert them to the target format. ETL processes also involve record consolidation—for example, customer records from various sources are integrated together into a best-of-breed record.

Data Warehouse

As data is gathered from various domains such as the ERP system and collected into a central data store, the storage facility begins to function as a data warehouse. A **data warehouse** is a large relational or multi-dimensional database that combines pertinent data in an aggregated, summarized form suitable for enterprise-wide data analysis, reporting, and management decision-making. It is *the* central point of data integration for BA, providing a single, comprehensive source of both current and historical information. Figure 12-5 lists the key characteristics of a data warehouse.

Figure 12-5: Key Characteristics of a Data Warehouse

Subject oriented	Organized by subject rather than process; domains include suppliers, customers, sales, and inventory
Stable and non-volatile	Once stored, data is not changed except for a compelling reason; updates are done periodically, which differs from ERP systems that processes transactions every second
Time variant	Reporting over a period of time
Integrated	Integrates data from CRM, ERP, legacy systems, POS data, economic data, and possibly unstructured data

Source: CIO Magazine

Data Mart

A **data mart** is a repository of data designed to serve a specific set of users. The data may originate from the data warehouse or the ERP system directly. The emphasis of the data mart is on meeting the specific needs of a particular group of employees in terms of analysis, content, presentation, and ease of use. Whereas a data warehouse combines data from across the enterprise, data marts are usually smaller and focus on a particular subject or data context for a limited audience. An example would be a data mart designed for retail buyers or logistics managers. Any number of data marts might support different target groups within a single organization, each one relevant to one or more business units for which it was designed. Figure 12-6 shows how data from several systems, including ERP, is stored into data warehouses and data marts for use in various types of BA.

Figure 12-6: Data Sources, Storage, and Business Analytics Uses

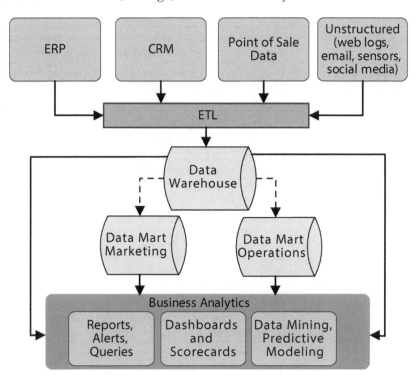

Business Analytics Best Practices

A BA solution can provide many organizational benefits, although as with other enterprise systems, problems often surface during the implementation process. The majority of these issues arise from inadequate planning and requirements gathering and people issues (we've all heard these before in the context of ERP systems!). Other obstacles to implementing BA include lack of IT know-how, lack of business know-how (knowing what questions to ask), data retention, data cleanup, increased data center work-loads, and growth in data storage requirements. Researchers have identified a number of best practices that will add value to a BA initiative. Figure 12-7 lists some of these.

Figure 12-7: Business Analytics Best Practices

Best Practice	Explanation
Collaborate to identify the "hard" questions	Form an interdisciplinary team to review the business and lay out all the questions that have been hard or elusive to answer.
Avoid the temptation to merely convert the "top 20" reports to the BA solution	The goal should be to create new and better reports that analyze information in different ways so the organization can achieve greater competitive advantage.
Plan for the impact that running real-time analytics has on the data center	Real-time analytics (such as giving instant promotions while customers are buying online) means that IT resource usage and procedures may need to be modified.
Have in-house talent design and run BA	Consultants may need to be hired to "get up and running." But make sure you have a plan to hand over the operation of the BA solution to those in-house.
Say goodbye to dirty data	Ensure the quality of data that analytics will be operating on. Scrub data before analyzing it.
Design analytics that deliver summary and drill-down capabilities	Top managers generally want a dashboard view of activity, whereas middle management and line personnel need drill-down capabilities.
Don't let BA do all the thinking for the organization	BA should make companies "get smarter" about how they do business. However, there will be times that instinct is the purest form of intelligence.

Source: M. Shacklett

Corporate Performance Management

Corporate performance management (CPM) is the area of BA that enables organizations to efficiently collect, aggregate, and analyze data from multiple sources in order to take the best course of action in line with strategy. Analytics vendors help automate CPM through dashboards and scorecards; thus, CPM focuses more on the reactive, lower-level types of intelligence, but it still has a solid foothold in the major corporations of the world. Used mainly within the accounting and finance departments, CPM analyzes income statement and balance sheet numbers and measures such as revenue, return on investment, overhead, and operational costs.

CPM, also known as **enterprise performance management (EPM)**, requires the alignment of business activities to tactical and strategic objectives in order to manage performance and make more informed decisions. When properly implemented, CPM bridges the gap between long-term strategies and day-to-day operations by aligning business metrics with critical success factors identified by management. A CPM interface, typically a scorecard, includes key performance indictors so that employees can keep track of their individual and team performance relative to corporate or enterprise goals.

Key Performance Indicators

It's commonly stated that you can't manage what you don't measure. Chapter 5 discussed business metrics, which represent a snapshot in time of a company's performance. Every area of an organization has specific business metrics that should be monitored—marketers track campaign and program statistics, sales teams monitor new opportunities and leads, and executives look at big-picture financial metrics, such as the overall profitability of a business unit. When a metric reflects a driver of strategy, it becomes a **key performance indicator (KPI)**. Thus, a KPI is a metric, but a metric is not always a KPI. A metric could represent the measurement of any business activity, but a KPI puts that performance in a strategic context. Figure 12-8 presents 10 characteristics of a good KPI.

Figure 12-8: Characteristics of a Good Key Performance Indicator

Indicator	Explanation
Reflects strategic value drivers	A **value driver** represents an activity that, when executed properly, increases the probability of an organization achieving its financial and organizational goals.
Defined by executives	Executives typically define KPIs in strategic planning sessions.
Cascades throughout an organization	Top-level KPIs cascade throughout an organization; data captured by lower-level KPIs rolls up to top-level KPIs.
Based on corporate standards	The only way cascading KPIs work is if the organization has established standard measurements across all business units.
Based on valid data	Before executives finalize a KPI, they need to make sure the data exists to calculate the metric. If not, they need to allocate funds to capture the KPI or revise the KPI.
Easy to comprehend	Employees must know what's being measured, how it's being calculated, and what they should do (and shouldn't do) to positively affect the KPI.
Always relevant	To ensure that KPIs continually boost performance, they need to be audited at least quarterly to determine usage and relevance. If a KPI isn't being looked at, it should probably be discarded or revised.
Provides context	Metrics always show a number that reflects performance, but a KPI puts that performance in context. KPIs evaluate performance according to expectations (positive or negative).
Empowers users	It's critical to revamp business processes when implementing KPIs to empower users to take the appropriate action in response to the KPIs. To be effective, KPIs must also have incentives attached to them.
Leads to positive action	KPIs should generate the intended action. Unfortunately, many organizations allow groups to create KPIs in isolation, which can lead to KPIs undermining each other.

Source: W. Eckerson

Historically, companies tended to focus more on financial KPIs, such as return on equity (ROE) or the price-to-earnings (PE) ratio. More recently, as firms have embraced business process reengineering, the focus of CPM efforts is on driving future performance. Consequently, while financial KPIs are still important, other measures have been identified that supplement the financial perspective. This concept of balancing financial KPIs with other types of KPIs is now an established method to drive future performance. The balanced scorecard, discussed next, is a well-known methodology to organize and manage all type of KPIs in line with strategic value.

The Balanced Scorecard

As discussed earlier, scorecards, as a valuable component of a company's BA toolbox, play an essential role in helping management teams make better strategic decisions. The **balanced scorecard (BSC)** is a popular scorecard methodology used to measure a company's performance against strategic goals and determine whether its business operations are aligned with its objectives, vision, and strategy. Developed in 1992 by Drs. Robert Kaplan and David Norton, the BSC concept is a type of CPM methodology. To put the BSC to work, companies should articulate goals for various aspects of their operations and then identify appropriate KPIs to measure performance toward those goals. The KPIs generally include both corporate targets and business unit targets, which are then translated into individual and departmental measures and targets.

When the BSC was introduced, it began to refocus companies that previously had relied solely on financial metrics to measure performance. The concept behind the BSC is that good performance in financial KPIs does not necessarily translate into future success because they are **lagging indicators**, providing knowledge of past activity and thus, in isolation, describing an incomplete picture of organizational performance. **Leading indicators** are needed to "balance" financial KPIs and set expectations for future activities. Poor performance in leading indicators may signal a future decline even though financials may look good. Figure 12-9 presents explanations of the four perspectives of a BSC. A perspective is a grouping of high-level strategic areas. While the financial perspective includes lagging KPIs, the remaining three perspectives contain leading KPIs.

Figure 12-9: Four Perspectives of the Balanced Scorecard

Perspective	Question	Description
Financial	"How do we look to shareholders?"	KPIs based on this traditional perspective have to do with profitability, growth, and shareholder value.
Customer	"How do our customers view us?"	KPIs based on this category relate to customers' concerns including time, quality, service, and cost.
Internal Processes	"What can we do better than anyone else?"	KPIs based on this perspective tell managers how the business is operating, focusing mainly on core competencies.
Learning and Growth	"Can we continue to improve and create value?"	KPIs included in this perspective capture growth in intellectual capital.

Source: Balanced Scorecard Institute

A BSC can be built using vendor-supplied BA tools, or organizations can purchase software such as QuickScore, which is specifically designed for the BSC. The main tool used in the BSC for visualization and communication is the **strategy map**, which shows cause-and-effect relationships among the perspectives and tells the story of how value is created in the organization. Improving performance in the objectives of the Learning and Growth perspective (the bottom row) should improve performance in the Internal Processes perspective (the next row up), which should improve Customer and Financial perspectives (top rows). Objectives are broken down into KPIs that are measured against benchmarks or targets. For example, improved CRM skills might be measured with how many training days on the CRM system marketing employees receive a year compared to target training days. Figure 12-10 shows an example of a strategy map.

Figure 12-10: Example Strategy Map for the Balanced Scorecard

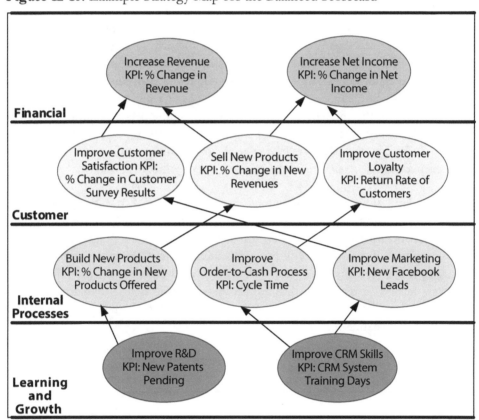

Benefits of the Balanced Scorecard

Since its introduction in 1992, the BSC has become a standard planning technique. Organizations have embraced the BSC's call for focus on both leading and lagging measures and the interplay among them. There are many benefits of using the BSC as a performance management tool. First, the BSC helps put an organization's mission at the center and translates it into tangible measures and actions. It also helps to mobilize employees to channel their energies, abilities, and knowledge toward achieving the company's mission. The BSC promotes a forward-looking, proactive organization instead of a reactive organization, which only changes course when things go wrong. Finally, the BSC provides a comprehensive and balanced view of performance by looking at the four perspectives. Companies can also add other perspectives salient to their operations.

Drawbacks and Limitations of the Balanced Scorecard

Implementing the BSC can be a costly and time-consuming process and may involve the use of consultants. Maximum effectiveness is attained when the whole organization understands the theory behind the BSC and the importance of achieving balance across the measures, which requires training and communication. Overcoming employee resistance may be a factor if they believe the BSC is just the "flavor of the month" or doesn't really work. Also, the usefulness of the BSC is dependent on the value of the data that is driving the process—thus, again, data quality matters. If the information used to evaluate progress is incomplete, inaccurate, and irrelevant, or uninformative, the BSC is not effective. For example, in evaluating training efforts, the number of people being trained is not as relevant as the type of training they received.

The BSC also has limitations. It is a framework to assist with CPM, but it's up to management to make sure the organization has followed through with converting KPIs to actual performance improvements that positively impact the bottom line. Also, implementing the BSC will not add value if the company's initial strategy is not a profitable one. Companies must have a winning long-term strategy; performance measures and management frameworks only help them achieve it. Organizations must also recognize that the business environment is dynamic and should alter their mission, vision, and performance measures in the face of changing customer preferences, competition, and other market forces.

Data Governance

When data lacks high quality, its use is diminished. This is where data governance comes in. **Data governance** involves the creation and management of the organizational structures, policies, and processes needed to define, control, and ensure the quality of enterprise data. A sound data governance program includes establishing a **data governance committee**, which is typically a cross-functional committee empowered by senior management that has a defined set of procedures for data quality and a plan to execute those procedures.

Analytic projects are large, time consuming, and expensive, and users are often disappointed about the outcomes or are not trained enough to appreciate the outcomes. Also, regarding data storage, it is often the case that large sections may go unused, and response times are unacceptable. The data governance committee should minimize risks that users will be unhappy once the system in place and should be especially mindful of data quality. This is a daunting challenge for many organizations, as research suggests that data stored in databases deteriorates at a rate greater than 20 percent per year.

The data in data warehouses and data marts must be managed over time, and various conflicting factors should be balanced. For instance, increasing capacity comes at a cost. Storage performance is also affected by data volume and hardware. Analytics needs historical data, so this affects capacity. There are also retention regulations on certain types of data. Archiving, backup and restoration all have performance, capacity, and cost implications as well. The data governance committee should be in charge of how data stored in the data warehouse and data marts is managed over time. This process is known as the **data life cycle management** and begins when data is created, to initial storage, to the time it becomes obsolete or deleted. The committee should also put in place processes for identifying and resolving problems with data quality.

Summary

ERP systems are adept at processing transactions, but ERP reporting is operations-based and the data may be too granular for high-level strategic decision-making. Additionally, many companies are gathering large volumes of data that ERP systems simply cannot deal with, such as social media and sensor data. Business analytics has the potential to give companies a competitive edge through the collection of data, both structured and unstructured, so that better, smarter decisions can be made both now and in the future. Business analytics includes reports, queries, alerts, dashboards, and scorecards, but it also encompasses more advanced types of analyses such as data mining and predictive modeling. More reactive types of BA include traditional business intelligence and corporate performance management techniques. An example of a framework for CPM is the balanced scorecard, which many companies use to help stay focused on mission across various perspectives including learning and growth, internal processes, customer, and financial. To gain valuable insights, various data sources are often integrated to form a data warehouse and perhaps data marts. Technologies are used to extract data from various sources, reformat it and cleanse it, and load it into a BA data store. A data governance committee must set forth appropriate policies and procedures to ensure data integrity and currency.

Keywords

Alert

Balanced scorecard (BSC)

Big data

Business analytics (BA)

Business intelligence (BI)

Corporate performance management (CPM)

Dashboard

Data

Data governance

Data governance committee

Data life cycle management

Data mart

Data mining

Data quality

Data visualization

Data warehouse

Enterprise performance management (EPM)

Key performance indicator (KPI)

Knowledge discovery

Lagging indicator

Leading indicator

Predictive analytics

Predictor

Report

Query

Query by example (QBE)

Scorecard

Strategy map

Structured data

Unstructured data

Value driver

Quick Review

1. True/False: Whereas a data mart combines databases across an entire enterprise, data warehouses are usually smaller and focus on a particular subject or department.

2. True/False: The balanced scorecard is a methodology for corporate performance management.

3. _____ is the statistical analysis of large pools of data to find hidden correlations and trends.

4. _____ is the central building block for business analytics.

5. Analytics makes use of _____ which helps users understand the significance of data by placing it in a visual context.

Questions to Consider

1. Give an example of a lower-level analytic and a higher-level analytic and explain each.

2. What are the four characteristics of a data warehouse?

3. Explain the importance and tenets of big data.

4. List the four perspectives of the balanced scorecard and describe each.

5. Explain the importance of leading and lagging measures in the context of the balanced scorecard.

References

Bertolucci, J. (2013, August 26). Big data: A practical definition. Retrieved from http://www.informationweek.com/big-data/big-data-analytics/big-data-a-practical-definition/d/d-id/1111290

Carr, J. (2013, April 25). 5 questions about ERP dashboards. Retrieved from http://www.ultraconsultants.com/5-questions-about-erp-dashboards/

Davenport, T. H. (2010). The new world of "business analytics." Retrieved from http://www.sas.com/resources/asset/IIA_NewWorldofBusinessAnalytics_March2010.pdf

Eckerson, W. (2008). *Ten characteristics of a good KPI.* Retrieved from http://www.bpmpartners.com/GuestColumnist.shtml

Elegant MicroWeb.com. (n.d.). Exceptions and alerts. Retrieved from http://www.elegantjbi.com/bi-suite/exception-reports-alerts.htm

Evans, M. H. (n.d.) Balanced scorecard 101. Retrieved from http://www.exinfm.com/workshop_files/scorecard_101.pdf

Goeke, R., & Faley, R. (2007). *Leveraging the flexibility of your data warehouse.* Communications of the ACM *50*(10), 107–111.

Hernandez, P. (2012, January 23). Reports vs. dashboards and balanced scorecards: Differences in theory and practice. Retrieved from http://hernandezpaul.wordpress.com/2012/01/23/reports-vs-dashboards-vs-balanced-scorecards-differences-in-theory-and-practice/

Jain, K. (2013, June 11). What is business analytics and which tools are used for analysis? Retrieved from http://www.analyticsvidhya.com/blog/2013/06/business-analytics-spectrum/

Kenyon, J. (2014, July 30). Business intelligence or business analytics? Retrieved from http://blog.optimizationgroup.com/business-intelligence-or-business-analytics

Klipfolio Inc. (2014). What are business metrics? Retrieved from http://www.klipfolio.com/resources/articles/what-are-business-metrics

Logi International, Ltd. (n.d.) BI encyclopedia: Automated business alerts. Retrieved from http://www.logianalytics.com/bi-encyclopedia/automated-business-alerts

Microsoft. (n.d.) What is the difference between a dashboard and a scorecard? Retrieved from http://office.microsoft.com/en-us/sharepoint-server-help/what-is-the-difference-between-a-dashboard-and-a-scorecard-HA101772797.aspx

Oz Analytics. (2009, July 14). 10 Signs That You Need Analytics. http://analytics.typepad.com/oz-analytics/2009/07/10-signs-that-you-need-analytics.html

Richards, L. (n.d.). Balanced scorecard drawbacks. Retrieved from http://smallbusiness.chron.com/balanced-scorecard-drawbacks-4602.html

Rouse, M. (2009). Predictive analytics. Retrieved from http://searchcrm.techtarget.com/definition/predictive-analytics

Rouse, M. (2010). Business intelligence dashboard. http://searchbusinessanalytics.techtarget.com/definition/business-intelligence-dashboard

Rouse, M. (2012). Data visualization. Retrieved from http://searchbusinessanalytics.techtarget.com/definition/data-visualization

SAP. (2012). Data warehouse solutions from SAP: Strategic direction and evolution. Retrieved from http://www.saphana.com/servlet/JiveServlet/previewBody/2164-102-2-3987/

SAS. (n.d.). What is data mining? http://www.sas.com/en_us/insights/analytics/data-mining.html

SAS. (n.d.). Big data: What it is and why it matters. Retrieved from http://www.sas.com/en_us/insights/big-data/what-is-big-data.html

Shacklett, M. (2012, July 12). 10 ways to optimize business analytics in your organization. Retrieved from http://www.techrepublic.com/blog/10-things/10-ways-to-optimize-business-analytics-in-your-organization/

Siegel, E. (2010). Seven reasons you need predictive analytics today. Retrieved from https://www14.software.ibm.com/webapp/iwm/web/signup.do?source=swg-BA_WebOrganic&S_PKG=ov3589&S_TACT=101KR4SW&dynform=114&lang=en_US

Siegler, M. (2010). Eric Schmidt: Every 2 days we create as much information as we did up to 2003. Retrieved from http://techcrunch.com/2010/08/04/schmidt-data/

Songini, M. L. (2004, February 2). QuickStudy: ETL. Retrieved from http://www.computerworld.com/article/2575153/business-intelligence/quickstudy---etl.html

Walker, D. (2012, March 26). Data management and business intelligence governance process: What we can do for your business. Retrieved from http://www.slideshare.net/datamgmt/implementing-bi-dw-governance

Index

A

Account, *151*
Accounting cycle, *134*
Accounts payable (AP), *136*
Accounts payable (AP) subsidiary ledger, *136*
Accounts receivable (AR), *135*
Accounts receivable (AR) subsidiary ledger, *135*
Active tag (RFID), *190*
Activity, *66, 139*
Activity-based costing (ABC), *139*
A la carte approach (use of consultants), *116*
Alert, *241*
Application controls, *4*
"As is" process, *47*
"As is" process map, *65*
Asset Management module, *142-144, 188*
Association, *163*
Associative entity, 25. See *junction table*.
Audit trail, *218*
Authentication, *224-225*
Authority ambiguity, *46*
Authorization, *220-221*
Authorization testing, *111*
Availability, *226*
Available to promise (ATP), *151*

B

Back-office systems, *3, 156*
Balanced Scorecard, *250*
Balance sheet, *133*
Balanced approach (use of consultants), *116*
Bench strength, *205*
Benchmarking, *55*
Benefits Administration module, *202*
Best of breed, *32*
Best practice, *6*
Big bang implementation strategy, *118*
      See *direct cutover strategy*.
Big data, *244*

Bill of lading, *152*
Bill of material (BOM), *138, 184*
Bin, *180*
Biometric software, *225*
Blocked stock, *187*
Bolt-on, *108*
Bottleneck, *46*
Business analytics (BA), *238*
Business case, *84*
Business case rationales, *84*
Business intelligence (BI), *239*
Business logic, *19*
Business metrics, *85*
Business performance management (BPM), *254*
Business process, *2, 44,*
Business process improvement (BPI), *52*
      See *business process reengineering*.
Business process management (BPM), *54*
Business process reengineering (BPR), *47*
      See *business process improvement*.

C

Capacity plan, *185*
Cardinality, *23*
Career and Talent Management module, *205*
Cash management, *136*
Cash-to-cash cycle, *175*
Casual user licensing, *87*
Catalog management, *179*
Center of Excellence (COE), *123*
Certified Information Security Manager
      (CISM), *230*
Certified Information System Auditor
      (CISA), *230*
Certified in Risk and Information Systems
      Control (CRISC), *231*
Certified in the Governance of Enterprise IT
      (CGEIT), *231*
Change agents, *8, 113*
Change management, *8, 112*

Change requests, *84*

Chart of accounts (COA), *133*

Chief Knowledge Officer (CKO), *166*

Clean slate reengineering, *47*. See *technology enabled reengineering.*

Client, *18*

Client-server computing, *18*

Cloud computing, *34*

Compensation Management module, *203*

Composite key, *25*

Concatenated key, *25*

Concurrent user licensing, *87*

Conference room pilot (CRP), *108*

Configuration, *31, 105*

Configuration data, *30*

Configuration tables, *105*

Constrained reengineering, *49*. See *technology-enabled reengineering.*

Consultants, *115-117*

Contact, *151*

Contract management, *178*

Contact-to-contract-to-cash process, *150*

Control account, *135*

Conversions, *106*

Coordinate, *180*

Core competency, *9, 47, 55*

Core ERP, *3*

Corporate performance management (CPM), *248*

Corporate social responsibility (CSR), *189*

Cost accounting, *138*

Cost allocation, *139*

Cost center, *141*

Cost drivers, *139*

Cost object, *138*

Cost pools, *141*

Create, read, update, delete (CRUD), *221*

Credit management, *136*

Cross-functional, *2*

Cross-functional flowcharts, *64*

Customer-drive approach (use of consultants), *116*

Customer exits, *107*

Customer independent requirements, *184*

Customer relationship management system (CRM), *154*

Customization, *32, 106*. See *RICEF.*

Cycle counting, *181*

Cycle time, *46*

D

Dashboard, *241*

Data, *245*

Data access logic, *19*

Database normalization, *27*

Data center controls, *226*

Data cleansing, *109*

Data collection, *109*

Data duplication, *46*

Data extraction, *109*

Data governance, *252*

Data governance committee, *252*

Data harmonization, *109*

Data life cycle management, *253*

Data loading, *109*

Data mapping testing, *110*

Data mart, *246*

Data migration, *109*

Data migration testing, *110*

Data mining, *243*

Data owner, *110, 201*

Data quality, *245*

Data scrubbing, *109*

Data visualization, *241*

Data warehouse, *245*

Decision point (process map), *66*

Demo days, *92*

Dependent demand, *182*

Determinant, *28*

Development (DEV), *33, 224*

Direct costs, *138*

Direct cutover strategy, *118*. See *Big bang implementation strategy.*

Distributed computing, *18*

Dual-factor authentication, *225*

Dynamic cycle counting, *181*

E

EDI translator, *191*

Edit checks, *218*

Electronic data interchange (EDI), *191*

Employee performance management (EPM), *206*

Employee self-service (ESS), *207*

Enhancements, *107*

Enterprise performance management (EPM), *248*

Enterprise resource planning (ERP) systems, *2*. See *Core ERP*. See *Extended ERP*.

Enterprise space, *11*

Entity, *22*

Entity integrity rule, *22*

Entity relationship diagram (ERD), *23*

Environmental, Health, and Safety (EHS) module, *189. See Corporate Social Responsibility.*

ERP selection team, *90*

ETL (extract, transform, load), *109, 245, 247*

Event monitoring, *163*

Explicit knowledge, *164*

Extended ERP, *3*

F

Fat client, *19*

Field, *22*

Field service, *158*

Financial accounting, *132*

 Financial Accounting module, *132*

First normal form (1NF), *27-28*

Fit/gap analysis, *94*

Fixed asset life cycle, *143*

Flow time, *70*

Foreign key (FK), *23*

Forms, *107*

Front-office systems, *156*

Full-time equivalents (FTE), *88*

G

General ledger (GL), *134*

Generally accepted accounting principles (GAAP), *132*

Goods/services receipt, *176*

Graphical user interface (GUI), *19*

Group interview method (process map), *67*

H

Handoffs, *46*

Heavy user licensing, *87*

Human capital, *200, 211*

Human capital management (HCM), *200*

Human Capital Management (HCM) suite, *202-207*

Hybrid approach, *161*

I

Identification, *224*

Identity and access management (IAM), *88, 224*

Impact analysis, *224*

Income statement, *132*

Incremental implementation strategy, *118*

Indirect costs, *138*

Industry solutions, *7*

Information Systems Audit and Control Association (ISACA), *229*

Implementation strategies, *117-119*

Input controls, *219*

Inspection lot, *186*

Instance, *33*

Integration partners, *4*

Integration testing, *111*

Intellectual capital, *164*

Interface control, *219*

Interfaces, *106*

Intermediaries, *46*

Internal controls, *45, 216*

International Financial Reporting Standards (IFRS), *132*

Inventory status report, *185*

Investment center, *142*
Invoice, *153*
IT application controls (ITACs), *219*
IT auditor, *4*. See *CISA*.
IT control, *216*
IT general controls (ITGC), *221*
IT governance, *231*
IT risk management, *231*

J

Job pricing, *203*
Junction table, *25*. See *associative entity*.

K

Key performance indicator (KPI), *249*
Knowledge, *164*
Knowledge base, *164*
Knowledge discovery, *243*
Knowledge management (KM), *164*
Knowledge management (KM) system, *164*

L

Lagging indicator, *250*
Lead, *150*
Leading indicator, *250*
Lead management, *151*
Legacy systems, *2*
Liquidity forecast, *137*
Logical access controls, *224*

M

Mainframe architecture, *18*
Maintenance, *123-125*
Management accounting, *137-142*
Management Accounting module, *137*
Manual steps, *46*
Manufacturing module, *182-186*
Manufacturing resource planning (MRP II) systems, *10*
Many-to-many relationship, *25*
Master data, *30*
Master production schedule (MPS), *184*

Material, *186*
Material requirements planning (MRP) systems, *9, 182*
Middleware, *32*
Mobility, *36*
Modifications, *107*
Modules, *2*
Multi-factor authentication, *225*

N

Named user licensing, *87*
Negative test, *228*

O

Off-page connector (process map), *66*
Old ways, *46*
Onboarding, *205*
One-on-one interview method (process map), *67*
One-to-many relationship, *23-24*
One-to-one relationship, *24*
On-page connector (process map), *66*
On-premise, *35*
Opportunity, *151*
Oracle *7, 8, 12, 22, 125, 240*
Order acknowledgement, *151*
Order fulfillment, *152*
Order-to-cash process, *150*. See *quote-to-cash process*.
Organizational knowledge, *164*
Output controls, *219*
Outsourcing, *208*
Overhead costing, *138-139*

P

Packing slip, *152*
Paper records, *46*
Parallel accounting, *135*
Parallel implementation strategy, *119*
Partial dependency, *28*
Partner channel management, *159*
Passive tag (RFID), *190*

Payroll module, *203-204*
PeopleSoft, *12*
Performance load testing, *111*
Personalization, *163*
Personnel Administration module, *202*
Phase (process map), *66*
Phased implementation strategy, *118*
Physical access controls, *225*
Planned independent requirements, *184*
Planned trip-to-payment process, *144*
Plant Maintenance (PM) module, *188-189*
Point of sale (POS) system, *153*
Post-go-live audits, *123*
Power users, *115*
Predictive analytics, *243, 254*
Predictive modeling, *163, 240*
Predictor, *243*
Presentation logic, *19*
Pricing, *163*
Primary key (PK), *22*
Process-centered, *2*
Process evaluator, *68*
Process flow line (process map), *66*
Process implementer, *68*
Process inventory, *53*
Process map, *64-66, 76*
Process map facilitator, *67*
Process mapping roles, *67-68*
Process map symbols, *66*
Process owner, *68*
Processing controls, *219*
Procure-to-pay process, *176*. See *purchase-to-pay process*.
Product costing, *138*
Production (PRD), *33, 224*
Profiling, *163*
Profitability analysis, *140*
Profitability segment, *140*
Profit center, *142*
Program change controls, *222*
Program manager, *82*
Project charter, *83*
Project governance, *98*

Project manager (PM), *82*
Project team, *81*
Prospect, *151*
Purchase order acknowledgment, *176*
Purchase order (PO), *176*
Purchase requisition, *176*
Purchase-to-pay process, *175*. See *procure-to-pay process*.
Purchasing module, *91, 136, 144, 175-176, 178, 188*
Purchasing plan, *185*

Q

Qualify, *150*
Quality assurance (QA), *33, 56*
Quality Assurance (QA) module, *186-187*
Quality control, *46, 56*
Query (-ies), *29, 241*
Query by example (QBE), *241*
Quotation, *151, 178*
Quote-to-cash process, *150*. See *order-to-cash process*.

R

Radio frequency identification (RFID), *190*
Record, *22*
Recruitment Management module, *204*
Recruit-to-retire process, *200*
Reference visit, *95*
Referential integrity rule, *26*
Relational database management systems (RDBMS), *21*
Relations, *22*
Reliability, *226*
Remittance advice, *153*
Reports, *106, 240*
Request for proposal (RFP), *92*
Request for quote (RFQ), *176*
Requirements analysis, *90*
Requirements document, *91*

Restricted stock, *186*
Retro-fit, *107*
Rework, *46*
RICEF (Reports, Interfaces, Conversions, Enhancements, Forms), *106-107*
Risk management, *120, 231*
Role, *64, 222*
Role ambiguity, *46*
Role-based access control (RBAC), *220*
Routing, *138, 186*

S

Sales module, *134, 135, 150*
Sales order, *151*
Sales pipeline, *158*
Sandboxes, *33*
SAP, *7, 8, 12, 18, 20, 32, 87, 89, 105, 107, 120, 124, 133, 202, 240*
Sarbanes-Oxley Act of 2002 (SOX), *5, 59, 217*
Scope creep, *84*
Scope management, *84*
Scope statement, *83*
Scorecards, *242*
Second normal form (2NF), *28*
Segmentation, *163*
Segregation of duties (SoD), *45, 220*
Segregation of duties violations, *46*
Self-generate method (process map), *67*
Serpentine picking, *180*
Server, *18*
Service level agreement (SLA), *35*
Service provider, *208*
Shared services, *44*
Small-to-medium sized enterprises (SMEs), *11*
Social CRM, *160*
Social media, *160*
Social media monitoring, *160*
Software as a service (SaaS), *35*
Software contract value, *89*
Software implementation, *104*
Software installation, *104*
Source document, *134*

Sourcing, *176*
Spend analysis, *178*
Stabilization, *122*
Start/stop (process map), *66*
Statement of cash flows, *133*
Statement of retained earnings, *133*
Steering committee, *83*
Strategy map, *251*
Structured data, *239*
Structured Query Language (SQL), *29-30*
Subject matter expert, *68*
Subscription-based licensing, *87*
Subsidiary ledger, *135*
Succession planning, *205*
Super user, *115*
Supplier performance management (SPM), *178*
Supplier relationship management (SRM), *178-179*
Supply chain, *174*
Supply chain management (SCM), *174*
Swim lanes, *68*
Swim lane diagram, *64*
System, *64*
System implementation assurance (SIA), *226*
System landscape, *33*
Systems diagram (SD), *64*

T

Table, *22*
Tacit knowledge, *164*
Talent profile, *206*
Technology enabled reengineering, *49*. See *constrained reengineering*.
Thin client, *20*
Third normal form (3NF), *28*
Three-tier client-server architecture, *20*
Three-way match, *177, 216, 218, 222*
Tier (ERP vendors), *11*
Time and Attendance Management module, *202-203*
Time period principle, *134*
"To be" process, *47*
"To be" process map, *65*